Castles of England

For My Wonderful Parents,
who ignited my interest in castles.

Castles of England

John Paul Davis

First published in Great Britain in 2021 by
Pen & Sword History
An imprint of
Pen & Sword Books Ltd
Yorkshire – Philadelphia

Copyright © John Paul Davis 2021

ISBN 978 1 39901 369 7

The right of John Paul Davis to be identified as Author of this work has been asserted by him in accordance with the Copyright, Designs and Patents Act 1988.

A CIP catalogue record for this book is
available from the British Library.

All rights reserved. No part of this book may be reproduced or transmitted in any form or by any means, electronic or mechanical including photocopying, recording or by any information storage and retrieval system, without permission from the Publisher in writing.

Typeset by Mac Style
Printed and bound in the UK by CPI Group (UK) Ltd,
Croydon, CR0 4YY.

Pen & Sword Books Limited incorporates the imprints of Atlas, Archaeology, Aviation, Discovery, Family History, Fiction, History, Maritime, Military, Military Classics, Politics, Select, Transport, True Crime, Air World, Frontline Publishing, Leo Cooper, Remember When, Seaforth Publishing, The Praetorian Press, Wharncliffe Local History, Wharncliffe Transport, Wharncliffe True Crime and White Owl.

For a complete list of Pen & Sword titles please contact

PEN & SWORD BOOKS LIMITED
47 Church Street, Barnsley, South Yorkshire, S70 2AS, England
E-mail: enquiries@pen-and-sword.co.uk
Website: www.pen-and-sword.co.uk

Or

PEN AND SWORD BOOKS
1950 Lawrence Rd, Havertown, PA 19083, USA
E-mail: Uspen-and-sword@casematepublishers.com
Website: www.penandswordbooks.com

Contents

Introduction   ix
Preface: The Castle in England   xv

Chapter 1	The Isles of Scilly, Cornwall and Devon	1
	Lyonesse	1
	The Isles of Scilly	3
	Pengersick	5
	St Michael's Mount	8
	Tintagel	10
	Berry Pomeroy	13
	Lydford	16
	Okehampton	18
	Tiverton	22
Chapter 2	Dorset and Somerset	25
	Corfe Castle	25
	Sherborne Old Castle	28
	Cadbury	29
	Dunster	32
	Farleigh Hungerford	34
	Nunney	36
	Taunton	37
Chapter 3	Gloucestershire and Wiltshire	40
	Berkeley	40
	Sudeley	43
	Old Sarum	47
	Old Wardour	49
Chapter 4	Hampshire and the Isle of Wight	52
	Odiham	52
	Portchester	53
	Carisbrooke	56

Chapter 5	Sussex	60
	Arundel	60
	Bodiam	63
	Bramber	66
	Hastings	68
	Herstmonceux	70
	Pevensey	72
Chapter 6	Kent	76
	Dover	76
	Hever	79
	Leeds	80
	Rochester	82
	Scotney	87
Chapter 7	Surrey, Berkshire and Oxfordshire	89
	Farnham	89
	Donnington	90
	Windsor	91
	Oxford	95
Chapter 8	Essex, Cambridgeshire, Suffolk and Norfolk	97
	Colchester	97
	Hadleigh	100
	Woodcroft	102
	Bungay	103
	Orford	104
	Burgh	106
	Castle Rising	108
	Framlingham	110
	Norwich	111
Chapter 9	Warwickshire, the West Midlands and Staffordshire	113
	Kenilworth	113
	Warwick	115
	Dudley	120
	Tamworth	121
	Tutbury	123

Chapter 10	Northamptonshire and Leicestershire	127
	Barnwell	127
	Fotheringhay	128
	Rockingham	130
	Belvoir	132
Chapter 11	Nottinghamshire, Derbyshire and Lincolnshire	135
	Newark	135
	Nottingham	137
	Bolsover	140
	Peveril	141
	Lincoln	143
	Tattershall	145
Chapter 12	Yorkshire	147
	Bolton	147
	Clifford's Tower (York Castle)	148
	Conisbrough	152
	Helmsley	153
	Knaresborough	155
	Middleham	156
	Pickering	158
	Pontefract	159
	Richmond	163
	Ripley	164
	Scarborough	166
	Skipsea	170
	Skipton	172
Chapter 13	Cheshire and Lancashire	174
	Beeston	174
	Lancaster	176
Chapter 14	Cumbria	180
	Carlisle	180
	Muncaster	183
	Pendragon	185
	Sizergh	187
Chapter 15	County Durham	189
	Barnard Castle	189

		Bowes	190
		Durham	192
		Lumley	194
		Raby	196
		Walworth	198
Chapter 16		Tyne & Wear	200
		Featherstone	200
		Hylton	202
		Thirlwall	204
		Tynemouth	205
Chapter 17		Northumberland	209
		Alnwick	209
		Bamburgh	212
		Chillingham	214
		Dunstanburgh	217
		Lindisfarne	221
		Prudhoe	224
		Warkworth	225
Chapter 18		Best of the Rest	229

Postscript	244
Appendix A: Royal Castles in the Middle Ages	246
Appendix B: Important Private Castles in the Middle Ages	247
Bibliography	248
Index	255

Introduction

Ever since I was a young boy, castles have fascinated me. As the child of history enthusiasts, who brought me up on the stories of England's vibrant past, my passion was not long in the making: albeit on a far more child-friendly level compared to the blood-soaked tales that have come to enthral me in adulthood.

Visits to castles were par for the course throughout my primary school years – not that I had much reason for objection. Holidays also tended to be castle related. Accompanying the usual rummage around Britain's historic towns, shops or, if the weather held, sandy beaches, a trip to the local medieval fortresses was rarely far from the top of the itinerary. On the occasions when it wasn't, ancient forts, abbeys and priories were often the main alternative.

Some of my most vivid childhood memories occurred when I was 5 years old: a family holiday to South Wales. During our two-week stay, we devoured the castles of Pembrokeshire and Carmarthenshire, along with pretty much everything on the way back to our home near Bath. To this day, I still believe I learned more during those two weeks than in my entire years of schooling. In the years that followed, no matter where we ventured throughout England and Wales, it seemed no shortage of medieval fortresses needed visiting; dry moats that needed exploring; jagged walls that needed climbing. I loved them and will always be grateful for the influence that these magical places had on me. Even now, there are few things I enjoy more than wandering historic ruins on a warm summer's day, imagining what had taken place there long ago.

Looking back at those carefree years, it seems like destiny that my path as a writer would, in many ways, revolve around the subjects that captivated me during my youth. Sure enough, when I decided to become a writer, the first book I attempted was on castles. The topic I chose was the ghost stories: there was something about the tales of the living dead that seemed so oddly appropriate when placed in the context of sites that could themselves be described as relics of a lost time. From stories of epic feuds and battle-hardened warriors to the lamentations of wronged prisoners and ladies in white, there was no shortage of scope for exploration.

Though the commission of my first book, later published as *Robin Hood: The Unknown Templar* put the castle ghosts' book on long-term hiatus, in the twelve years that have followed, the stories of these mighty fortresses have rarely been far from my mind. No matter what area of history I choose to concentrate on, castles remain a consistent fixture of my life. The reasons for this, I now realise, are obvious. Even during those early visits, I somehow realised these remarkable buildings are the rare epitome of military might and noble grandeur. They are a fortress and a home. The private and the communal. It has often been said that to ignore their role in medieval history is to fail to understand history itself. I know I am not alone in thinking nothing symbolises medieval history quite like a castle.

As anyone lucky enough to grow up in the UK or Europe knows only too well, castles are an inescapable part of the landscape. For almost 1,000 years, their mighty walls have towered menacingly over the towns and countryside. Even in the modern-day, they remain key landmarks and often the heartbeat of communities: the fulcrum around which tourism and local economies run. Some have passed into public ownership; others are now the property of descendants of famous forebears whose spilling of blood has stained the pages of history. Some open their doors to tens of thousands of visitors a year; for many, the number is far smaller. Some occupied critical strategic points and became vital military structures; others were monuments to wealth and decadence. Many of Britain's castles could be regarded as similar, but no two are ever exactly alike. This begs an important question.

How does one define a castle?

For the majority of readers, especially those who enjoy visiting castles, the question may seem an obvious one. Even if articulating a precise and succinct definition that might satisfy the dictionary compilers eludes them, almost everyone will recognise a castle when they see one. The *Oxford English Dictionary* defines a castle as 'a large building, typically of the medieval period, fortified against attack with thick walls, battlements, towers, and in many cases a moat'. Though this definition is certainly not wrong, to go by this alone leaves much to the imagination. One of the things I love most about castles is that they can mean different things to different people. To some, they have become a symbol of Norman autonomy or feats of architectural genius. To others, they are ostentatious family homes: the setting of joyful feasts and balls in richly decorated great halls. They are the setting of long-running sieges and the catalyst of violent uprising – indeed, the chocolate shop for the military buffs. At various times, some have served as prisons of men, women and children – innocent and guilty. In more recent times, they have become the host of fascinating museums and art galleries. Is one definition more correct than others? Is the word 'castle' merely a voluntary label? Are some of these 'castles' not castles at all?

Throughout the planning of this book, my research has taken on many forms. Like any work of non-fiction, it has resulted from a combination of primary and secondary research. While the ability to visit the sights first hand – the restrictions placed on us due to Covid-19 aside – has been a true blessing, as always, much of the information has come from books and manuscripts. Of the many I have turned to, two I consider to be outstanding. The first was R. Allen Brown's 1976 edition of *English Castles*. The second: Marc Morris's, more recent, *Castle*. Had it not been for a mention of Brown by Morris, this gem of a book may even have passed me. During their introductory sections, both authors wrestled with their explanation of what a castle is. In Brown's eyes, the definition is a simple one: 'a fortified residence' and 'residential fortress'. English Heritage, the custodian of many of England's great castles, agrees with this and states prominently on their website that a castle is both a fortress and a place of residence. In his timeless work, Brown denotes the importance of this duality – the domestic and military – that separates it from other homes, not least stately homes. Castles were for defence: a demonstration of strength, but also beloved homes.

Had this book been focused on castles beyond England, namely France and Switzerland, where the term 'chateau' has come to denote both military residences and country estates, I might have been taken in by the temptation to dig deeper. In truth, in England alone, there is no shortage of evidence to be unearthed. Accepted it should certainly be that a castle is both a home and a fortress, in reality, many cover several functions. Writing in the Elizabethan era on the Tower of London, the famed antiquarian John Stow succinctly illustrated how this unique structure that began life as an imposing early Anglo-Norman keep in time developed into a site of many purposes: a royal palace; a public records office; an armoury; a museum; an observatory; a minting office; a military barracks; a bank vault; a zoo.

Unique the Tower of London may be among the castles of England – indeed, the castles of the world – the realisation is an important one. Even in the case of the most basic castle, the multitude of purposes was astounding. Like the great abbeys and priories, they were often self-sufficient. Vegetables flourished among the verdant gardens that were frequently dotted with fishponds and fruit trees. Ploughmen toiled in the uneven fields, their sweaty brows a necessary price for the promise of a productive harvest. Bags of grain filled the castle stores and kitchens, from which the aroma of baking bread would waft daily as the ingredients mixed with water from the castle well. Though life was hard and often simplistic, castles were the sites of living communities where even the smallest would rarely consist of less than 30,000 tonnes of stone and a household of anything between twenty and several hundred.

On deciding to return to my earlier unpublished work on the castles of Britain, one of the big decisions was precisely where to focus. An Englishman by birth and a frequent visitor of her castles, the decision to focus on England was an easy one. From here, however, the choices became far tougher. To understand how these once-primitive structures evolved into the mighty bastions we know and love today is merely one part of the journey. If a castle is a site of dual – if not multi – purpose, then there are at least two main points of evolution relevant to this book. Is this to be a book concerning the history of the castle as a fortress or as a home – or perhaps a combination of the two? Similarly, how can the history of the castle focus solely on the stonework – or in earlier cases, woodwork – and not the people? Having already encountered such questions during my work on the Tower, the answer here was obvious. Had it not been for the people who frequented them, the story of the stonework is meaningless.

By accepting the definitions mentioned, I start with a clear focal point. In contrast to the works of historians such as Brown and Morris, this book is not primarily concerned with matters of engineering or how they were constructed. Nor is it a detailed study into their makeup. Instead, I intend to present the history of these beautiful buildings through the eyes of those whose lives took place there. Of particular importance are those whose actions contributed to the castle's development and survival. The same is true of those who have often been unfairly maligned or those about whom questions remain unanswered. Just like with the Tower, finding such tales was no great challenge. Even for the smaller sites, the number of people involved was incredible. Beside the lords and their usual retinue of knights and squires, a working castle invariably employed a second army: one whose expertise ranged from carpentry, woodcutting, masonry, tile making, carting and blacksmithing to farming, cleaning, cooking, fishing, hunting and all other forms of domestic activity. To this day, their legacies survive in the furnishings of the great halls, kitchens, chapels, moats, bedrooms, walls and towers. While the names of some have slipped into obscurity, many stories are recorded. It is for them that this book has been written. The builders, defenders, wreckers and destroyers. The inheritors, purchasers, sellers and restorers. The beneficiaries of good luck, usurpation, privilege and status. The victims of war, famine, mistreatment, misogyny, murder, mystery and legend.

In many ways, I see this book as the successor, if not the reincarnation, of that first effort of 2008. As I begin this quest, I am already faced with a bizarre irony. Like the story of the castle itself, what started as a basic premise has evolved into something far more structured and ambitious. Building on my initial hope to provide an in-depth insight into the stories behind the castles of England and Wales, this book will not be a one-off. The castles of Wales will follow. Including my previous book for Pen&Sword, *A Hidden History of the Tower of London: England's Most Notorious Prisoners*, one could say this is part two. For that reason, I have decided not to include the Tower in this one.

As was true of that book, it was never my intention to play to melodrama or distort the legends further. Nor was it my intention to write solely on white mists and grey ladies. It has famously been said that when the legend beats the facts, print the legend. A better objective is to enjoy the legend but investigate the facts. When the legend is false, we can still take enjoyment in the fiction. Far more important is to benefit from the truth.

For such reasons, I have chosen to concentrate on castles that have what I consider to be the most enthralling stories instead of being the most magnificent structures. As a devoted visitor of medieval citadels, there was a temptation to concentrate on my personal favourites, such as stone ruins; however, it is not the author's job to be guided by personal preference alone. I have made a particular effort to concentrate on castles whose status as a castle is clear – or at least accepted. For this reason, I have avoided grand houses whose castle label I consider dubious. I have, by and large, concentrated on castles in state ownership. English Heritage owns many. Some operate under the direction of lesser-known, often more local trusts. A handful remain in private hands. Some now serve as museums or hotels. Though I thoroughly enjoy staying in such locations and often broke my research trips in historic coaching inns, it was not my intention to tout others for business; worse still, deprive them. It was also not my intention to use private places that cannot be visited. Occasionally I have broken this rule, but only because the stories were so compelling, it was impossible to leave them out. Concerning those that have been converted into guesthouses or hotels, I have focused on those particularly accessible to guests. One of the great privileges of visiting a castle is being able to walk in old footsteps. It is a far rarer treat to sleep in the same rooms.

Not only have I tried to focus on locations that can be visited, but I have also tried to use only those that are easily accessible. Many reading this will undoubtedly agree with me that castles are beautiful locations, and I'm quite sure many readers will have a desire to research their stories independently. I hope you do. It is only by uncovering the secrets of the past that we can truly understand in whose footsteps we follow. As much as I would love to say this book highlights every mystery, in truth, such things are, alas, not possible. Though stories of legendary figures, unsolved murders, mysteries and ghosts can stand the test of time, the facts belong to history – our understanding of which remains a never-ending journey. Future revelations will undoubtedly come to light. Besides my hope that this work will encourage others, it is also something I plan to revisit. This book is something of a pioneering effort, revision of which will almost certainly become ongoing and lead to further works. History is itself only of benefit if we learn from it. And the more we know, the more necessary the revision.

If there is one thing that castles teach us, it is that the past shaped our identities. Within their walls occurred some of the most fascinating and strangest stories to have happened in British history. For that reason alone, their importance transcends their physical beauty. Their stories are echoes of a lost world. On every level, they are irreplaceable. When we visit them, we are awarded the opportunity to see that world. We can explore them. Learn from them. Reflect on what happened. Enjoy it.

And, if our imagination allows it, see a world that no longer strictly exists but will never truly die.

Preface: The Castle in England

The word 'castle' did not exist in Anglo-Saxon England. The same was not true about the concept of military defence.

Innovative ways to combat an enemy was, of course, an ongoing process throughout ancient times. As the age of the hunter-gatherer gave way to that of permanent Neolithic settlement in around 4000 BC, a new type of hilltop fortress began to materialise, complementary of the new culture of animal husbandry and crop farming that would go on to dictate much of European history ever since. Before the Roman invasion, fortifications in England had developed little beyond the hill forts of the Iron Age: which defined much of the European landscape 800 BC–100 AD. By the time Edward the Confessor was crowned in 1043, the age of the hill fort and cliff castle had given way to the Anglo-Saxon burh, more or less a direct upgrade on the hill forts, which proved useful in withstanding Viking raids.

Writing in 1051, when the burh was still a regular feature of many a Saxon settlement, a monk at Canterbury sensed something far more groundbreaking was at hand. Included in his writings that would eventually form part of the *Anglo-Saxon Chronicle*, the chronicler referred to the formation of a strange establishment in Herefordshire by French members of the king's party. More sophisticated than the burh, the word he used was alien to his vocabulary. In Latin, its builders had christened it: *'castellum'*.

Fifteen years after the monk of Canterbury made a note of this military marvel, the offspring of the first *castellum* were sprouting up all over England's south coast. While their exact appearances remain something of a mystery, the Norman poet Robert Wace appears to shed a little light on them. In an ad hoc passage from his commentary on William the Conqueror's landing at Pevensey, he recorded the invaders' ships contained far more than just horses and men:

Then they cast out of the ships the materials and drew them to land, all shaped, framed and pierced to receive the pins which they had brought, cut and ready in large barrels, so that before evening had well set in, they had finished a fort.

Doubtful though it is that the chronicler of Canterbury ever truly knew what he had described, all the signs point to what we would now recognise as a motte and bailey castle. That the concept was a mystery to Wace, who lived a century later, is perhaps less likely. No less than four early French castles are depicted in the Bayeux Tapestry, all of which possess an unmistakable resemblance to those erected in England. As history would later show, these solid yet flammable assemblies of wooden posts arranged around small hills and designed to provide for small communities was still a long way from being the last word on the castle in England. Within thirty years of William the Conqueror's landing, many of motte and bailey status had already been superseded by structures created in stone. Indeed, some were built that way from the very beginning.

From here, a transformation began that would forever alter England's landscape and shape her history for centuries to come. Though for a short time after William's death, the importance of such structures declined, during the 'Anarchy' of Stephen and Matilda, their need became critical. Practically everywhere in England revolved around the baron and his castle, all of whom employed mercenary forces, as well as sergeants and serfs to administer the lands. In feudal England, the power of a baron became inexorably connected with his castle. As such, castles, and their misuse, dictated the ebb and flow of this nineteen-year civil war. Empowered by the construction of 'adulterine' castles – those built without royal permission – be it of wood or stone, the minor lord flourished.

Building on their original purposes as military vehicles following William's landing in 1066, it is no surprise castles developed a reputation as settings of rebellion or oppressors of the people. Nor would this change in a hurry. As the twelfth century gave way to the thirteenth and fourteenth, sites that had begun life as Dark Ages mounds had developed into something far grander. For monarchs like John and Henry III, the fortifications founded by their forebears provided effective forms of defence, yet with plenty of room for improvement. For their descendants, such as Edward I and Edward III, their importance as vehicles of conquest intensified. Only when the long years of domestic and foreign conflict slowly gave way to relative stability, made possible by the development of law and order, did the fortified residence give way to the country estate; the crenulations gave way to the gardened courtyard. What had started life as an instrument of protection had become soft – spoiled by great exposure to wealth and exuberance.

How far the castle had come.

True to the evolution of the castle in England, many of the structures included in this book were involved in the transition. Many started life as Iron Age hill forts or Roman temples or villas. Others as Saxon burhs. In many cases, it was on the site of these former forts and burhs that the Normans put down motte and baileys. Some of the castles were listed in the *Domesday Book*; some were not. The fortresses that survived into the twelfth century or whose origins date to that period saw years of sustained development at the hands of stonemasons. Those that weren't have largely disappeared from history; their foundations rotted away or burned to ash. Due to the lack of information that survives from this period, the stories of few are known today. Indeed, the Pipe Rolls, which owe their origin to the reign of Henry I, has only one survivor from that particular period.

For this reason, most of the castles included are stone ruins and owe at least some part of their existence to the Norman or Plantagenet eras. Some started life as royal castles; others baronial. In many cases, the site has witnessed the construction of two if not multiple castles: what began as a motte and bailey or medieval stone structure now stands as a rebuilt Georgian or Victorian country estate. In the cases of the great ruins, many owe their destruction to siege or slighting – deliberate sabotage to render it useless – either during or after the English Civil War. Though their interiors have long been deserted, many performed a valuable military service and offered protection for their community until their walls became irreparable. In such cases, the story is a familiar one: all was well until the castle's all-time nemeses – gunpowder and cannonballs.

As the following pages will show, similar though many of England's mighty fortresses may be in appearance, the stories of no two are ever exactly alike. In some cases, a castle conceived out of the need to perform a valuable military duty became redundant when its community moved on. In others, the community was wiped out by the fortress's inability to protect them. In some instances, the buildings thrived on their ability to adapt. In others, the trail ends. Regardless of how they met their end – if indeed their end has been met – their impact on English history should not be forgotten.

In the following pages they tell their story.

Chapter 1

The Isles of Scilly, Cornwall and Devon

Lyonesse

Charles Dickens wrote that he knew of no experience comparable to watching the sunset over Land's End. Should the great novelist have looked out to sea from there at the end of a calm summer's day, he might well have been rewarded with the sight of a burning ball of golden yellow, glistening off an endless stretch of calm blue, beyond which the mystery of creation awaited discovery. On certain days, a ghostly mist crosses the headland: a phenomenon that appears all the more portentous when mixed with the noise of a strong tide lapping against the rocky shoreline or the dreary calling of a foghorn resonating through the haze.

There is an old legend that before the Norman Invasion, a great landmass existed beyond the tip of Land's End and stretched out far across the Celtic Sea. Most accounts place its destruction between the midtenth and eleventh centuries, yet the exact date has become the subject of intense conjecture. Other reports from the Middle Ages claim this mysterious land veered south and joined with the equally legendary city of Ys that reputedly existed off the north coast of Brittany. It is generally accepted that the origin of the legend is no later than Celtic times.

Of all the lost lands said to have sunk beneath the waves, evidence for this particular landmass is at least interesting enough to consider. Not only do vague accounts appear in various Saxon writings, but early literature also includes a partial list of its kings, which has since become inextricably intertwined with Arthurian legend. It was written that the lost land, usually known as Lyonesse, was a fabled country made up of beautiful towns and buildings, among which the bells of 140 ancient churches tolled. Scant evidence for the claim is supported by the remains of a fossilised forest visible at low tide. Timeless reports also speak of

Cornish fishermen dredging up ancient masonry or glass among their wares. To this day, stories also abound that the ghostly tolling of those long lost bells continues to be heard, seemingly originating from beneath the waves.

Thanks to Alfred Lord Tennyson, Lyonesse's home in Arthurian lore has long been settled. His epic work *Idylls of the King* pinpointed Lyonesse as the location of Arthur's fateful Battle of Camlann, in which he succumbs to wounds inflicted by nemesis Mordred. The same landmass has also become famed as the birthplace of Tristan, whose love affair with Iseult was destined for tragedy. Tristan was himself a knight of the round table, and his father a king of Lyonesse.

Such stories are just two of many that connect Lyonesse to the Cornish mainland. Located near Fowey, the Tristan Stone is said to mark his grave. Though unlikely to be factual, the stone possesses a strange aura: the type somehow typical of Cornwall in general. The coat of arms of the Trevelyan family also celebrates the tale that their forebear was the lost land's one survivor after being galloped to safety by his trusty white steed.

In recent times, stories of Lyonesse have generated new interest. In 1998, researchers from the Institute of Metahistory in Moscow claimed that the lost continent of Atlantis had at last been located, approximately 100 miles into the Atlantic, on the edge of the Celtic Shelf. Consideration has also been made that this could fit the description for Lyonesse, albeit far further away from the tip of Land's End as it had appeared in the earliest legend. Indeed, potentially more in keeping with Plato's descriptions of Atlantis.

Should a kernel of truth exist in the old legends, a prime contender is the Isles of Scilly. The possibility that this small archipelago of over 100 islands and islets, located 28 miles from Land's End, really are the mountaintops of land that disappeared beneath the waves is doubtful. Nevertheless, for more than 1,000 years, a combination of rumour and old documentary evidence has spoken of the Isles of Scilly as a single landmass.

At the time of the Roman occupation of Britain, sources told of the Scillonia Insula, which implies a more substantial landmass than mere islands. Similarly, the Greeks spoke of the Cassiterides – Tin Islands. So important was the location to them and the seamen of Gades – modern-day Cádiz in Spain – and their trading with the Phoenicians that the site of the Cassiterides was a closely guarded secret. The reference is curious. Tin mining is practically unheard of there in the modern day. Contrastingly, the process was highly lucrative in Cornwall. Tradition named the most extensive island Ennor, which had a large settlement and at least one port.

Reference to one land mass also compares with accounts left behind by the Vikings. In the tenth century, a combination of Norse oral tradition and later writings spoke of farming communities, large monasteries – or at least some form of religious foundations – and several town-like communities, raids of which yielded the theft of several cattle. Sadly it can no longer be claimed with certainty that any of these accounts concerned a single landmass, nor one separate from mainland England.

Though evidence of petrified wood and the historical veracity that some ports have indeed fallen into the sea does potentially offer credence, the story of Trevelyan has a certain Noah and the Great Flood feel about it. Similarly, the idea that God smote the wicked with a single stroke compares well with the tales of Sodom and Gomorrah and Atlantis. Of perhaps even greater intrigue is suggestion in Arthurian literature that the land was mostly underwater, akin to the Low Countries, and effectively plugged using dams and tidal barriers. In one version of the Arthurian tradition, Mordred's deputy, Maelgwyn, occupied Lyonesse for several months after the Battle of Camlann and ordered its opening in about 538 AD. Until further evidence comes to light, the story of Lyonesse, though fascinating, must be considered more myth than history.

The Isles of Scilly

As marine traffic developed, defence of the inhabited islands from hostile raids became more pressing. The first of the Isles's castles were built on the largest island of St Mary's and named Ennor in honour of the single island spoken of in Saxon texts. Available evidence suggests it probably consisted of little more than a shell keep and a walled courtyard. The earliest reference is found in a deed from 1244.

In 1306, Edward I appointed Sir Ranulph de Blanchminster constable in return for an annual rent of 6s 8d or 300 puffins. The Isles were a natural habitat of the creature: technically a fish, thus rendering it edible during Lent. By 1337, the islands and its assets formed part of the Duchy of Cornwall. After garrisoning some 150 men at arms during Tudor times, its influence and prosperity waned under Elizabeth I and was soon in disrepair. Before this time, led by the government of Edward VI and under the watchful eye of Sir Thomas Godolphin, work began on a castle on the second-largest island of Tresco, itself reputedly a haunt of mermaids and mysterious cave passages that link it to St Mary's. Due to its poor positioning on the west side of the island, the defensive capabilities of what was then named Castle Down were severely limited. It was later renamed King Charles's Castle.

A new castle was built on St Mary's, named the Star Castle in honour of its unique eight-pointed shape. When Tresco and its neighbouring island, Bryher, fell to Admiral Blake's Parliamentarians during the Civil War, the Royalists were forced to surrender St Mary's too. A second castle was built on Tresco in 1652, known as Cromwell's Castle. After operating as a prison under the Commonwealth and Charles II, from 1669, the Star Castle hosted a garrison of 200. It later became the Governor's mansion before opening its doors as a hotel in 1933 in a ceremony involving the then duke of Cornwall, later Edward VIII. The hotel remains open to guests and offers some of the best views of the locality. Ennor Castle's stone keep also survives in part, while nearby earthworks provide a reminder of its use in the Civil War. The gunpowder-battered remains of King Charles's Castle have been reassembled. Close by, Cromwell's Castle still stands guard over Tresco harbour, three centuries after helping to ensure the Isles never fell to the Dutch.

A small side note to their existence is that during the latter days of the English Civil War, Admiral Maarten Tromp's Dutch navy found themselves at war with the Royalists. In league with the Parliamentarians, the Dutch navy was blighted by Royalist raids at sea. So precarious was the Royalist position by this time, its navy had retreated to the Isles, their one remaining stronghold. After initial talks came to little, Tromp declared war on the Isles on 30 May 1651. Due to the Isles's enforced surrender to the Parliamentarians in 1651, the war came to little and would have been instantly forgotten had all concerned remembered to sign a peace treaty. This mishap was finally remedied in April 1986 after the Dutch ambassador flew over for talks. Thus ended one of the longest wars in history: officially lasting 335 years and suffering not a single shot or fatality.

Pengersick

Located close to Land's End, the ruins of Pengersick are easily among England's most picturesque. Contrary to its name, which means 'head of a marshy place', the castle is a magical place over which a strange atmosphere often hangs.

The original site probably dates back to the Bronze Age. Excavations have confirmed the presence of earthworks predating the Norman Conquest. A more tangible mark survives from the twelfth century, at which time the Pengersick family constructed the original Norman castle in stone to defend Mount's Bay from sea raiders. Three centuries later, a combination of fruitful marriage and the spoils of a Portuguese vessel, the *San Antonio*, enriched the future owner and later governor of St Michael's Mount, John (Job) Militon, who used the extra wealth to expand the castle. In 1899, the Devonshire Reverend Sabine Baring-Gould wrote of Militon's father of the same name:

> near Germoe, but nearer the sea is a very fine remnant of a castle, Pengersick. It was erected in the time of Henry VIII by a man named Millaton ... He had committed murder and to escape justice he fled his native country and hid himself in the dip of land facing the sea at Pengersick, where he constructed at tower amply protected with means of defence. The basement is furnished with loops for firing upon anyone approaching, and above the door is a shoot for melted lead. The entire building is beautifully constructed. Here Millaton remained in concealment until he died, never leaving his tower for more than a brief stroll. The land had not been purchased in his own name, but in that of his son.

That the older John Militon had a reputation for murder before he constructed the castle is plausible, albeit again, there is no clear proof of this. Evidence that he stuck to the castle appears supported. This may also be behind the rumour that his ghost haunts the modern house. Most of what survives dates from the sixteenth century, when a fortified manor house was built more in line with the standards of Tudor living. Writing in 1814, the English antiquarian and engraver, Samuel Lysons, composed of the site:

There are considerable remains of an ancient castellated mansion on this estate, called Pendersick Castle, the principal rooms in which are made use of as granaries and hay-lofts; one of them, which is nearly entire, is wainscoted in panels; the upper part of the wainscot is ornamented with paintings, each of which is accompanied with appropriate verses and proverbs in text hand.

Few places compare with Pengersick concerning the number of legends. Indeed, the castle has a reputation as one of the most haunted castles in England. Prevalent among the old yarns are those that surround the original twelfth-century owner, Henry Pengersick. Henry appears by all accounts to have been possessed of a violent temperament; he may even have been psychopathic. Local legend also states he participated in Devil Worship. Indeed, the castle is reputedly the setting of both Satanism and witchcraft. One of the estate's more famous legends concerns his killing of a monk of Hailes Abbey, who presented himself at the castle to collect tithes. The murdered monk is synonymous with the hooded spectre alleged to haunt the grounds. Finding proof of the murder, however, has been difficult. Better evidence surrounds his assault of the diligent brother. A similar report concerns a local vicar.

Henry's hand is also alleged to have been involved in another life cut short: that of his beautiful wife, Engrina Godolphin, whose family were wealthy magnates. Henry is known to have been violent to Engrina, who reputedly haunts the modern tower house's main bedroom. How she died is a mystery, though there is some evidence that her tale may have merged with another of the castle's darker stories. A ghostly woman has been seen clutching her stomach in agony. Often the apparition of a maid or nurse accompanies her. How the ghost of this thirteenth-century lady haunts the more modern sixteenth-century fortified house seems mysterious in its own right without proving the existence of ghosts. Yet, an interesting solution has been put forward based on the knowledge that the modern castle was built using the same stones as the original. Proponents of the 'stone tape theory', that events of some importance become deeply entrenched into the local ether due to the physical properties, have long advocated this as the reason for the hauntings.

Another candidate for the strange haunting concerns the castle in its present form. More specifically, Job Militon's son, William. Stories of a ghostly woman may also lend to the story that William sought to poison his wife. Baring-Gould again picks up this fascinating account:

> According to local legend, William Millaton lived a cat and dog life with his wife Honor. They hated each other with a deadly hate and at length each severally resolved this incompatible union must end. William Millaton said to his wife, 'Honor, we have lived in wretchedness too long. Let us resolve in a reconciliation, forget the past, and begin a new life.'
>
> 'Most certainly do I agree,' she said.
>
> 'And,' continued William, 'as a pledge of our reunion, let us have a feast tonight.'
>
> So a banquet was spread in Pengersick Castle for them twain and none others. And when they had well eaten, William said,
>
> 'Let us drink to our reunion.'
>
> 'I will drink if you will drink,' she said.
>
> Then he drained his glass, and after that, she drained hers. With a bitter laugh she said, 'William, you have but three minutes to live. Your cup was poisoned.'
>
> 'And you,' he retorted, 'have but five, for yours was poisoned also.'
>
> 'It is well,' said Honor. 'I am content. I shall have two minutes in which to triumph over your dead carcass, and spurn it with my foot.'

Highly plausible it is that the marriage was an unhappy one, a brief check of the records is enough to confirm this story as false. Rather than dying within minutes of one another, Honor survived her husband's death in 1571 by a further eight years.

That the reputed ghosts of a black cat and dog are intended as symbolic of this unhappy union is another intriguing suggestion. The Black Shuck is a famous one in England's south-west. Another possibility is that this infamous stretch of coast that became the domain of smugglers in the eighteenth and nineteenth centuries saw the Shuck's creation as a cover.

The spirit of a teenage girl is alleged to haunt the battlements, tempting others over. A mischievous boy also pulls at women's skirts. Encasing the strange stories of suspected murder and tragedy is the sudden appearance of ghostly mists that cloak the ancient stones in obscurity.

St Michael's Mount

Few places in Cornwall epitomise the magic of this beautiful county better than St Michael's Mount. Located just south of the mainland at the heart of Mount's Bay between Marazion and Penzance, the mount is a tidal island accessible via boat travel or a causeway at low tide.

Like much of England's south-western tip, legends abound. Synonymous with the tale of Lyonesse, a large forest once spread along the coast around the mount: it is here the fossilised remains can still be seen at low tide. Prior to its modern naming, locals dubbed the mount 'Carreg luz en kuz', meaning, 'the white rock in the wood'. The origins of the mount itself are even more mysterious. The early stories centre around a giant named Cormoran, who chose the peak to keep watch over his neighbours. The giant had a preference for the white granite rocks that could be found in the surrounding hills, much to the displeasure of his wife, Cornellian, who collected greenstones in her apron. Legend tells that Cornellian's perceived laziness irked her husband, leading to his kicking her in frustration, causing one of the stones to fly up and onto the sand. Chapel Rock still occupies a spot on the beach and is cited as the stone in question.

For many years, the giant plagued the locals by rustling sheep and cattle from the mainland. One morning a young boy rowed out to the mount when the giant was asleep and sought to end his reign of terror by digging a deep hole, which he disguised with twigs and straw. When the giant awoke, he unwittingly fell into the well-laid trap, after which Jack-the-giant-killer returned home a hero. Despite the clear mythology at play, an ancient well is still visible at the present site and is celebrated as the spot into which the giant fell.

Prehistoric myths are not the only tales to have graced this isolated spot. The name itself owes its origins to a legend involving St Michael the Archangel and his visitation to a group of local fishermen in the days of early Christianity. Writing his revered 'Lycidas', the famous poet John Milton also played on local lore that St Michael sat atop a stone seat at the mount's summit. During the fifth century, St Keyne, a daughter of the Welsh king, Brychan of Brycheiniog, made a pilgrimage to the mount. The nearby well of St Keyne marks the place where she settled.

A monastery is believed to have existed on the mount from the eighth century until the early eleventh. In honour of St Michael, Edward the Confessor founded the chapel in 1044 and granted it to the Benedictine order. The chronicler John of Worcester recorded that on 3 November 1099, the mount suffered from an overflowing sea, drowning many people and animals. The *Anglo-Saxon Chronicle* states of an identical tragedy, dated 11 November, that 'the sea-flood sprung up to such a height, and did so much harm, as no man remembered that it ever did before'. It is likely the forest's fossilisation and the legend of Lyonesse both connect with this event.

Thanks in large part to the juxtaposition of the castle and priory, the mount has enjoyed a colourful history. By no means an obvious military citadel, the site has nevertheless proved an effective guard of the harbour. Bernard le Bec, also abbot of Mont-Saint-Michel in Normandy, founded the medieval priory in 1135. Though much of the present site dates from the fourteenth century, due to the circumstances of its foundation, the island has long been regarded as the Norman abbey's counterpart and shares many attributes, physically and spiritually.

During Richard I's captivity in 1193, Sir Henry de la Pomeroy, a supporter of John, took the mount, craftily feigning entry Trojan-horse-style by disguising his men as pilgrims. The priory was surrendered on the Lionheart's release, and the disgraced Henry committed suicide – see also Berry Pomeroy. The priory maintained its links to the French monastery until around 1423, when control passed to Sion Abbey of Twickenham. In 1473, when the Wars of the Roses were at something of a cooling point, the Lancastrian earl of Oxford, John de Vere, entered the mount by repeating Pomeroy's method. Furious at Oxford's audacity, the king ordered the castle be retaken. Twenty-three weeks of toil by some 6,000 men followed before Oxford was defeated and exiled. In September 1497, when the Rose Wars were over, Lady Catherine Gordon – wife of the pretender, Perkin Warbeck – stayed there while her husband marched on Exeter. She was subsequently taken prisoner following his defeat.

Like most pilgrimage sites in the British Isles, the mount's importance declined with the Dissolution of the Monasteries. One of the few notable events to occur in the century that followed was the lighting of a beacon to warn of the coming of the Spanish Armada in 1588. The mount was sold to Parliamentarian Colonel John St Aubyn in 1659 and remains the seat of his descendants.

Being a site of such importance and associated with so many legends, it is no surprise it is also reputedly haunted. Among the most peculiar phantoms is a tall man who reputedly stalks the priory church. Renovations in the nineteenth century revealed a small dungeon below the church in which the skeleton of a man over 7 feet tall was found. Exactly who this gentleman was is unknown. That he offers a point of origin for the giant is unlikely, albeit plausible.

Tintagel

Of all the castles mentioned in this book, very few compare with the magic of Tintagel. With every footstep, one runs the risk to get lost among reality and legend.

On both visits made in recent years, I can honestly say I loved every second. Though the village has become overly commercialised with new-age trinkets, the area's natural aura remains undiminished. Without question, there is a vibe about this particular stretch of coastline that is difficult to explain without witnessing it personally. It is not an injustice to say, Tintagel ranks not only among my favourite castles in England but also one of my favourite places on the planet.

Perhaps unsurprisingly, the vast majority of the tourist trade surrounds its connection with the 'once and future king'. No place in Britain, with the possible exception of Glastonbury, has formed a deeper attachment to the legends of King Arthur. Exactly how this happened is a story worthy of further investigation. Though parts of the tale are relatively modern, their origins go back to the twelfth century.

The originator, somewhat bizarrely, was not a local, but a Welshman. Writing his *The History of the Kings of Britain* around 1136, Geoffrey of Monmouth was the first chronicler of the Norman age to write of Arthur. Indeed, no other narrator has played such a role in the legend's development. Of intrinsic importance was his claim that Arthur was conceived at Tintagel: the unholy culmination of a deceitful union between Arthur's father, Uther Pendragon, and Igraine, wife of Gorlois, Duke of Cornwall. Among Geoffrey's conjecture was how Uther entered a conspiracy with Merlin, who used his magic to alter Uther's appearance to match that of Gorlois. Unsuspecting that the man Igraine made love to was not her husband, Arthur was conceived, and destiny fulfilled.

That the modern traditions are deeply intertwined with the circumstances surrounding Arthur's birth is perhaps unsurprising. Below the present-day ruins lies an impressive sea cave that runs through to the other side. From no later than the Victorian era – more specifically the work of Tennyson – this tidal inlet has been known locally as 'Merlin's Cave'. It has often been claimed that those who enter the cold desolate basin at low tide are in danger of being overcome by feelings of oppression. Ironically, this author found the opposite to be true. Had it not been for the tide coming in, I would have happily spent the night there. Again, perhaps unsurprisingly, the cave has developed a reputation for being haunted. In the Arthurian legends, Merlin frequented the cave while Uther performed his deceitful deed in the castle above.

That a historical Arthur or Merlin possessed any genuine connection to the castle is doubtful. Though evidence that both existed, at least as more simplified Anglo-Roman leaders, has some credence, none of the Tintagel links predate Geoffrey's chronicle. Claims that some form of Roman presence existed here are supported by tangible evidence. In 1998 the foundation stone of a much earlier fortress was uncovered close to Tintagel Castle. Inscribed in Latin, the term has been translated 'Artognou father of a descendant of Col has made this'.

Whether this mysterious inscription should be considered proof of the existence of the legendary king or a startling coincidence remains unclear. Tintagel may have been occupied, or at least visited, by the Romano Brits but the evidence isn't conclusive. That Dark Age Celtic kings of Dumnonia held court there, slightly more evidence exists. More non-English fifth and sixth-century pottery has been found at Tintagel than the rest of the country put together. The evidence that has survived confirms Tintagel was important for trade well before the present castle was built. Close by, the beautiful St Nectan's Glen conceals a waterfall that cascades into the rock basin below. So beautiful and serene was the site, the fifth-century Saint Nectan created a hermitage there. Legend says that he threw a silver bell into the bedrock on his deathbed, declaring it would only reappear when the true religion was restored.

Of what survives of the castle, the evidence is easier to gauge. Second son of King John and younger brother of prolific builder Henry III, Richard, Earl of Cornwall, acquired Tintagel around 1225 on being granted the earldom. Less than eight years passed before construction of the new fortress was underway. In stark contrast to the design of most post-Conquest citadels, Tintagel never possessed a keep and was instead laid out with long halls. The castle is also unique as it is set out in two distinct parts: one, located on the mainland; the other, on a small isthmus that juts out into the sea. Despite its coastal position, the castle has little defensive value: a move probably used by Richard to curry favour with his Cornish subjects.

By 1337, Tintagel formed part of the duchy of Cornwall, the first recipient of which was the 7-year-old Edward of Woodstock, later the Black Prince. Edward was influential in adding other halls to replace parts, including one section of the great hall, that had fallen into the sea. The castle was already in decline by then, and by comparison, the rebuilds were modest. The one exception was on the orders of Edward's son, Richard II, who feared a French attack. In later years, the castle was used as a prison, and by the Tudor age had become increasingly decrepit.

Although only parts have survived of the sea-battered thirteenth-century structure, the castle remains shrouded in mystery. People passing by the ruins at night have often talked of experiencing feelings of dread and foreboding. In keeping with the myth of Lyonesse, the eerie sounds of muffled bells have apparently been heard coming from the water. According to local legend, once a year, the slender remains are replaced by the inexplicable appearance of the magnificent fortress that supposedly once existed.

That a fortress mightier than the one that survives now, its ancient vestiges clinging like ivy to the cliff edges, ever existed sadly belongs solely to myth. As time has passed, the area has become what a sponge is to liquid. Even in its early days, Richard, Earl of Cornwall took a serious interest in the legend of Lyonesse. Indeed, a square walled garden was established on the isthmus in honour of Tristan and Iseult, close to where the modern statue of Arthur now stands. In the Victorian era, Tennyson famously added his own contributions, while Charles Dickens and William Makepeace Thackeray also saw Tintagel as worthy of inclusion. As the influence of the great writers promoted interest in the site, the village itself capitalised. For centuries the local hamlet carried the name Trevena. Only around 1900 did it change its name to Tintagel.

Though the present ruins have no connection with a historical King Arthur, this should not detract from this beautiful spot's magical atmosphere. While the closest one will get to Arthur and his knights is the popular tourist site 'King Arthur's Great Halls', Tintagel is well worthy of recognition and a place most deserving to be the home of King Arthur and his knights of the round table.

Berry Pomeroy

Situated on a craggy outcrop overlooking the Gatcombe Brooke, a crumbling shell is all that survives of what some regard as one of the most sinister places on earth.

If appearances alone are anything to go by, the reasons for such a reputation are self-explanatory. On first viewing, the depleted ruins of Berry Pomeroy Castle present every dark, evocative image necessary for a cult horror film, albeit a natural phenomenon created by a broad array of beech trees that cast deep shadows and starve the area of light. Even on sunny days, the lush valley fed by abundant rain and moist warm air provides an imposing covering to the charred remains of an enigmatic fortress damaged by fire, war and exposure to the elements.

Two families are known to have occupied the castle. The first were the Pomeroys after William the Conqueror presented the land to Ralph de la Pomeroy shortly after the Norman invasion. The family occupied the area for several centuries and eventually cemented their status with a Norman-style castle. The castle's exact age has long been a matter of discussion. A record in the *Domesday Book* confirms William granted the de la Pomeroys the feudal barony of Berry Pomeroy before 1086. In 1207, a deer park was also enclosed.

Though a manor almost certainly existed nearby, much of the castle dates from the fifteenth century, which tallies with the first written reference from 1496. After serving as the baronial seat of the family for over 200 years, the castle was sold to Edward VI's Lord Protector Sir Edward Seymour, 1st Duke of Somerset, famously brother of Henry VIII's unfortunate third queen, Jane. During Edward's reign, Seymour lavished £20,000 on a fine Tudor home within the old walls.

This blend of Norman and Tudor architecture is rare and can only be found in a small number of other castles in England and Wales.

Following Henry VIII's death in 1547, Seymour's lot improved dramatically on being appointed Edward VI's guardian and protector of the realm. Then, somehow inevitably, corruption by power resulted in his downfall. Arrested for treason in 1551, his beheading soon followed. Thanks in part to a lengthy legal battle, Seymour's family regained the castle under Elizabeth I; however, financial limitations forced them to desert it at some point between 1685 and 1694. Local legend tells that a dramatic thunderstorm hit the castle, destroying what was left of the roofs and mullioned windows that were already suffering from years of neglect. The fourth Seymour baronet, Sir Edward, relocated to Wiltshire on his mother's death in 1694.

With this, what was once the stronghold of two powerful families has become little more than a grim shell. In the centuries since, stories have circulated of bizarre happenings within the remains, especially at night. Many experiences are similar: citing shortness of breath and the dreadful belief that they are being watched. The tormented cries, believed to be of a murdered baby, killed in vile circumstances many centuries ago, are claimed to reverberate. Lining the cold walls of the ancient keep, ominous silhouettes also continue to appear, accompanied by strange mists that further shroud the fortress in uncertainty.

That these strange sounds and sightings are mere tall tales concerning a ruined castle in a verdant area seems logical enough. Yet, intriguingly many compare well with what is known of the castle's past. One of the most menacing spirits said to haunt the castle is a horrifying woman in white. The phantom is reputedly Margaret Pomeroy, a resident during the fifteenth century. Margaret was a beautiful woman who met a sad and premature end due to the envious conspiring of her sister, Eleanor. Forever in the shadow of her lovely sister and fearing Margaret's affection for the man she loved, Eleanor imprisoned Margaret in the dungeon. Adding to the torture, the conceited Eleanor would regale her sister with tales of passionate lovemaking.

More than four centuries have passed since the Pomeroys occupied the castle, but the lady in white reputedly still resides among the ruins and has even been known to seek human company. Local legend tells that on certain nights, usually when the moon is full, her terrifying apparition rises from the ruined Margaret's Tower, before drifting up the ramparts to call passers-by to enter her domain. Those who accept her invitation are rewarded, not by tangible worth, but by a fate of madness or death by suicide.

Joining Margaret, the ghost of a lady in blue is also reputed to haunt the ruins. Local legend has long told that she, too, has been known to lure visitors to the location where her life ended in such despair. In common with the latter, the reason for her post-life habitation is the result of a heinous crime. Supposedly the daughter of a Norman lord, the girl was raped by her father and fell pregnant. When the child was born, it was brutally murdered.

Famous though the tale is, the exact circumstances of the butchering are unclear. Whether the girl's father murdered the unfortunate child, or else she was personally responsible, perhaps during a fit of post-natal depression, or her furious mother smothered the poor baby, all seem plausible. Consistent with her awful lot, witnesses describe the blue lady's face as a portrayal of suffering. Legend has it that sightings of this mournful apparition precede a death in the Seymour family. In the nineteenth century, when Sir Walter Farquar was attending to the wife of one of the castle stewards, he apparently witnessed the spirit, shortly after which Seymour's wife died.

According to one of the castle's more colourful legends, the destiny of two Pomeroy brothers was decided one fateful day. Exactly when and why the change of ownership occurred is another matter of uncertainty. In one particular version, Edward VI ordered the seizing of the family's assets after their role in the Prayer Book Rebellion of 1549. While the fortress was under siege, the brothers made the drastic choice to don full battle armour and drive their horses from the castle battlements, falling to their deaths in the deep ravine below, rather than suffer a long drawn out defeat and execution. Known today as 'Pomeroy's leap', the area where the brothers are said to have jumped is thought to be haunted by a vivid reconstruction of their drastic action. Screams and thuds have also been heard in the vicinity of the 'leap'. Another story tells that, before this, they hid the family treasure. That either event ever occurred remains unverified. The Prayer Book Rebellion post-dates Seymour's purchase of the castle. If there is any truth in the tale, it is far more likely to concern the apparent suicide of Sir Henry de la Pomeroy during the reign of

Richard I – see St Michael's Mount. Tradition also states that Henry poisoned himself.

In addition to those already mentioned, other inexplicable happenings are also reputed to have left visitors uneasy. Mysterious lights have been witnessed. Voices have also been heard in areas that appeared to be deserted. Isolated cold spots, the slamming of doors and inexplicable gusts of wind continue to elude rational explanation. A lady in grey is also said to appear from time to time, accompanied by the occasional visitation of a Cavalier soldier. Far more harmlessly, the spirit of a playful black dog has been seen running through the ruins and into the woodland. Incidentally, many visitors complain that their dogs refuse to pass beyond specific points.

Precisely what occurred at Berry Pomeroy remains challenging to determine. Similarly, why these spirits continue to haunt the castle is unclear. Yet, as far as many locals and believers in the paranormal are concerned, so long as the ghosts of the castle's past continue to reminisce the dark days, God's wrath at Berry Pomeroy will remain unabated.

Lydford

Seven miles north of Tavistock, the village of Lydford has changed much over the centuries. Once a town of some local economic importance, the modern dwelling is peaceful by comparison.

Established as one of the four Saxon burhs of Devon by Alfred the Great, the town had its own mint in the reign of Æthelred the Unready and by the coronation of Edward the Confessor was arguably the most important settlement in the county after Exeter. Yet, come the compiling of the *Domesday Book*, Lydford's importance had diminished. No less than forty houses were destroyed following the Norman Conquest. It is a measure of its lost significance that until the following century, those from across Dartmoor were buried at the parish church of St Petrock, whose origins, it would appear, are seventh century. The path used to mark the deceased's final journey is locally known as the 'lych way' and is said to be haunted by a procession of monks in white habits.

Close to the village, the beautiful Lydford Gorge has transfixed locals and passersby for centuries. Of its many waterfalls, the largest has endearingly been christened 'the white lady', while a series of whirlpools are known as the 'Devil's Cauldron'. A more personal name concerns a far smaller waterfall, that of 'Kitty's Steps'. There is an old tale that an ageing woman of that name took a shortcut home through the gorge one evening and mysteriously disappeared, despite her familiarity with the area. Several days later, the discovery of her red headscarf offered the first clue to the site of her disappearance. Her ghost is said to return on the anniversary of her death. Her head bowed, eyes on the pool.

The town's significance may have declined after the Norman Conquest, but it was still regarded highly enough to warrant upgraded fortification. One corner of the old burh was used as the foundation of the original castle: a small fort or ringwork more fundamental than a motte and bailey. Like the castle in Exeter, the local revolt of 1068 prompted its formation. By the middle of the following century it was abandoned.

When the second stone castle was founded in 1195, again for law and order purposes, it included a tower and surrounding bailey. Throughout the Middle Ages, it was used as a prison and law court and became an administrative office for the Royal Forest of Dartmoor and the Devon stannaries. Redesigned as a motte and bailey by Richard, Earl of Cornwall, it became the property of the duchy of Cornwall under Edward the Black Prince and was used as a royalist gaol during the Civil War. Though its use as a site for stannary and forest administration continued into the Victorian era, its condition varied and ultimately descended into ruin. Throughout the fourteenth century, the castle also developed a reputation for injustice. It was described during the reign of Henry VIII as 'one of the most heinous, contagious and detestable places within the realm'.

Famed as a location where justice was meted out, it is no surprise that the ghost stories concern this. Most prominent among the hauntings is that of the hanging Judge George Jeffreys. Famous for his role in the 'Bloody Assizes' – a trial concerning hundreds of supporters of the king's nephew and would-be usurper, James Scott, 1st Duke of Monmouth – local tradition states that it was at Lydford that much of his dastardly justice was done. Though Jeffreys's presence among the towns of Devonshire is known, there is no direct proof he was ever at Lydford. It says much about the man's loathed reputation that he is said to appear in the guise of a black pig instead of the smartly attired and periwigged professional who watched over such proceedings in life.

Strangely, the darkened swine is not the only creature linked with the area. Indeed, as opposed to being a ghostly prison for those who suffered its often cruel administration of justice in life, the site seems to be more of an ethereal menagerie. A black hound is said to haunt the ruins – a somewhat ubiquitous apparition in Devon. Even more bizarrely, other claims have been put forward that a ghostly bear haunts the grounds. Unlike the Tower of London, the area has less reputation for holding animals.

Completing Lydford's story is a more traditional spirit: a tall, dark and misty phantom that lurks in the dungeon. Some who have visited the site have spoken of a certain air of oppression, independent of the underground location. To the willing believer, the idea that the spirit of a long-ago prisoner remains bound to his site of incarceration may well be an adequate explanation. Of the man's identity, no clue has yet been found.

Okehampton

Constructed by the Normans between 1068 and 1086 as a motte-and-bailey on the northern border of Dartmoor, Okehampton would develop into the largest castle in Devon. Mentioned in the *Domesday Book*, the castle became the home of the evocative Baldwin de Brionne (FitzGilbert), who served as sheriff of Devon in the late eleventh century. The Courtenay family, future earls of Devon, acquired the site through marriage in 1173 and upgraded it substantially from 1297 onwards.

Throughout the fourteenth century, the timber structure was fortified and enjoyed a relatively uneventful existence. This changed in 1538 when Henry Courtenay, 1st Marquess of Exeter abandoned the family home after being convicted of treason by Henry VIII. Due to his opposition to the Dissolution of the Monasteries, Courtenay was held in the Tower of London and gruesomely executed. Coupled with the confinement in the Tower of his wife, Gertrude, and son, Edward, later first earl of Devon, the castle was abandoned and the stones quarried by locals.

Perhaps unsurprisingly, several centuries of being uninhabited have resulted in this once stunning fortress becoming a desolate yet romantic ruin. Situated on the borders of a wooded valley and overlooking the picturesque River Okement: a vibrant yet isolated area of the Devonshire countryside, the depleted shell developed a reputation as 'picturesque' and featured in the art of J.M.W. Turner and Thomas Girtin. Although Okehampton appears a postcard ruin with a history free of bloodshed, it is said to be plagued by the bizarre antics of a cursed woman. Even more intriguing, the haunting is said to have originated after Okehampton's desertion.

The crux of this unique legend concerns one Lady Mary, daughter of the much-loathed Sir John Fitz. After inheriting a vast fortune aged 21, Fitz, a resident of Fitzford House near Tavistock, lived with his daughter at the family home and wasted much of his wealth before committing suicide after his debts spiralled out of control. With no other family, the 9-year-old Lady Mary inherited what remained of the family fortune and was made a ward by King James I of the earl of Northumberland. She eventually married the earl's brother, Sir Alan Percy.

As fate had it, only a short time passed before her husband passed away, reportedly of a fever. Still a young woman, Lady Mary then became free to follow her heart. Much to the Percy family's dismay, her second choice of husband was one Thomas Darcy. Strangely, Darcy also died shortly afterwards. Widowed for the third time in 1622 following the death of Sir John Howard, she married a fourth, Sir Richard Grenville, in 1628. A victim of cruel mistreatment, she returned to Tavistock after their divorce and peacefully lived out her days.

Although the evidence suggests that her first three husbands died of natural causes – and the fourth ended in divorce – having profited from four separate marriages, rumours began to circulate in Tavistock that the deaths were not without suspicion. Though the authorities never charged the wealthy heiress and widow with any such offence, according to local legend, the spirit of Lady Howard remains doomed to seek penance for her sins. In what must surely rank among the more bizarre stories of a haunting ever recorded, Lady Howard is said to ride off in a ghostly carriage, constructed from the bones of her four husbands, pulled by phantom horses and a headless driver.

Why on earth the phantom of this particular lady appears bound to the depleted ruins of a castle that she never owned is itself the best place to start. True, Lady Mary was of the Courtenay clan, who owned the castle for much of its history, yet this does not account for her own connection.

According to one popular version of events, she does not ride within the carriage, but rather alongside it: not in human form, but the guise of a black dog. Throughout the Dartmoor countryside, the appearances of such creatures have been reported for centuries, terrifying residents out on the moors. But unlike the beasts that haunt the Devonshire moors, this particular large slobbering dog is said to be cursed to deliver a single blade of grass from the castle grounds to her home in Tavistock, at which time her soul shall be at peace. Surrounded by lush greenery, the task for the doomed lady is unlikely to be completed anytime soon. Legend tells that she is bound to make this 30-mile round trip every night, beginning at the stroke of midnight, to the ruins and back to her former home. Once returned, the grass is laid on a large slab of granite alongside what she has assembled over the years. Her home in Tavistock, Fitzford House, was destroyed in the 1800s, though the gatehouse was rebuilt in 1871.

Weird as this may sound, many claim to have witnessed the death coach on its phantom journey and laid testament to the murderous woman's appearance. Accompanied by the rattling of the skeletal framework, an icy chill pervades, similar to the feeling of standing in a butcher's meat locker. The sound of the horses' hooves on the ground reverberates like thunder before the demonic sight appears inexplicably from the darkness: four headless horses, whipped by the violent lashings of the bloodstained whip brought down by the hideous form of a headless driver. Once passed by, the monstrous apparition of a woman, dressed in an ethereal shade of white, deep eye sockets lying empty within a colourless and tortured face, is said to appear from the rear of the coach. Although many possessed of an interest in the paranormal have searched for the honour of seeing the ghostly carriage, it is regarded as an ill omen should the coach stop. For if that happens for someone, or it stops at a place of residence, legend has it that the occupant would be destined to join the lady on the endless journey.

That the ghost of Lady Howard embarks on her eternal torture is, of course, highly unlikely. In reality, the poor woman appears to be the product of both mistaken identity and two stories blended as one. The real Lady Mary Howard was born in 1596 and did indeed marry four times. In life, she enjoyed travel by a magnificent coach with four pineapples located at the corners of the roof. Her first step on the road to fortune came from her father's murder of an innkeeper. In due course, he also passed, either killed or by his own hand. Rumours of foul play most likely stem from her insistence that the relatives of her first husband would not possess any claim to her wealth following her second marriage.

While no evidence has yet come to light that Mary was a murderess, a better case exists against the wretched Frances Howard, once the wife of Robert Devereux, son of the famous second earl of Essex, *ipso facto* third earl on his father's execution in 1601. Repulsed by a series of strange occurrences, including his wife practised necromancy, Essex had the marriage annulled. Following Howard's second marriage to Robert Carr, 1st Earl of Somerset, a favourite of James I, Frances is believed to have conspired with family head, Henry Howard, 1st Earl of Northampton, for the murder of Carr's bosom buddy, Sir Thomas Overbury, who fortune had placed in the Tower. Over the coming months, Overbury's health declined rapidly due to repeated poisonings. When the conspiracy was uncovered, Howard was spared the death penalty due to her timely pregnancy but was initially doomed to share the Bloody Tower with her husband, whom she now hated. A similarly depressing existence followed outside the walls.

Regardless of the truth behind this strange tale, the castle itself is often regarded with apprehension at night. The shadow of the dog is said to continue to haunt the ruins, irrespective of the carriage. The apparition of a white shape has also been seen in an empty void that was once a window.

As for Lady Howard, passers-by on the road at night continue to walk with caution, fearing the offer of a lift from the death carriage that would spare them their walk in the cold. For as long as the grass continues to grow, it seems Lady Howard will forever cast a shadow over the ruins. No better legacy honours the story than this old ballad, whose authorship has been lost in the mists of time.

> My ladye hath a sable coach,
> And horses two and four;
> My ladye hath a black blood-hound
> That runneth on before.
> My ladye's coach hath nodding plumes,
> The driver hath no head;
> My ladye is an ashen white,
> As one that long is dead.

'Now pray step in,' my ladye saith,
'Now pray step in and ride.'
I thank thee, I had rather walk
Than gather by thy side.
The wheels go round without a sound
Or tramp or turn of wheels;
As cloud at night, in pale moonlight,
Along the carriage steals.

I'd rather walk a hundred miles
And run by night and day
Than have the carriage halt for me
And hear the ladye say:
'Now pray step in, and make no din,
Step in with me and ride;
There's room I trow, by me for you,
And all the world beside.'

Tiverton

Built by Richard de Redvers in the first decade of the twelfth century, Tiverton grew to be a mighty fortress under the ownership of the family's successors both in the home and title – the Courtenays.

As recalled in the section on Okehampton, the Courtenays owned significant property in Devon, of which Tiverton was 'head and chief mansion'. On gaining the property around 1293, the family remained there until the last member died in 1556 – ironically one of many prominent Catholic families to perish under Mary I. Of some note, in 1495, William Courtenay married Princess Catherine Plantagenet. As the ninth child of Edward IV and Elizabeth Wydville, Catherine was the youngest sister of the missing 'Princes in the Tower' and Elizabeth of York, queen of Henry VII.

Since the Courtenays' decline, the castle has experienced something of a chequered history. After being passed for a time between William Courtenay's lesser descendants, it became the property of the Giffard Family and was a Royalist stronghold in the Civil War. Besieged by the Parliamentarians, the persistence of General Fairfax was rewarded in

1645 when a lucky shot struck the drawbridge chain. After the war, the ruined fortress was rebuilt as a fine country house by the West family, wealthy wool magnates. In later years, it entered the Carew and Campbell families.

Having endured the highs and lows of English life for more than 900 years, several changes of ownership, conquered yet never destroyed, it is no surprise that the castle's history has given rise to many stories. Among the most bizarre is that of an eighteenth-century bride who wished to entertain herself before her wedding with an epic game of hide and seek. Sadly for all concerned, the clever bride chose her hiding place too well. One can only imagine the bolt of despair that shot through her when the chest in which she had decided to conceal herself locked shut. Extreme though her cries for help must have been, her muffled pleas failed to attract attention. Her skeleton was not discovered until many years later. The validity of the story is open to question, albeit honoured with a placard on the stairs.

Far more famous is the tragic occurrence that surrounded the daughter of one of the governors. In the early seventeenth century, the governor in question was one Sir Hugh Spencer, who desired his daughter Alice to marry one Sir Charles Trevor, a wealthy man many years her senior. Aged just 21 and renowned for her beauty, Alice viewed the match as uninspiring, not least as Trevor was famed for being possessed of a violent disposition.

Complicating proceedings, Alice was also desired by the castle manager, Maurice Fortescue – a lowly man by comparison. According to one account, Trevor was suspicious of Fortescue's intentions and sought to rub his good fortune in the humble manager's face. One fateful day, a jubilant Trevor celebrated his excellent mood by throwing his hat into the air ceremoniously. Unfortunately for all concerned, Fortescue's dog leapt upon the hat and ripped it to pieces. In the chaos that followed, Trevor slew the dog and Fortescue punched him in the face. Furious at this slighting, the older man challenged Fortescue to a swordfight.

Realising a moment of destiny was upon him, Fortescue recognised he had no option but to defend his honour. On informing Alice of his predicament, he declared his love, useless though it may be. On hearing this, the young beauty tearfully told him she had always felt the same way. Embracing her love, she declared that should he fall, her heart would die with him.

When the hour came, Fortescue met Trevor in the local woodland. Their swords drawn, the ancient trees echoed to the sounds of combat. Despite wounding the older man, a sharp jab to the neck killed the young manager, after which Trevor booted his body unceremoniously to the river. Only later did Trevor realise his mistake. As Fortescue's carcass became swept up in the currents, the hysterical Alice plunged herself into the depths after him. Whether she clung to the hope that her love was not beyond resuscitation or she was overcome by emotion and committed suicide is unclear.

Since that time, local tradition tells that whenever the River Exe floods, the duo's ghosts, including the loyal dog, can be seen embarking on a merry saunter through the woods – enjoying the freedom that their spirits were denied in life.

Chapter 2

Dorset and Somerset

Corfe Castle

The large village of Corfe Castle has changed little over the centuries. Situated in a peaceful area near the Dorset coast, the survival of many of its original buildings and the surrounding beauty has made the village a firm favourite among holidaymakers. Even at the height of the tourist seasons, it is difficult to imagine that such a pleasant setting once witnessed the relentless onslaught of the Roundhead army during the English Civil War.

Protected by the rugged cliffs of the Isle of Purbeck and located on a large hill overlooking the village, the castle after which the village was named remains a formidable sight. One of the first in England to be built in stone, the locally quarried material from Purbeck remains famed for its strength and beauty. At its prime, this mighty citadel of towering turrets, solid walls and long high windows comprised the ideal blend of defence and reconnaissance. For such reasons, this magnificent fortress was one of the most critical Royalist strongholds ever built. None of the devastations that occurred to England's castles was so crucial as the Parliamentarian destruction of Corfe. Now a picturesque ruin, whose leaning walls bear the scars of bombardment and plundering, the castle remains an imposing presence. Legend holds that so long as the castle stands, so too will the village.

Built by William the Conqueror, the castle underwent a series of changes in the reigns of Henry I and John. John's obsession with improving the defences made Corfe his personal favourite. It has long been believed that John stashed the Crown jewels there during the First Barons' War. Throughout its long history, several prisoners were held within the sturdy walls. Indeed, many are known to have died there. Uncovering a logical reason for the oppressive atmosphere some speak of on visiting the dungeon is rarely viewed as problematic in the context of the enormous loss of innocent life sustained here. Nor is it a surprise that Corfe has a reputation as being haunted.

According to ancient tradition, the local area was plagued by murder before the Norman walls were built. While hunting a stag in Purbeck Forest in 978, King Edward the Martyr was killed by his stepmother, Elfrida (Ælfthryth). Legend places his death either at or near the mount on which the eleventh-century castle was built. Postholes once belonging to a Saxon hall can still be found at the site. How Edward met his end is sadly unclear. Some versions of the event refer to his being set upon while dismounting his horse. Of the early sources, the *Anglo-Saxon Chronicle* goes into the most detail: claiming that when he visited his stepmother, the unsuspecting king was stabbed in the back as Elfrida handed him a goblet of wine. Regardless of the exact circumstances, history recalls that on Edward's death, Elfrida's biological son usurped the throne: henceforth Æthelred 'The Unready'.

Though the ghost of the murdered king is, somewhat surprisingly, not among those reputed to haunt the area, since the Saxon days, the spectre of death has rarely been far from Corfe Castle. Around the time of King John's troubles with Ireland 1209–10, the king pursued a vendetta against the prominent Norman magnate William de Braose, leading to the imprisonment of his wife, Maud, and son. After being imprisoned at Windsor, both would see out their wretched days at Corfe, apparently starved to death – see also Windsor Castle. Six years earlier, John had imprisoned the Poitevin lord Savari de Mauléon at Corfe, who escaped by getting his gaolers drunk. Also held were hostages of Margaret and Isabel of Scotland.

During both John's reign and that of his son, Henry III, the castle was the enforced residence of John's niece, Eleanor of Brittany. The reasons for her imprisonment were mostly political: Eleanor herself having possessed a claim to the throne as the daughter of John's late brother, Geoffrey. During Eleanor's time at the castle, twenty-two of her loyalist French men at arms were purposely starved to death as a consequence of their failed escape. Stories have long abounded that their tormented cries remain audible under certain conditions. In 1221, the governor of the castle, Peter de Maulay, a key supporter of John years earlier, was stripped of the castle for his apparent involvement in a plot to free Eleanor. Humiliated and stripped naked before his peers, de Maulay was later cleared and returned to some form of station. In the early years of Edward I, it also served as the prison of Amaury de Montfort, son of the rebellious Simon de Montfort, 6th Earl of Leicester, who died in the Battle of Evesham in August 1265.

Corfe's status as a royal castle remained until 1572 when Elizabeth I sold the fortress to her Lord Chancellor, Sir Christopher Hatton. In 1635, it changed hands again. Its penultimate years of occupation were under the ownership of Chief Justice Sir John Bankes, a staunch Royalist and attorney general to Charles I. When the Civil War broke out, most of Dorset was under Parliamentarian control, rendering Corfe vulnerable. When Bankes departed for Oxford with the king, Corfe briefly operated under the stewardship of his determined wife, Lady Mary, who lived there with their children. After the Roundheads failed to infiltrate the castle during the garrison's participation in a May Day hunt, they were left little choice other than lay siege. After successfully extending her garrison to eighty, Lady Bankes oversaw a six-week defence against some 600 Roundheads before a detachment of Royalist troops finally came to her aid.

Sadly for the stubborn heroine, in 1645 – at which time Parliamentarian control of the area was almost absolute – the collaboration of Royalist Colonel Pitman with Roundhead Colonel Bingham ensured the garrison's betrayal. After convincing Lady Bankes of his ability to bring in reinforcements from Somerset, their arrival revealed them to be Parliamentarians in disguise. When the siege resumed, the garrison faced attack from both outside and within. Rather than suffer execution, Lady Bankes and her troops were granted safe passage. Though the castle's time as a residence was over, fortunately, parliament's decision to slight as opposed to destroying it has ensured its survival in the dramatic fashion seen today.

Shortly after that time, stories began to circulate that the newly ruined fortress was haunted. Apparitions of phantom horses and strange flashes of light to soldiers adorning Civil War uniforms and even those of Roman legionnaires have been reported stalking the vicinity. Claims of a headless apparition in white haunting the grounds have also gathered pace. According to local lore, the spirit belongs to a woman who betrayed the Royalists during the onslaught. How she lost her head remains a mystery. That Lady Bankes haunts the remains has also been mooted. Whether her spirit remains restless and earthbound or not, her tenacity in the face of a formidable enemy is deserving of memory.

Sherborne Old Castle

Visitors to the modern 1,200-acre park will notice that Sherborne Castle does not look like a castle. This fine Tudor mansion, located close to the market town of the same name in the parish of Castleton, was not always known as such. Originally called Sherborne Lodge, tradition holds that a certain Sir Walter Raleigh passed by the site on his way from London to Plymouth and fell in love with it. On leaving the road to explore the area on horseback, it was later recalled that the dashing privateer and explorer fell from his horse and landed in the dirt. On the unfortunate mishap, the antiquarian Sir John Harrington in his *Nugae Antiquae* told that his 'very face, which was then thought a very good face, ploughed up the earth where he fell'. On making his love of the site known, either directly or by subtlety, to Queen Elizabeth, Raleigh got his wish. In January 1592, Elizabeth awarded him a 99-year lease on the property. Raleigh completed the four-storey rectangular lodge two years later.

Why Sir Walter Raleigh fell in love with the area has much to do with the reason this humble lodge is now known as a castle. Located in the grounds of the far grander mansion are the ruins of the same twelfth-century fortress that had first averted Sir Walter's eye. Built by the swashbuckling Bishop of Salisbury, Roger de Caen – also known as Roger of Sarum or Roger le Poer – the castle remained in possession of the bishops up to Raleigh's time. There is an old legend that another former bishop, St Osmund, Earl of Dorset and lord chancellor, placed a curse on the site during the late eleventh century that any non-cleric who took possession of the building would meet their doom. As fate would have it, Raleigh lost his son in 1592 and endured a stint in the Tower for marrying Bess Throckmorton without the queen's permission. It has previously been argued that Raleigh was himself a victim of the curse.

Condemned to a far longer second stint in the Tower for his alleged connection with the Catholic plots against James I, Raleigh was deprived of his beloved Sherborne. Ironically, James granted the estate to his favourite, Robert Carr, who would also later take over Raleigh's lodgings in the Bloody Tower when the latter was off on his final expedition to the new world. On Carr's fall from grace, James sold the estate to John Digby, 1st Earl of Bristol. Ironically the sale coincided with Raleigh's doomed final voyage that preceded his execution.

Though use of the castle in Raleigh's time had largely come to an end, the onset of the Civil War saw it come out of retirement. At the time of the outbreak, the garrison was staunchly Royalist and remained so until its capture by the Roundheads in September 1642. A Royalist revival the following February saw the castle recaptured before siege from the 'hound' General Fairfax in 1645 led to the Royalist garrison's surrender in August. Ruined by a combination of military bombardment and mining, the remains were slighted in October and left to the elements.

Close by, Raleigh's lodge survived far better. Described initially by the antiquarian John Aubrey as 'a delicate Lodge in the park, of Brick, not big, but very convenient for its bignes, a place to retire from the Court in summer time, and to contemplate etc', the Digby family left their mark with the addition of four more wings of similar style to the original.

Though Digby's descendants continue to own the impressive estate, even after 400 years, it is the legend of the gallant privateer who still holds the most sway. Tall tales tell that every Michaelmas Eve – 28 September – Raleigh's headless ghost returns for a merry saunter around the estate where he enjoyed the rural life between 1593 and 1603. Of Raleigh's escapades there, few draw more amusement than one involving the master and one of his servants one sunny day as he smoked without care under a great oak tree. Mistaking the flame of Raleigh's pipe for a fire, the servant rushed towards him with a full pitcher of beer.

One can only imagine Sir Walter's reaction to being doused from head to toe.

Cadbury

Nestled in ancient hillside in the heart of Somerset, the scattered remains of Cadbury Castle hardly give the appearance of a fortress steeped in history. Five miles north-west of Yeovil in an area known as the Somerset Levels, the site that began life as a prehistoric fort is one of the oldest in England. Excavations carried out at the site have confirmed its existence in the Neolithic, Bronze and Iron ages. Connections were also established with the Durotriges: an early Celtic tribe who occupied parts of England before the Roman invasion. It is thought that the Romans, and possibly the Saxons, later used it as a fort and, temporarily, a mint.

Little visual evidence remains of the ancient fortress now. Unlike many Norman conversions, the castle was never rebuilt as a motte and bailey. Though the *Domesday Book* labels it as part of the feudal barony of North Cadbury, the best evidence suggests that the site was at least partially deserted around 1020.

Despite its somewhat bare appearance, there is something genuinely magical about Cadbury. When twilight descends in the spring and summer months, strange shadows cross the hillside: a transfixing sensation, albeit a natural one. As the evening sun retreats ever further behind the horizon, observers will be treated with unrestricted views from the summit: field upon field of unspoilt greenery in all directions the reward for the arduous climb. In the absence of nearby cities, the surrounding towns and villages are unobtrusive by comparison: a clear day will allow views to extend to well-known landmarks like Glastonbury Tor. For one with a vivid imagination, the sights of the ancient landscape deliver the impression of timelessness. A perfect reminder of what the land would have looked like when Neolithic civilisation flourished.

Yet as some locals have long claimed, it is not just the appearance of the land itself from which a sense of timelessness pervades. Indeed, not only is Cadbury one of the oldest hillforts in England but quite possibly the oldest haunted one. On 21 June, the apparitions of ghostly horsemen are reputedly a common appearance near the castle. Due to limited knowledge of 'The Dark Ages', the identity of the castle's former inhabitants is unknown. However, modern tradition connects it to one of the greatest legends in existence.

Of all of England's longstanding mysteries, King Arthur remains one of the most hotly disputed. Tales of a warrior king assisted in his quest to protect the Holy Grail by a brotherhood of loyal knights bonded together by freedom, equality and mutual respect, continue to enthral both old and young, despite historical evidence remaining somewhat inconclusive. Many areas claim some degree of affinity with Arthur. Few, however, predate the Middle Ages.

A particularly prominent hypothesis is that Cadbury is itself the legendary Camelot. Unlike the mystery concerning the identity of the king himself, any suggestion linking Camelot and Cadbury does appear to have an exact point of origin. A clear record of Cadbury's importance lies with the renowned antiquary John Leland, who enjoyed an extensive tour of the country throughout the 1540s. Of his findings, Leland noted: 'At the very south end of the church of South-Cadbryi standeth Camallate, sometime a famous town or castle ... the people can tell nothing there but that they have heard say Arthur much resorted to Camalat.'

The reference is an intriguing one. Sadly, Leland himself concedes the tale is almost solely of local lore. In recent times, renowned author Geoffrey Ashe and historical researcher and author Graham Phillips have accepted the Camelot suggestion. If the legendary king did exist, the best hypothesis places him around 540 AD. Evidence gathered over the last century confirms that Cadbury was in use at the time. Better yet, the earthworks were reinforced with timber and stone. There is no doubt that the fort could have been used as an effective defence against attackers. Should Arthur have indeed been conceived at Tintagel – no record of which predates Geoffrey of Monmouth – it certainly stands to reason that Arthur, as a prince of Dumnonia, could have seen Cadbury as an important stronghold.

Unlikely it may be that the spirits who reputedly haunt the ruins are those of the 'knights of the round table', apparitions of mounted knights are still said to appear there. Carrying lances as the legendary knights are often depicted, their way through the night lit by ghostly torches, the phantom horsemen ride from the castle to a spring near Holy Trinity Church, Sutton Montis, where they water their horses. Local legend tells that the knights rise from their graves in a cave under one of the nearby hills, guarded by an iron gate that opens for one night every seven years.

Perhaps unsurprisingly, the ghostly horsemen aren't the only Arthurian legend associated with the castle. A nearby dusty track is mostly unused in the modern day. Local tradition tells that the track was once known as King Arthur's Lane and continues to play host to an ethereal hunt. Led by Arthur, the knights are said to gallop on their phantom horses before disappearing without a trace.

Enticing though the stories are, concrete evidence connecting Camelot and Cadbury is non-existent. True it may be that any historical Camelot from the fifth or sixth century would have been no more sophisticated than a hill fort, there is no evidence that the written tradition predates Leland and the reign of Henry VIII. The exact site of the legendary king's grave, alas, remains elusive. Local tradition also tells that the mysterious cave gate that guards the tombs is destined to reopen at such a time when England's need is greatest. In such ways, the legend, one could argue, takes root deep in the longings of every patriotic Englishman. How reassuring would it be to know that in our hour of greatest need, the greatest king of all will be there to save us?

Dunster

Situated atop an ancient tor in the village of the same name, Dunster is one of those rare castles that could have been lifted straight from a European fairy-tale. When viewed from a distance, the imposing rose-shaded towers and magnificent battlements create the alluring illusion of floating among the clouds as they rise above a sea of verdant treetops. For this, the modern tourist must reserve their gratitude for the famous British architect Anthony Salvin: the man responsible for updating many medieval structures in the Victorian era, including the Tower of London. Though some medieval purists will turn up their nose at Salvin's work, the village and county are rightly proud of a site that could easily be regarded as the quintessential English Gothic revival castle. Indeed, one of the most picturesque ever conceived.

Enchanting though the modern walls may appear from the outside, even the briefest peek into Dunster's history is enough to confirm that all is not what it seems. Originally fortified during the Anglo-Saxon period, the tor's earthwork defences enjoyed a significant upgrade following the Norman invasion when William de Mohun constructed a motte and bailey to help pacify Somerset. So feared was de Mohun's son and namesake, not least his love of fire and plunder, he earned himself the inauspicious title 'Scourge of the West'.

Like many castles of the period, a shell keep was constructed around the motte during the reign of Henry I, which helped it survive the nineteen-year winter. After being taken over by the Luttrell family in the late fourteenth century, subsequent owners expanded the castle several times, including constructing an impressive manor house within the lower ward in 1617, which was modernised in the 1680s and 1760s. Fortunately, this new addition avoided destruction during the Civil War, in which the medieval walls were severely battered. On Salvin's arrival in the 1860s, endeavours to remodel the castle began in earnest. As a consequence, little remains of the medieval castle, which the National Trust now owns.

It should not be viewed as any great shock that the castle has become famous for its selection of legends, mysteries and a reputation for paranormal activity. Chief among the castle's alleged hauntings is the strange clicking sound that is said to reverberate on a full moon. Intriguingly, the second William de Mohun, owner of Dunster during the Anarchy, set up a mint at the castle, which is said to be the haunting's origin.

The castle is also reputedly the haunt of a lady in grey. Local legend tells that she was a serving girl who her masters sorrowfully abused. Joining her is a footman in Jacobean clothing, a Royalist soldier and a man in green who appears near the stables. A ghostly Roundhead has also been seen in the medieval gatehouse. Intriguingly, during the early-1700s, the remains of a chained-up, seven-foot-tall skeleton were found in an oubliette in the right-hand tower.

Of all the spectres said to haunt the castle, it is perhaps those of a Civil War pedigree whose stories intrigue the most. Though the Luttrells were initially possessed of Parliamentarian sympathies, in 1643, Thomas Luttrell changed sides after giving in to Royalist pressure. Further to being held by a Cavalier garrison, the future Charles II stayed at the castle in May 1645. The possibility that a captured Roundhead was left to rot cannot be ruled out.

Regardless of the unfortunate prisoner's exact identity, a fitting epilogue to the castle's long military history comes with the antics of the governor's spirited mother. After keeping the Roundheads at bay for 160 days, the enemy commander, Colonel Blake, threatened the Royalist Colonel Wyndham that he would place the man's mother in the line of fire unless he surrendered. True to her resilient nature, Mrs Wyndham urged her son to ignore the threat and stand firm. In April 1646, at which point the Royalist cause was lost, Wyndham finally stood down. Tradition tells that on nights when the air is heavy, the courageous mother wanders the corridors, keeping watch over a castle she was so determined to protect.

Farleigh Hungerford

In the village of the same name in the glorious Mendip district of Somerset, the ruins of Farleigh Hungerford serve as a tangible reminder of the lost glory of a once-powerful family. After finding fame as the steward to the wealthy John of Gaunt, third son of Edward III and first duke of Lancaster, Sir Thomas Hungerford reached the pinnacle of an impressive career by being appointed Speaker of the House of Commons in the so-called 'bad parliament' of 1377. Though he was by no means the first to hold the position, he was seemingly the first to be officially recorded by name.

Aided by Gaunt's influence and his developing wealth, Hungerford purchased the manor of Farleigh Montfort in 1369, later named Farleigh Hungerford in his honour. After beginning the inner court in 1377, the ambitious knight found himself in trouble for crenellating without a licence. Pardoned in 1383, he passed on an already impressive fortress to his son, Sir Walter, who in turn extended the castle with an additional court after making his fortune in the Hundred Years' War. As a reward for his exploits, not least his performance alongside King Hal at Agincourt, Henry VI created him Baron Hungerford in 1426.

After Baron Walter died in 1449, the castle enjoyed relative stability up until the Civil War. The one exception was Walter's grandson, Robert, 3rd Baron Hungerford, who was captured by the French in the Hundred Years' War and joined the Lancastrian cause after his mother paid his 7,966-mark ransom. After surrendering the Tower of London with Lord Scales to the Yorkists, he was on the losing side at Towton and was attainted in Edward IV's first parliament of November 1461. His efforts to rally the northern Lancastrians encountered some success before his capture at the Battle of Hexham in May 1464 led to his execution at Newcastle. Ironically, his son, Walter, was on the winning side at Bosworth and was knighted by Henry VII on the field of victory. He was also returned the castle by an act of attainder.

Hungerford control of their beloved fortress continued until the rise of Cromwell. The devout puritanism of the latest owner, Sir Edward Hungerford, great-nephew of the previous magnate who died in 1607, placed him firmly in the Cromwell camp. In 1643, the Royalists took the castle when Sir Edward's half-brother, Colonel John Hungerford, installed a Royalist garrison, which supported itself by regularly plundering the countryside. After successfully withstanding Parliamentarian raids throughout 1644, the Royalist garrison fell in 1645. Due to Colonel John's acceptance of Sir Edward's terms, the castle was spared slighting. On Edward's death in 1648, it passed to another half-brother, Anthony, and later his son, another Sir Edward, in 1657. A notable spendthrift, in 1686, Sir Edward was forced to part with it, and by 1730, the castle had fallen into disrepair. A survivor of the Civil War and the wrath of parliament, it remains an almost unspeakable tragedy that this wonderful castle was partially broken up because of poor financial management.

For any modern visitor, the present-day remains are not without charm. Much of the medieval castle has survived intact – a fact much pleasing to this author who enjoyed countless visits during his youth. A visit to the crypt reveals many strange body-shaped lead coffins, some of which include moulded faces or death masks. Exactly whose they were is a mystery, though it is probable that they were laid down during the flamboyant ownership of Sir Edward. Such coffins were expensive and illustrated the family's wealth and extravagance. Four men, two women and two children are believed to have been embalmed that way: the latter are thought to be mothers who died in childbirth. Somewhat poignantly, the tiny baby-sized coffins have been placed beside them, which visitors can still see behind the grille.

Perhaps unsurprisingly, these coffins are not the only mysterious story associated with the castle. In 1516, Sir Walter's son, Edward, inherited the castle and held it until his death in 1522. The owner's death was of double misfortune for his widow, Lady Agnes, who was subsequently arrested on suspicion of murdering her first husband, John Cotell. Among the accusations against her were strangulation and disposing of his body in the castle kitchen. Found guilty, she was hanged at Tyburn in 1523. Her ghost is reputed to appear close to the chapel.

Similarly awful luck awaited her stepson, another of Farleigh Hungerford's Walters. Married three times, Walter endured a trip to the gallows on being found guilty of trying to poison his final wife. The unravelling of this strange episode began when the lady in question wrote to Henry VIII's chief minister, Thomas Cromwell, complaining that her husband had imprisoned her in a tower for three years and subjected her to poison. Cromwell, with whom Walter was well known, ignored the lady's pleas. However, on Cromwell's fall from grace, Walter's guilt was swiftly confirmed, and Lady Hungerford enjoyed a far happier marriage to Sir Robert Throckmorton, during which she mothered at least four children.

Nunney

Dating from around the same time as Farleigh Hungerford, fourteenth-century Nunney is another of those splendid fortifications that appears like something from a time slip.

Constructed by the adventurous Sir John Delamare – another who made his fortune during the Hundred Years' War – questions over the castle's design has spawned many a debate. Clearly of French influence, something of comparison to nearby Old Wardour, the distant views of its mighty walls looming over the nearby village are enticing. Up close, the epic battlements and towers, surrounded by its picturesque moat in which carp swim freely, possess a nice, picturesque quality. Indeed, as the architectural historian Sir Nikolaus Pevsner observed, Nunney is 'aesthetically the most impressive castle in Somerset'.

Though the castle avoided military action prior to the Civil War, Roundhead cannon fire ensured its downfall. Initially successful in frustrating the Parliamentarians, in 1645, Colonel Richard Prater ran into complications. A committed Catholic, his stance was often at odds with the Protestantism of the villagers. Tradition tells that at least one such local passed on what he knew of the castle's weaknesses to the Roundheads, who subjected it to vigorous cannon fire.

Ever determined to withstand the siege, Prater even hoisted a flag with a crucifix as a sign of his faith. After two days, however, the brave resistance was broken. Though the castle escaped slighting, Prater's family remained deprived of it until the restoration. In 1700, his descendants sold it, and in 1789 the present custodians were ordered to be ready to house prisoners of the French revolution. It is unclear if they ever arrived.

Gutted by war and exposed to the elements, Nunney never regained its former glory. Its walls clad in ivy, ownership continuously changed hands before finally falling into the hands of preservers. Though within the silence of the empty chambers, few stories of paranormal activity have arisen, a bizarre legend has survived concerning the manner of its fall. One of the women who made up the garrison is reputed to have conducted an affair with a Puritan minister. The consequences of this may have betrayed the weak point in the north wall. She was accused of witchcraft on the garrison's surrender and made to suffer trial by ordeal. Tied up and thrown into a nearby stream, her ability to float was seen as proof of damnation. On returning to land, she was burned at the stake in the castle's shadow. Local legend suggests that her restless spirit is forever destined to wander the nearby villages.

Taunton

Taunton is among the oldest castle sites in western England. The *Anglo-Saxon Chronicle* states that a defensive structure was built back in the early eighth century by the Saxon rulers of Wessex. Though confirmation remains elusive that the site was the same as that on which the castle now stands, the evidence suggests it is likely. The chronicle refers to King Ine of Wessex 'timbering him a burgh', which his consort, Æthelburg, destroyed twelve years later in response to its being conquered. A few years later, Queen Frithogyth, wife of Æthelheard, king of Wessex 726–40, is believed to have ordered an ecclesiastical minster or priory on the site, after which the bishops of Wessex constructed a manor house to oversee their vast estates. Archaeological excavations have confirmed both buildings, including the graveyard, did once lie on the site of the present castle.

According to the *Domesday Book*, legal records placed Taunton under the ownership of the bishops of Winchester. An Augustinian priory had superseded the minster by this time, which may well have used some of the older buildings. In 1107, Bishop William Giffard, also lord chancellor to Henry I, began creating the castle with the conversion of the bishop's hall. This was developed around 1138 by Henry of Blois, King Stephen's brother, and successfully defended by his successor as bishop, Peter des Roches, in 1216. Two years earlier, des Roches briefly served as justiciar and regent to King John. He was also a tutor and later advisor to Henry III.

It was probably under the guidance of keen builder des Roches that the castle was reconstructed and extended during the thirteenth century. In 1282, it was used as a prison for the tenacious Amaury de Montfort, son of the late baronial rebel and sixth earl of Leicester, Simon. In 1451 it was besieged by the earl of Devon.

By 1600, a combination of previous military encounters, several centuries of weathering and poor management had left the castle in a state of ruin. A Royalist garrison remedied this during the Civil War until a Parliamentarian onslaught forced them to surrender in 1644. Throughout the following year, the Parliamentarians found themselves defending a Royalist counter manoeuvre, which was eventually relieved following a Roundhead victory at the Battle of Naseby on 14 June 1645.

As to be expected, the ongoing siege did severe damage to the walls. Though it avoided slighting or destruction in the aftermath, in 1662, the keep was demolished. Later that century, it became the location of the assizes court and in 1873 purchased by the Somerset Archaeological and Natural History Society. Visitors can now enjoy the sights of a fascinating museum.

Consistent with many castles of a pre-Norman Conquest pedigree, Taunton comes with its fair share of legends and ghost stories. A man in period dress and wig has reputedly been seen. The same is true of a fair-haired woman and a fiddler named Tom. Yet of all the stories connected with the building, the most alluring must concern the events that plagued Somerset in 1685.

Nephew of the new king, James II, as the bastard son of the late Charles II and his famously licentious mistress, Lucy Walter, James Scott, 1st Duke of Monmouth had his own ambitions to be king. Exiled to the Low Countries on his father's orders in 1679, Monmouth returned to England on 11 June 1685 with a meagre force of some eighty men. From there, the duke swiftly took command of Taunton Castle and was proclaimed king by his followers. Fresh from their exploits in the West Country, the night passed with feasting, singing and merriment. Many girls danced for the royal guest and his soldiers, who enjoyed the companionship and consumption of wine.

As with most ill-considered uprisings, this would be the height of Monmouth's glory. On meeting his enemy at Sedgemoor on 6 July, his forces, swelled to around 4,000, were soundly routed by the king's charges. Upon his capture and arrest, the king dismissed Monmouth's pleas for clemency out of hand. Monmouth's best attempts at making peace with his wife killed what precious time remained before his botched beheading on 15 July at the hands of the infamously incompetent Jack Ketch. Contemporary reports claim Ketch required no less than five blows before he severed what remained with a sharp knife.

There are two colourful legends connected with this event. The first is that Monmouth had no portrait, therefore requiring his head to be stitched back on so he could sit for one posthumously. Intriguingly, a strange painting, once rumoured to be of the duke, is presently in possession of the National Portrait Gallery. Another, arguably even more mouth-watering, is that unable to bring himself to execute his nephew, James II arranged Monmouth's transfer to the Bastille, where he would go down in history as the Man in the Iron Mask.

Many years after that unique night in the castle's great hall on Monmouth's arrival, the spirits of that occasion are said to repeat their epic feast. In the nearby castle hotel, the sound of ghostly fiddle music has been heard, which may also be the source of Tom, the fiddler.

Incidentally, the pre-celebration banquet is not the only claim the castle has to the events of the Monmouth Rising. In response to his nephew's mischief, James II sent out his chief justice, the infamous 'Hanging' George Jeffreys, to mete out his legendary justice. The Bloody Assizes were held in the great hall: an ironic move in the context of the earlier celebrations there. Jeffreys sentenced no less than 200 of Monmouth's supporters to death there; approximately 800 were also sold into slavery. A bizarre side note is the castle now possesses a privy Jeffreys is believed to have used, built specifically for the Bloody Assizes.

In addition to the sounds of merriment, the ghostly memories of the courtly proceeding are also said to resonate throughout the great hall. Sounds of stomping boots and strange dragging noises are believed to represent the unfortunate defeated of Sedgemoor, whose fates were sealed there. Similar also concerns those of heavy whipping and gentle screams. According to local lore, they are the sounds of those who had danced for the duke and his supporters being scourged by the sadistic judge as punishment for their licentiousness that fateful night.

Chapter 3

Gloucestershire and Wiltshire

Berkeley

Erected by William FitzOsbern around 1067 as one of a clutch of motte and baileys to endorse William the Conqueror's authority in the south, Berkeley is a rarity among England's mighty fortresses. Upgraded to stone in the following century under three generations of men, all named Roger de Berkeley, besides a brief period of royal rule under the Tudors, the castle, remarkably, has remained in the same family throughout its history. Though the final Roger lost possession of the fortress in 1152 for supporting Stephen over Henry of Anjou (later Henry II), his successor, Robert FitzHarding, a wealthy burgess from Bristol, is officially credited as the modern family's founder.

As expected of a castle whose origins date back to the Norman Conquest, the building has a rich history. It was there the rebel barons assembled in 1215 en route to Runnymede. In 1384, Lady Katherine Berkeley founded a school there, around which time England's final court jester, Dickie Pearce, died after suffering a fall from the Minstrel's Gallery. When an ownership dispute arose in 1470, matters were sorted with the Battle of Nibley Green. The battle is ironic for not being part of the Wars of the Roses and instead marks the last of England's battles fought between feudal magnates.

Its ownership sorted, Berkeley was in safe hands when Elizabeth I enjoyed a game of bowls on the green. During the Civil War, it was royalist garrisoned until the cannon fire of Colonel Thomas Rainsborough led to its surrender. Fortunately, it survived slighting due to an Act of Parliament that allowed the family to maintain it, provided they never repair the damaged keep and outer bailey. Such an act remains law to this day.

A site of many important happenings, it is Berkeley's role in the disappearance of Edward II that remains its most famous. When outnumbered by the forces of his angry queen, Isabella, later dubbed the 'She-Wolf' of France, and her accomplice – and alleged lover – Roger Mortimer, 1st Earl of March, the defeated Edward was placed in the custody of Thomas de Berkeley – Mortimer's son-in-law – and Berkeley's brother-in-law, John Maltravers. What became of the king has given rise to one of the greatest mysteries in England's history. In the castle keep exists a chamber in which the king is believed to have lingered. In addition to the king, the chronicler Geoffrey le Baker reported that local victims of Lord Berkeley's cruel justice to rotting animal carcasses were kept in the dungeon below. Modern visitors have often claimed to feel uneasy there, not least as the chamber gives off something of a lonely vibe. Protocol at the time was for imprisoned royals and nobles to be well treated, albeit usually at their own expense.

Exactly when Edward was transferred to Berkeley is also a point of contention. Most historians place the date as 3 April 1327, yet this is based primarily on one indenture. Luxury goods are also listed in the rolls as having been bought during his captivity. Whether Edward made use of them is unclear. A poem entitled 'Lament of Edward II' may have been autobiographical. Others have dismissed its authorship.

Of Mortimer and Isabella's intentions, speculation has again been rife. Like the events surrounding the equally unfortunate Richard II later that century, Edward II's abdication had already cleared the path for the king's son, Edward III, to take the throne. Yet, as was commonly the case in medieval England, the survival of the old king always left open the door for usurpation. Throughout 1327, a series of plots are reputed to have been considered by Mortimer's critics. These include those of the Dominican order and some of Edward II's household knights. At least one appears to have been successful in making their way inside the castle. It has also been suggested that the king may have been moved before returning to Berkeley around August.

Edward is known to have become ill during his imprisonment, yet he remarkably made a full recovery. Since that time, rumour has abounded that, on growing frustrated with Edward's longevity, Maltravers and Sir Thomas Gurney decided to take matters into their own hands. Whether the pair were acting on impulse or under orders from the new king's regents is unclear. Even more uncertain is the manner of their actions. So much so, it has given rise to one of the most significant controversies concerning an English king. Holinshed's Chronicles cites: 'a kind of horn or funnel was thrust into his fundament (anus) through which a red-hot spit was run up his bowels'. The Elizabethan playwright Christopher Marlowe used Holinshed as a primary source for his play on the king. Rather than arrange matters to ensure historical accuracy, however, in somewhat Shakespearean style, he presents Edward as a poor husband and neglectful ruler with a tendency towards homosexuality: suggestions that lie at the heart of the poker story. The final scene plays on his murder, which also states that he was held down 'with heavie feather beddes' after which the poker makes its first appearance.

Though many historians accept that Edward II met some form of end at Berkeley, the evidence is highly suspicious. The suggestion that Edward's death occurred on 21 September 1327, two days before the king learned of his father's passing, is often accepted. Yet contemporary sources can authenticate neither this nor the poker. Rumours of the king's alleged murder circulated slowly throughout the 1330s and beyond, not least courtesy of the colourful anecdotes of le Baker. That somebody murdered Edward is undoubtedly possible. Without question, the former king's death would have solved Mortimer's problem. Less than three years later, however, the teenage Edward III made moves to usurp his mother and regent – see Nottingham Castle. Mortimer was taken to the Tower and later executed at Tyburn. Intriguingly, Edward II's key gaolers, Sir Thomas Gurney, Maltravers and William Ockley, fled, fearing the king's wrath. Isabella, meanwhile, entered semi-retirement – see Castle Rising.

Confirmation that Edward II died in 1327 is itself a topic of some discussion. What is believed to have been the king's body was embalmed at the castle and displayed. A month later, on 21 October, it was taken to Gloucester Abbey – now the cathedral. On 20 December, the abdicated king was buried before the high altar. Speculation has been rife about the delay. Most arguments contend that it was to allow Edward III's attendance. The reasons for the king's burial at Gloucester, as opposed to Westminster, was probably of geographical convenience, yet this may also indicate the government of the time firmly believed that they were dealing with a dethroned king. The wooden effigy adorned with a copper crown constructed for his funeral is itself an oddity. Indeed, it was the first of its type in post-Saxon England. This may be explained by the fact that Edward had been dead for three months. His present effigy, of alabaster, depicts him as a king and apparently represents a likeness. Throughout the following decade, something of a cult of Edward arose, leading to rumours of miracles occurring at his tomb. The tomb was opened in 1855, at which point a wooden coffin revealed a second lead one.

Perhaps of greater intrigue is the possibility that Edward died many years later and was merely relocated in 1327. A letter dated January 1330 courtesy of the archbishop of York to the Mayor of London clearly states that 'Edward of Caernarfon is alive and in good health, and in a safe place'. A strange document, the 'Fieschi Letter', sent to Edward III by an Italian priest named Manuel Fieschi later tells the incredible story of how Edward II was liberated from Berkeley. On escaping, he made his way by land and sea to the town of Cecima in Italy and lived out his life as a hermit. Fieschi was a papal notary who was made bishop of Vercelli. Support for the letter comes in the knowledge that a French archivist discovered it in an official register that predates 1368. Furthermore, folklore in Cecima tells of an English king once buried in a local church. Diplomatic accounts also refer to a visit Edward III made to Koblenz to be made vicar of the Holy Roman Empire in 1338. At this point, he enjoyed a meeting with one William le Galeys or William the Welshman, who claimed to be the king's father. Born at Caernarfon Castle, Edward II was indeed a Welshman by birth. Whether the letter described the actual story of the king or was contemporary fiction remains a mystery.

Sudeley

Surrounded by the picturesque Cotswold Hills, restored Sudeley stands as a magnificent legacy of both the brutality of war and the committed efforts of restoration. A 'romantic ruin' after being slighted in the Civil War, the castle was saved in the nineteenth century by two glove-making brothers from Worcester. For the restoration that has followed, conservation lovers owe a great debt to the ambition and commitment of the Dent family, whose tireless efforts have been rewarded with the return of this historical fortress to its former glory.

Recorded in the *Domesday Book* and thought to date back to the Anglo-Saxons, the site has experienced a long and colourful history. The castle was likely established to combat the carnage of the Anarchy. In 1441,

Ralph Boteler, henceforth Baron Sudeley, inherited the site and built the present castle with proceeds amassed during the Hundred Years' War. Among his additions were serving quarters and a double courtyard surrounded by an impressive moat. Further additions included the chapel and state apartments. For failing to obtain a licence to crenellate, Boteler was briefly in trouble before receiving a pardon from Henry VI.

Boteler's loyalty to Henry VI would be of profound importance to the castle. In 1469, the Yorkist Edward IV forced the outcasted Lancastrian to sell Sudeley. On being led away, Boteler reportedly stated, 'Sudeley Castle, thou art the traitor, not I.' Compounding Boteler's woes, the fortress was subsequently held for nine years by Richard, Duke of Gloucester – later King Richard III. It was from here Richard travelled to the Battle of Tewkesbury in 1471. After swapping the fortress with brother Edward for Richmond Castle, making Sudeley a royal castle, Richard retook possession on his accession in 1483 and maintained it until his defeat at Bosworth. The newly crowned Henry VII gave the castle to his uncle, Jasper Tudor, who died in 1495. As Jasper had no legitimate issue, by 1509, Sudeley was again under royal ownership. In 1535, Henry VIII visited with Anne Boleyn, ending a somewhat barren run in the castle's history. On Henry's death, it passed to his son, Edward VI, from whose reign at least part of the ruins originates.

Thanks to a combination of Boteler's work and later care under royal ownership, the castle developed a reputation as one of the finest homes in England. Its fortunes declined, however, after its surrender to the Parliamentarians in the Civil War. A dormant wreck until 1837, its fortunes improved. Better still awaited when the castle was granted to the Dent brothers' nephew and heir, John Croucher Dent and his wife, Emma, in 1855. In 1877, Emma wrote of the castle:

> Few residences can boast a greater antiquity, or have witnessed more striking changes. A mansum, or manor-house, before the Conquest, a baronial castle in the time of Stephen, then alternately going to decay, or rising into additional magnificence, with stately towers to overlook the vale – again suffering from neglect, and once more right royally restored and beautified to receive the widowed Queen as Seymour's bride, with all her lordly retinue.

Though renovations remain ongoing, the beautiful restoration has re-established many important connections with its colourful past. Fine works of art and portraits of its former owners hang on the walls, all of which are laid out in a manner complementary to its former existence. According to numerous visitors, employees and former owners, the artwork is not the only reminder of the castle's past. Sudeley is reputedly one of the most haunted castles in England.

Although sightings of this apparition are rare, it has long been regarded that the spirit of the castle's most famous resident still lingers within its fine walls. Remembered by history as the only wife of Henry VIII to outlive the king, Queen Catherine Parr moved to Sudeley Castle in 1548 – a year after Henry's death. On taking the throne, the newly-crowned Edward VI – son of Jane Seymour and now *ipso facto* owner of Sudeley – offered no objection to a 'unfulfilled gifts' clause in his father's will, which entitled his uncle Sir Thomas Seymour to acquire Sudeley. Regarded by many as a treacherous villain, Seymour's lust for power inspired him to propose to the future Queen Elizabeth. After the princess wisely spurned his advances, he soon turned his attentions to the king's widow, who had previously been his mistress before marrying Henry.

Shortly after the wedding, Catherine moved to Sudeley already pregnant. At 36, this was a joyous miracle for Catherine, who had no other recorded children. Her dream came true on 30 August 1548 after a turbulent pregnancy that ended in her giving birth to a daughter: Mary. Unfortunately, seven days after the birth, Catherine died of a fever. She was laid to rest in the chapel of St Mary: interred in a coffin made entirely of lead. Incidentally, her funeral was the first royal Protestant one in England.

For more than 200 years, Catherine's body rested in peace in the chapel. But, after the castle fell into neglect, the chapel, too, became a sad ruin. In 1782, her casket was found and opened. The unfortunate discoverer was a local farmer named John Locust, who watched on in horror as her perfectly preserved remains decomposed before his eyes. The rector of Sudeley reinterred her in 1817, and her body now rests in the Chandos family vault: prominent Royalists who owned the castle during the Civil War. The coffin remains intact beneath an elaborate tomb erected in her honour. Sadly, the original remains have become somewhat grim due to repeated plundering.

Since the casket's exhumation, sightings of a lady in an elegant green dress have been reported from time to time. Reminiscent in appearance to a painting of the former queen hanging in the castle nursery, the lady's spirit has been seen looking distantly out of one of the windows. Why Catherine's ghost still haunts the castle is often rationalised to be due to the circumstances of her entombment. Others, however, believe that her appearance is of connection to the hauntings of the nursery itself.

Perhaps unsurprisingly, given the turbulent nature of England's history, the next part of the Seymour/Parr family story was not a happy one. Ever plagued by lust, Thomas Seymour again set his sights on Princess Elizabeth and met his downfall after conspiring against his brother, Edward Seymour, who served as regent to Edward VI. Thomas was executed on 20 March 1549 on the grounds of treason, to which Elizabeth commented: 'This day died a man with much wit and very little judgement.'

As for little Mary, the child sadly disappears from history. Over the years, many theories have been put forward as to her possible fate. Among the most outlandish, the Victorian author Agnes Strickland in her biography of Catherine Parr, made the intriguing case that Mary lived into adulthood and married one Sir Edward Bushel, a member of Anne of Denmark's household. Other claims have been made that she moved to Ireland and was raised a Protestant by the Hart family, who may have enjoyed a privateering profit-sharing scheme with Seymour. Reference to Mary has also been suggested in a more modern work by Parr biographer Linda Porter, regarding an epitaph written after her death aged 2. The author connects her burial and brief life to a Lincolnshire estate owned by the duchess of Suffolk.

Regardless of the truth about poor Mary, ghostly crying has been heard from the nursery for many years. Locals believe that the spirit of mother and child continue to linger within the magical fortress, hoping to one day be reunited. On Seymour's death, the castle passed to Catherine's brother, William Parr, 1st Marquess of Northampton. In 1554, Mary Tudor gave it to John Brydges, 1st Baron Chandos. Over the next half-century, Elizabeth was entertained there three times, including a three-day feast to mark the anniversary of the defeat of the Spanish Armada. Charles I stayed there after failing to take Gloucester. The Roundheads conquered it several times from 1643 and slighted it in 1649.

At least one apparition from this violent time is said to haunt the castle: not a former soldier but a phantom hound. Occupied by Prince Rupert before its fall, among his faithful was a large black hunting dog killed in the attack. Though the castle remained in Royalist hands until the third siege, it was not long until the ghostly manifestation of the deceased hound was witnessed at the castle. Reputedly an omen of ill tidings, the hound was often seen roaming the ruins of the banqueting hall before disappearing.

After its restoration, Sudeley was revamped into a splendid Victorian home. Many workers were employed to help run the gardens, kitchen and maintain the household. Although staff are no longer employed for such activities, it is said that one of the castle's former staff returns there. Known as Janet, the former mistress of the house was a firm and strong woman. For such a large residence, the task of carrying out the housekeeping duties was no mean feat, and many worked under Janet's leadership.

Local stories abound that the apparition of the former housekeeper still resides at Sudeley. She is often seen around August and September, patrolling the landing. Due to the number of young men and women who worked there, one of her main tasks was to keep the sexes separate. Even now, it is claimed she rules the roost, ensuring her standards refuse to drop.

Old Sarum

Of all the castles mentioned in this book, few possess a richer history than Old Sarum. Perched atop an ancient hill 2 miles north of the historic city of Salisbury, Old Sarum marks the site of the area's earliest recorded settlement. Though it may appear modern compared to the mega monoliths of Stonehenge and Avebury and other prehistoric fortifications that have been dated to around 3,000 BC, Old Sarum's roots can be traced firmly back to an Iron Age hillfort from as early as 400 BC. During its prime, the fort occupied a prominent position over the intersection of two ancient native trading paths.

In the centuries that followed, Old Sarum's importance intensified. Occupied throughout the Roman era, during which the old trading paths were developed into long, straight roads, the site was modernised throughout the Saxon era and proved an effective defence against the

Vikings. It was also from here that William the Conqueror conducted his conquest of the West Country.

Outdated by the architectural renaissance of the Norman Conquest, William replaced the old fort with a motte and bailey before a stone curtain wall was put down around the time of the city's first cathedral. In 1075, the Council of London oversaw the translation of Herman, previously bishop of Ramsbury and Sherbourne, thus creating Salisbury as a bishopric. After Herman's death in 1078, progress became the responsibility of his successor, Osmund, who the Catholic Church later canonised. The cathedral was consecrated on 5 April 1092, five days before it, somewhat inauspiciously, suffered storm damage.

Osmund's successor, Roger le Poer, was a far different man to the saintly builder. Having profited from a fortuitous layover from Henry I, who heard mass at Roger's church, the king was reportedly much impressed by the speed of his service, and therefore appointed him royal chaplain. Awarded the bishopric later in Henry's reign, along with being appointed lord chancellor, he rebuilt the first cathedral and refortified the motte and bailey in stone. Within the castle, the state apartments developed into a royal palace and were particularly enjoyed by Henry I and future monarchs. Sadly for the capable Roger, his hard-line policy and the promotion of his mistress – Matilda of Ramsbury – and son – another Roger le Poer – ensured his downfall. Ever loyal to Henry, he was dismissed by Stephen and charged with treason. He died in 1139, apparently of grief.

As a consequence of the capable, albeit selfish, Roger's removal, Old Sarum entered a period of decline. Around 1170, Henry II commissioned a series of improvements, after which it served as the setting of Eleanor of Aquitaine's house arrest. Ongoing disputes between authorities, religious and civil, combined with long-term questions over the site's vulnerability and a consistent water supply, inspired the dean and chapter to petition to move the site. Even worse, the lack of flourishing trees and vegetation caused the chalk to blow so hard and reflect so brightly it damaged the eyesight of many of the clergy. The only solution was to move onto the nearby plain below. On this, the present-day city has thrived.

There are many legends of the circumstances of the move. Among them is a wonderful Robin Hood-esque story that, on receiving permission, an archer shot an arrow from the top of the old tower, and on the spot where it landed, the new cathedral was built. One version of the story states that the arrow pierced the skin of a hart or another deer and on the spot where it perished, so the building work began. Regardless of the exact truth, in 1220, when Bishop Richard Poore occupied the see, the clergy vacated the old site, and the townsfolk followed. As for the castle, what had begun as a motte and bailey that developed into a royal palace frequented by many early Plantagenet monarchs became something of a ghost fortress. Stone from the old town was quarried for the new. In 1322, the dilapidated castle was finally abandoned and sold by Henry VIII in 1514. Despite being virtually deserted, the area continued to be represented at parliament and became a prominent rotten borough of the Pitt family.

For visitors in the modern-day, the sparse remains of former pathways and low walls do little to convey the full story of what was once among the most important places in the West Country. Indeed, a visit at the height of summer, when the setting of the sun creates atmospheric shadows across the ivy and bracken, does more to develop the area's aura of timelessness than its former use. Should one dig deeper, it should not be forgotten that many events that took place here had lasting effects on England's history. It was almost certainly at Old Sarum that William the Conqueror received the fully compiled *Domesday Book*. The original Salisbury Cathedral from the late eleventh century developed the 'Use of Salisbury' or the 'Salisbury rite', the church's Latin liturgical rite. Similar in most ways to the famous Roman rite, the 'use' was well respected throughout the medieval church and remained in use at English churches and many European ones until the Reformation.

Of equal importance, it was within the castle walls that William the Conqueror called his tenants in chiefs in August 1086 to swear him allegiance. As the following centuries would illustrate, the Oath of Salisbury would be of profound importance to European history. Feudal England was born in Old Sarum Castle.

Old Wardour

The death of Sir Lawrence de St Martin in 1385, the last of his line, was the first step of many that ultimately culminated in the first castle at Wardour. Now part of the civil parish of Tisbury, about 13 miles west of Salisbury, the St Martin's lands were acquired by John, 5th Baron Lovell, who was granted permission to construct a castle there seven years later by Richard II. Built throughout that decade using local greensand, the master mason was William Wynford: famous for his work on Windsor Castle and Wells Cathedral three decades earlier, as well as on Corfe Castle, Winchester College and New College, Oxford. For Old Wardour, Wynford devised a hexagonal blueprint inspired by the style of many castles of France. The six-sided shape and inclusion of several self-contained guest suites are both unique in Britain. Equally alluring are the gothic decorations, several of which appear atmospheric in the poor weather. It was here scenes from *Robin Hood: Prince of Thieves* were filmed, along with other movies and photo shoots.

For more than half a century, the Lovells lovingly oversaw Wardour's rise until the backing of the wrong horse in the Wars of the Roses saw the Yorkist usurper Edward IV confiscate the castle in 1461. Over the next eighty years, various toing and froing between owners finally led to some stability following its purchase by Sir Thomas Arundell in 1544. A prominent Catholic, Arundell married Margaret Howard, a sister of Henry VIII's doomed fifth wife, Catherine.

A family of ancient Cornish roots, the Arundells held several estates in Wiltshire, of which Old Wardour was arguably the finest. Despite Sir Thomas losing the castle – and his life – in 1552, after being executed for religious-based treason against Edward VI, his son, Sir Matthew repurchased it in 1570.

Like many of England's great castles, at Oliver Cromwell's hands, Wardour met its destiny. By this time, the castle had passed to Sir Thomas's great-grandson, the second Lord Arundell. Thomas was away when the castle was besieged; however, the Parliamentarians had not counted on the resolute determination of the 61-year-old lady of the castle, Lady Blanche. Neither her husband's absence nor the limited garrison of twenty-five against a Roundhead force of 1,300 initially proved a course for surrender. For six days, 2-8 May, she held out bravely until the threat of Roundhead mines beneath the walls forced her hand. As fate had it, her husband died a short time later from wounds suffered at the Battle of Stratton on 16 May. The following year, the third Baron Arundell, Henry, attempted a counter siege, during which mining of the walls convinced the Parliamentarians to surrender. Though the family successfully recovered the castle, the damage sustained during the two sieges put renovation into permanent abeyance. For a time, the family were forced to make do living in the corn store before a small house was built nearby.

Over the years, the ruins developed a reputation for being haunted. Most prominent of the spirits is Lady Blanche herself. Sadly, the terms offered to her to end the first siege were not honoured, and the brave widow was left destitute. She died in Winchester in 1649 after a time in Shaftesbury. Since that time, her likeness has been seen, her expression somewhat doleful, as though the weight of the world hangs heavily.

As well as its resident ghost story, there existed a strange legend that white owls appeared at the castle at times of tragedy. These harbingers of doom have not been seen since the 1940s when the final Arundell passed without issue. Committed royalists and Catholics throughout their lives, it is likely they took both to the grave. In so doing, in Old Wardour, we are left with a double treasure. A unique structure whose history of bravery, loyalty and devotion should forever act as positive reminders of the area's rich past.

Chapter 4

Hampshire and the Isle of Wight

Odiham

Little now remains of Odiham. Nestled in a secluded area, close to the historic village of the same name, the castle has long been known locally as King John's Castle due to his renowned love of the place. Indeed, it was one of only three castles constructed from scratch during his reign. John probably chose the location due to its being approximately midway between Windsor and Winchester. After lavishing more than £1,000 on the new building, it was most likely from there John set out on the road to destiny in 1215 that would ultimately lead to the water meadow at Runnymede and the signing of Magna Carta.

For John's children, control of Odiham was no less temperamental. Subjected to a two-week siege by the rebel barons and their foreign accomplice, the dauphin of France – later Louis VIII – in the First Barons' War of the following year, the garrison of thirteen held out admirably before surrendering peacefully in July. The royalists recovered the castle under the guidance of William Marshal, 1st Earl of Pembroke, regent to Henry III after John's death. Several modifications were later made, including the rebuilding of the keep and an inner moat around it. In 1236, Henry gifted the castle to his sister, Eleanor, who two years later married the soon to be infamous Simon de Montfort, 6th Earl of Leicester.

Further renovations began the following year, including a kitchen on a bridge over the inner moat and a new hall outside the keep. Work continued during Simon and Eleanor's occupancy up until Simon's rebellion against Henry 1263–65. As a consequence of Simon's imprisonment of the king after his victory at Lewes in May 1264 and Simon's death at Evesham the following year, Henry banished Eleanor and confiscated Odiham.

In the post-Montfort years, similar patterns repeated. The setting of a parliament in 1303, the castle also featured during the rebellion of the Despensers, committed supporters of the dethroned Edward II, against Roger Mortimer, 1st Earl of March, and Queen Isabella during the minority of Edward III. In 1346, the castle again achieved fame for becoming the involuntary home of David II of Scotland following his capture at the Battle of Neville's Cross. For more than eleven years, the royal prisoner endured house arrest, albeit allowed to keep a household and occasional hunting privileges. Throughout the following two and a half centuries, use as a hunting lodge became common. Before its being reported a ruin in 1605, the castle appears to have been commonly used as a prison and then solely as a hunting lodge. In 1792, the Basingstoke Canal was constructed through the southern corner of the bailey, which permanently changed the layout.

Although the sparse remains are little more than a shadow of the castle's former self, local legend tells that within the ruins, the soothing sounds of a lute can at times be heard, accompanied by the faint echo of a song. Precisely who the phantom minstrel is remains a mystery. An entertainer of past royalty or an unfortunate captive, one can only imagine. All that can be deciphered for sure is that within these walls built by John and inhabited by politicians, royalty and commoner alike, Odiham is a real gem prone to fly under the radar. Yet, if one should listen carefully enough, murmurs of its eventful past can still be heard like an echo on the wind.

Portchester

When visiting Portchester Castle without prior knowledge of its history, one is unlikely to guess that its imposing ruins exist within the confines of a Roman fort. Though no clear evidence exists as to who constructed it, the most plausible contender is the military commander Marcus Aurelius Carausius, near-namesake of the famous emperor, during the reign of Emperor Diocletian in the late third century. Roman history and lore have long been a critical influence on the area. There is an old legend that Pontius Pilate saw out his days in the locality after being brought on a galley as a final refuge. Sadly, like many legends of the time, a source is elusive.

Since the fall of the Roman Empire, the once-revered fort, located close to the market town of Fareham and around which the suburbs of Portsmouth grew, has endured a most eventful history. Believed to have been founded in the late eleventh century, Portchester probably served as a baronial castle throughout the Anarchy before becoming the property of Henry II, who granted it to Henry Maudit. The strong walls became a favourite of King John, who often used it as a hunting lodge and the usual purposes of sea defence. Like many in the area, the fortress was besieged by the dauphin of France during the First Barons' War and briefly taken in June 1216 before being relieved by William Marshal, 1st Earl of Pembroke the following year.

It was most likely at Portchester that Henry III lodged before setting out on his French campaigns of 1230, 1242 and 1253. More conclusive evidence concerns the starting point of Edward III and Henry V's campaigns, including those that culminated in their famous victories at Crécy and Agincourt. Also in 1415, the authorities apprehended a group of conspirators engaged in the so-called 'Southampton Plot'. Such events would help inspire Shakespeare's masterpiece *Henry V*. The three main conspirators, Richard of Conisburgh, 3rd Earl of Cambridge, Henry Scrope, 3rd Baron Scrope of Masham, and Sir Thomas Grey were all kept in the castle dungeons before being executed in August – a month or so after their initial arrest.

Consistent with the evolution of the castle throughout England, developing times saw even stronger walls. Following in the footsteps of Edward I, his son, Edward II, spent around £1,100 reinforcing its battlements to combat the threat of a French invasion. Yet this did not prevent the castle's condition from being described as ruinous in 1335. Further work was carried out during the reigns of Edward III and Richard II, including on the state apartments and at least one of the Roman walls that the sea had mercilessly battered.

Throughout the fifteenth century, a change in the local economy saw the nearby town of Portsmouth rise in importance. As a consequence, Portchester's heyday had passed. A survey from 1441 declared the castle 'ruinous and feeble'. However, this did not prevent it from being selected as the arrival port for Margaret of Anjou four years later.

Only by the beginning of the Tudor era was the castle the subject of improvement. The fruits of this were in place by October 1535 when

Henry VIII and Anne Boleyn visited the castle – its first visit by a reigning monarch in more than a century. In 1562–63, when England held the Normandy port of Le Havre, the castle operated as a makeshift military hospital, after which Elizabeth I ordered its preparation for an attack from the Spanish. In 1603, the ageing queen may have held court there, by which time its state was probably much improved. Documents from six years later describe it as being in stable condition.

Such improvements would not be enough, however, for the castle to remain in royal hands. In 1632, Charles I sold the now impressive fortress to Sir William Uvedale. A range of various successors among the Thistlethwaite family saw the castle house Parliamentarian dragoons – mounted infantry – in the Civil War. Due to its coastal location, the castle saw no military action, and in the post-civil-war period, operated mainly as a prison. Later that century, it is recorded as having housed some 500 prisoners of the Anglo-Dutch wars. The same was true of the Spanish war of succession in the early 1700s. The renewed threat of an invasion by Napoleon led to its refortification and the imprisonment of more than 7,000 French prisoners of the Napoleonic wars. With this, Portchester's purpose as a military fortress came to an end.

For the modern visitor, Portchester is a treat like few others. Set against the imposing backdrop of England's south coast, the combination of arguably the most impressive Roman walls in northern Europe juxtaposed with the towering square keep that stands guard over the nearby harbour offers a stunning example of a fortress subjected to ongoing transition. Accompanied by the soothing sounds of the waves breaking against the rocks and the salty fragrance delivered by the local breeze as it blows a moistening spray, it is easy to get lost in one's thoughts and become consumed with visions of the way things were.

Used consistently since the third century, it is hardly surprising that Portchester is reputedly the haunt of many of its former inhabitants. Due to the small amount of consecrated land and the high mortality rate among the prisoners, the dead were often buried in tidal mudflats. The sight of dismembered corpses and skeletons unearthed by storms has been reported over the years. Evidence has also been found for satanic witchcraft in the graveyard of the twelfth-century St Mary's Church.

Several apparitions are said to haunt the castle. A ghostly monk has been spotted walking the front of the castle before gradually disappearing.

A dark-haired woman has also been seen bending over a grave. Whether this is the same woman from the Victorian era, who is said to have fallen in a bid to save her baby or another, similar tale, concerning a young woman who threw herself from the walls on hearing that her fiancé had become lost at sea is unclear. Nor does any evidence survive to offer any insight into either woman's identity.

Of all the apparitions said to haunt the castle, none are so terrifying of a spectral rider on a black horse. The strange being has been known to instil a horrible feeling in the castle staff. Regardless of the exact source of the strange apparition, with a history that stretches back to ancient Rome and a purpose inexorably linked with naval matters, criminality and defence, it is surely no surprise that many connected with the castle believe they share it with many of its former inhabitants. Together, their individual life stories encapsulate so much of Portchester's history. By remembering those of the past, the illusion is created that we still co-exist with that ancient time. Even if just momentarily.

Carisbrooke

The medieval castle in the village of Carisbrooke, near Newport, has much in common with its nearby cousin of Portchester. Not least that the site's importance is said to date back to before the birth of Jesus Christ.

A combination of historical sources and archaeology investigations offer persuasive evidence that at least one of the ruined walls is of Roman origin. The *Anglo-Saxon Chronicle* also records that Wihtgar, the cousin of King Cynric of Wessex was buried there in 544. A Saxon stronghold was still present on the site in the eighth century: a century after the Jutes may have occupied the Roman fort. Further additions were put in place around 1000, most likely as a defence against the Vikings.

After the Norman Conquest, the history of the castle becomes easier to catalogue. The Earl of Hereford, William FitzOsbern, is believed to have begun a motte and bailey forfeited to the Crown after his death and later updated in stone. From 1100, Carisbrooke became the property of the powerful de Redvers family, who built much of it throughout the following two centuries. In the fourteenth century, the iconic double-towered gatehouse followed, after which other defences were added by the Wydvilles and Elizabeth I to help combat the threat of the Spanish. Fortunately for the English, and in later times, the British, the castle never fell. Nor did the Isle of Wight. For such reasons, it was generally accepted that whoever held Carisbrooke held the Isle of Wight.

Considering its military importance and the number of attacks it has suffered over the centuries, Carisbrooke is in a surprisingly good state. Indeed, there are few such impressive examples of juxtaposed constructions anywhere in the United Kingdom. A critical military structure, the castle has also served as the home of many noblemen and their families, several of who made significant impressions on its rich history. Among the most prominent is Queen Victoria's daughter, Princess Beatrice, who was governor of the Isle of Wight before her death in 1944. At that time, the castle entered public ownership.

Having witnessed more than 2,000 years of military struggles, acts of deceit, despair, murder and tragedy, the castle is unsurprisingly steeped in legend. While under siege from the French in 1377, it is said that a bowman named Peter de Heyno defeated the enemy single-handed by killing the French commander, causing the shepherd-less sheep to retreat.

Even more compelling is the tale concerning King Charles I. Charles initially sought to escape Cromwell's wrath by fleeing to Carisbrooke. However, on handing himself over to the governor, he soon realised he had made a dreadful mistake. Despite this, his fourteen months in captivity were far from unbearable. Twenty-course meals were prepared for him, either side of which the king busily attempted to escape. During his time at Carisbrooke, Charles made two unsuccessful attempts at flights. On the first occasion, he suffered the embarrassment of getting stuck between the bars of his window, something the large banquets were unlikely to have helped. Much the wiser from the experience, next time, the king destroyed the bars with acid, only to be disturbed by his gaoler, Colonel Hammond. On visiting the king, Hammond commented, 'I am come to take my leave of your majesty, for I hear you are going away.'

Go away, Charles soon would. He left Carisbrooke on 6 September 1648, some four months before his execution on 30 January 1649. Intriguingly, some of the messages that the king delivered to his supporters still survive, written in code. To this day, the cypher has never been broken.

As fate would have it, Charles's imprisonment was not the last of his family's connection with the castle. After his death, his son, Henry, Duke of Gloucester, and daughter, Princess Elizabeth, were forced to endure similar circumstances. Before her arrival, the educated young lady penned an emotional memoir of her final meeting with her father on the eve of his beheading. Sadly, her lot would be equally heartbreaking. On catching a cold during her crossing, she was downed with pneumonia and perished after three days. Tradition tells that she was found with her head laid on an open bible that her father had gifted her. Two centuries later, Queen Victoria commissioned a sculptor to honour Elizabeth, which rests in the church of St Thomas in Newport, where the unfortunate girl was buried.

Although the castle is now unoccupied, save the employees of English Heritage and members of the general public who visit every year by the tens of thousands, it has long been reported that the spirits of Carisbrooke's turbulent past still reside within its strong walls. Since at least 1690, the well house has served as the primary water source for the castle. The original features are popular among modern-day visitors as a rare opportunity to see the large wooden treadwheel draw up buckets from the well. For much of its existence, donkeys were used to pull the wheel. Yet before the furry animals' arrivals, such menial work was the harsh reality for the castle's prisoners.

Though the days of human incarceration in the well house may be over, local lore tells that reminders of the well's past occasionally show themselves. Among the most disturbing are reports that the spirit of a drowned girl has been seen in the well, staring aimlessly from the water. Officially, no such records of a drowning exist; however, there is one possible candidate for the poor child. Elizabeth Ruffin was the daughter of the mayor of Newport and lived at the castle around 1632. Though the well house was specifically highlighted in J. Meade Falkner's novel *Moonfleet*, an unsubstantiated journal entry that Ruffin 'threw herself down a well at the castle' seemingly served as the inspiration. Witnesses of the apparition often report that the ambience of the room is replaced with an overwhelming sense of grief that seems consistent with the circumstances of her alleged death. Whether she was pushed, jumped or fell, the events have never been known, despite a longstanding belief that she perished. The apparition of the young woman has reputedly been seen on many occasions: her face a deathly pale, her clothing soaked.

Elizabeth Ruffin is not the only ghost thought to haunt the castle. During the summer months, the area is a popular tourist attraction. While walking their dogs near the castle moat in 1994, a man and a woman were caught off guard by the strange appearance of a young woman wearing a white dress. The couple initially assumed that she was also merely out walking her two dogs, yet as they got closer, they were shocked as her body became transparent before fading from sight. It may well be that the story is connected to a similar account of a woman in a long, heavy dress seen walking four lapdogs. Also usually seen in the summer months, her ghost tends to originate from the courthouse before making her way across the grounds in a dress out of season for the warmth.

A male phantom is also said to join the cloaked lady in her ghostly endeavours. The man, who has been seen near the moat, appears dressed in brown trousers and a short sleeveless jacket, again reflective of the style of days past. Standing isolated, he has been known to communicate with at least one eyewitness with two indistinguishable words, 'Reet Graveley.' What exactly he means and why he haunts the castle remains unclear.

Chapter 5

Sussex

Arundel

Gutted by fire during the English Civil War, Arundel Castle was rebuilt in the eighteenth century by the eleventh duke of Norfolk and subsequently improved by his descendants. Regarded as one of England's finest ancestral homes before the fire, the present fortress once again lives up to its earlier reputation. Indeed, Arundel is a rare example of a castle that provides present-day occupants and visitors with an appealing blend of Norman style architecture mixed with delightful Victorian gardens set against the picturesque backdrop of the Sussex countryside.

Like many of England's castles, its origins lie far back in the mists of time. Parts of the site may date to St Edward the Confessor (1042–66); however, there is no conclusive evidence for this. Of the castle itself, the first owner was Roger de Montgomery, 1st Earl of Arundel: a key advisor to William the Conqueror and seemingly a relation due to his being a grand nephew of Duchess Gunnor, the wife of William's ancestor, Richard I of Normandy. Montgomery started the castle on Christmas Day 1067 as part of a broader package that included several manors. On Montgomery's watch, work began on a large Norman motte and bailey. Unlike many of that time, Arundel included a double bailey that developed into one of the finest in southern England. Despite his death nearly a millennia ago, it has often been claimed that his ghost returns to check up on the castle where he resided for so long.

From 1138, the castle has remained, except for temporary interruptions, the ancestral home of the dukes of Norfolk – continued at times in lineage by the female heiresses. The year after its acquisition by the original ancestors, Empress Matilda was invited to stay at the castle; the state apartments created for her visit have survived. When the castle returned to the Crown on the death of William d'Aubigny, 1st Earl of Arundel, in 1176, Henry II spent vast sums improving it. Richard I later offered the castle to William d'Aubigny, the third earl, whose family retained it until the fifth earl, Hugh d'Aubigny, died in 1243. Inherited by his sister, Isabella, her descendants maintained the estates, with two interruptions, until 1580, during which time, further renovations and additions were made.

Among those interruptions was the castle's confiscation following the execution of Edmund FitzAlan, 2nd Earl of Arundel in 1326, for rebelling against Edward II. Consequently, the castle was granted to the king's half-brother, Edmund of Woodstock, 1st Earl of Kent – a legitimate son of Edward I by his second marriage. Roger Mortimer executed Edmund for his continued support of Edward II after his abdication – see also Berkeley Castle. His daughter, Joan the Fair Maid of Kent, future wife of Edward the Black Prince and mother of Richard II, and her children were placed under house arrest there.

By 1346, all was forgiven, at which time Richard FitzAlan, 3rd Earl of Arundel fought alongside the king and Black Prince at Crécy. Family fortunes changed, however, in 1394 when Richard II assaulted the eleventh earl of the same name with a pole in retribution for the earl's late arrival for the funeral of the queen, Anne of Bohemia. On the earl's execution, the castle was granted to John Holland, Duke of Exeter; however, on the duke's execution, Henry IV returned Arundel to the FitzAlans. They would hold the castle until the days of the nineteenth earl, Henry FitzAlan, whose daughter Mary married Thomas Howard, 4th Duke of Norfolk. Though Norfolk lost his life in 1572 for his Catholic conspiracy against Elizabeth I and his desire to marry Mary, Queen of Scots, his descendants still hold the earldom.

From the time of Norfolk's execution to the early 1640s, Arundel's fortunes proved fair. Yet, as the wind of change blew over England and Scotland, the long march to civil war led to the castle's downfall. For eighteen long days from 19 December 1643, the sturdy walls suffered the pounding of Cromwell's cannons, culminating in a Royalist surrender. Despite boasting an impressive garrison, the severe winter weather proved decisive, as poor road conditions prevented it from being relieved. During the siege, the prominent Roundhead lieutenant-colonel John Birch was shot in the stomach. Ironically, the effect of the cold weather stemming the blood flow may have saved his life. Taken by the Roundheads, parliament decreed the castle's slighting in 1653; however, most of the damage was weather inflicted.

Though the castle remained in the Howard family, a preference for their other properties saw them pay it little attention. This changed in 1787 thanks to the efforts of Charles Howard, 11th Duke of Norfolk, who helped restore the castle to its former glory. So significant was his work, coupled with that of descendant Henry Charles Howard, thirteenth duke, that Queen Victoria and Albert visited it in 1846. Despite remaining in private ownership and officially still the home of the dukes of Norfolk and earls of Arundel, Arundel is now open to the public.

Renovated and rebuilt in the original style, modern-day Arundel has succeeded in inheriting the character of days gone by. Indeed, it has long been said that the castle's long, illustrious past is not only illustrated in its fine art but also the ghosts of former inhabitants.

One of the castle's most famous ghosts is a young lady. Dressed in an ethereal shade of white, she has been seen on many occasions, drifting through the late-eighteenth century Hiorne's Tower. Her spectre has also been seen standing atop the tower, her face illuminated by the pale shining of the full moon. Although her name is long forgotten, after falling victim to a tragic love affair, she is believed to have committed suicide by jumping off the tower.

The woman in white is not the only sad spectre reputed to haunt the castle. While working predominantly in the kitchens 200 years ago, a young boy was battered to death by his masters. Since that time, his apparition has been seen slaving over the hot stove as he did in life.

Another said to haunt the castle is the 'blue man': so named for his frequent appearances wearing blue silk garments. Believed to have lived at the castle during the reign of Charles II, the man has been seen on countless occasions, usually perusing the historical literature of the castle library. Like the lady in white, who he was, why he reads and for what he searches remains unclear. Eyewitness reports suggest that the man appears to be actively searching for something and that the peace he seeks shall only come when his mission is complete.

It might well be the same man who is also known to haunt the castle in the guise of a Cavalier soldier. Traditionally the home of committed Royalists, Arundel, despite being attacked by Oliver Cromwell's army, never left the family. That this spirit is one of the hundreds of loyal men who made up the garrison, perhaps stricken by the attacks or sickness that ravaged the castle in the cold winter of 1643, seems a logical conclusion.

Of all the hauntings said to occur at Arundel, it is that of nonhuman entities that are perhaps the most compelling. At least one small white bird has plagued the castle for several centuries. Local legend states that if a white bird is to be seen hovering around the castle windows, someone associated with Arundel will shortly die. The exact source of the legend remains unclear; however, it may connect with certain characteristics from the castle's past. Before the restoration of the keep, the dukes of Norfolk kept a colony of American owls as pets.

Throughout its history, stories of brushes with the paranormal have become almost part and parcel of day-to-day life. In 1958, an employee spoke first hand of his witnessing such an entity in the servants' quarters. On walking along the corridor to turn off the exterior lights, he became aware of a man with long hair walking in front of him, dressed in a light grey tunic. Who he was is another of Arundel's many mysteries. All the witness could describe was that the man was reminiscent of a figure in an old photograph.

Bodiam

Of all the castles included in this book, few have featured more in works of art and appeared on the front cover of castle calendars and magazines than beautiful Bodiam. Renowned for its pleasing appearance and symmetrical design, round towers intersected by parapet walls and surrounded by lush greenery and a moat, Bodiam has often been described as the quintessential medieval castle.

Located near the East Sussex village of Robertsbridge, few who have ever gazed upon its attractive façade have failed to be impressed. Should one stand before its walls on a crisp winter's morning or a late summer's evening when the light is just perfect, it is easy to let the mind wander and imagine one has slipped into a real-life fairy tale. Thanks to the clearness of the moat, in such conditions, the castle casts a complete reflection, thus furthering the illusion of grandeur. From a defensive standpoint, the view would have been incredibly imposing. To the artist, highly romantic.

There is no denying that Bodiam is among the most picturesque castles on the planet.

To the surprise of many, a designation that Bodiam should even count as a castle is an area of contention. To make sense of this, we must return to the original definition of a castle: a home, yet also a fortress. That it meets the criteria of the former, there is no doubt. From its creation in the late fourteenth century to its dismantlement in the Civil War, Bodiam was a beloved residence. Less convincing, however, is evidence for the latter. Scratch beneath the surface, Bodiam is the perfect example of a medieval extravagance. A castle built for the surface as opposed to substance.

Nevertheless, in this author's view, its inclusion in this book is easily merited. In no uncertain terms, Bodiam is a turning point castle. While England's forces continued to engage in combat with French troops on the continent, the days where England needed massive bastions to augment the royal or baronial power appeared to be over. As the need for defences against conquest dwindled, the case for smart homes developed. Nothing represented this change more than Bodiam. Nor did anybody represent this change more than Sir Edward Dalyngrigge.

A man of lesser stock than the typical castle owner, this ambitious social climber made his mark in the Hundred Years' War as a knight of Edward III. After setting off in 1367 to become a mercenary in the free company of Sir Robert Knolles, Dalyngrigge returned ten years later and married his beloved Elizabeth, heiress of the original manor of Bodiam – other sources suggest that the marriage preceded his departure. Like many English of lower gentry, a commander of the wars, his plundering of the French brought him great riches. Until 1388, he served as a knight of the shire in ten parliaments.

This rising influence put him in direct conflict with the new king's influential regent, John of Gaunt, 1st Duke of Lancaster. Dalyngrigge lost a lawsuit to Gaunt in which he performed petulantly and ordered to part with around £1,000. Fortunately for the hot-headed knight, an intercession from his patron, Richard FitzAlan, the earl of Arundel, after Gaunt's departure spared him the anguish of paying the fine. Gaunt's loss would prove Bodiam's gain. Due to their tremendous cost, the average knight could rarely afford more than a traditional manor. Yet, past successes had made Dalyngrigge a highly wealthy man, from which Bodiam's future was assured.

Though beloved for its luxury, Bodiam was one of several castles built on the south coast in the 1380s for defensive purposes. Officially, the old reason of defence of the realm was still necessary to be granted a licence to crenellate. Yet, in reality, the Hundred Years' War was merely an excuse by the flamboyant owners to chance their hands. When Dalyngrigge put his builders to work, England had already entered the age of Geoffrey Chaucer. For men like Dalyngrigge, it was a time of great opportunity, where rags to riches were possible, regardless of social class.

Putting together his plans for Bodiam, he carefully designed a castle fit for his personal preferences. Still an enclosure castle, yet more square than the traditional, the walls are far thinner than those of earlier centuries. From a defensive standing, the lack of keep is an interesting omission. Similarly, the moat and battlements are far from perfect. Past tests have proven that the digging of a trench could drain the moat in under a day. As previously mentioned, the reflection creates the illusion that the castle is double its true size, a picture more for admiration than actual use. Sir Edward Dalyngrigge would have known this and probably requested it.

Supported, nevertheless, by the claim that French attacks against towns in the south of England warranted the building of a castle, Dalyngrigge got his way and set to work on his masterpiece. Ironically, Arundel was one of the Lords Appellant, thus a key conspirator against Richard II in 1388, and the following year subsequently crushed. Initially on his patron's side, Dalyngrigge defected and sought the protection of the royalist earl of Huntingdon. By backing the king when he needed to most, Dalyngrigge narrowly escaped treason. As the records show, over the coming years, no one attended more councils than Sir Edward.

As a consequence, time at his new castle became a rarity. He died around 1394 and was succeeded by his son, John. No obituary for Sir Edward or Elizabeth has survived. Nor an effigy. Records confirm that while his parents, Roger and Alice, were buried in a nearby parish, Edward and wife were interred in the abbey of Robertsbridge west of Bodiam. Any remains were destroyed in the Dissolution.

Following the days of the ambitious social climber, Bodiam enjoyed a mostly peaceful existence, reflective of its calm exterior. This would end in the Civil War when the Royalist owner, Lord Thanet, was forced to sell the castle to a Parliamentarian to pay off fines levied against him. At this time, Bodiam was partially broken up and left to rot. The bridge and parts of its interior were dismantled. The barbican was also demolished, rendering it non-defendable. Purchased by the squire and politician John 'Mad Jack' Fuller in 1829, the castle was gradually restored under a series of owners, before entering public ownership in 1925 when Lord Curzon gifted it to the National Trust.

Today, the appealing walls conceal little more than a hollow shell, whose interior is often the venue of familial enjoyment during the day. Yet, despite its relatively quiet history, at night, the castle is reputedly far livelier. Strange sounds have been heard from within: songs sung, oaths recited – often in French. Further to the ethereal sounds, the ghost of a lady in red has been seen stalking the battlements. Who she is, is unclear. Elizabeth Dalyngrigge, the wife of Sir Edward, perhaps? Or possibly one of their descendants.

Joining the lady in red, the ghost of a young boy in Dickensian style clothing has been seen running towards the moat. Local lore conjectures that the boy had an unfortunate accident and drowned.

Bodiam's existence as an opulent residence has long been over. Likewise, its status as a castle is hotly disputed. What should not be questioned, however, is what the castle represents. Critics of capitalism and the history of the class system may easily argue that this building of surface grandeur, yet little substance, is a prime example of a monument to decadence. Yet should one take a closer look, it is also the prime example of what can be achieved through hard work and following a dream to its conclusion. The adventurous, at times dishonest and dubious, antics of Dalyngrigge aside, Bodiam also represents a significant turning point in the history of the castle. An era when the Norman bastions' time was fading, and the moated manor house style of Herstmonceux was soon to begin. In such ways, Dalyngrigge may hold the distinction of being among the most important planners of his day. The man who not only saved the castle but made it accessible to the average knight.

Bramber

Once the opulent home of the powerful de Braose family, little now remains of Bramber Castle. Lying near the quaint Sussex village of the same name, the pleasant setting close to the sea and surrounded by mature trees provides a charming point of interest for the villagers.

Put down shortly after the Norman Conquest, the castle was designed to act as a defensive port overlooking the River Adur. Construction was overseen by the prominent Norman, William de Braose, who built the original motte and bailey and nearby church around 1070. In the following century, the timber defences were heavily fortified into a Norman stronghold, which provided residence for the family until 1326.

Famous among their number was another William de Braose: a key supporter of King John until the king sought a vendetta against him, officially for unpaid debts. Paying for his luxurious lifestyle, John instructed that Braose's four youngest children would be taken into royal custody as a form of collateral to ensure William refrained from abusing his power. Refusing to be manipulated by this desperate act, William ignored John's implausible demand. Learning of a plot to kidnap them, Braose fled to Ireland with his family. Though William managed to escape, eventually settling in France, a worse fate awaited his wife Maud and eldest son, another William. Imprisoned for a time at Windsor, the sorry pair were starved to death at Corfe Castle – see Corfe Castle.

Little is known of the castle's role after the male line of the de Braose family died out. From 1326, the fortress appears among the property of the de Bohuns, and from 1330, the Mowbrays. However, due to it being located in a relatively deprived part of the county, they never lived there. The recurring threat of French raids ensured the castle remained of some importance. In 1355, two captured French pirates are recorded as having escaped. However, by the 1450s, Bramber's purpose had declined. An interesting record from around 1555 refers to 'the late castle', which was used for grazing. During the Civil War, what remained of the fortress was garrisoned by the Roundheads and destroyed in 1644 by the Cavaliers. The castle's destruction appears to have followed a skirmish in which the latter attempted to gain control of the local bridge. According to local lore, marksmen were also stationed at the nearby church.

Now a meagre ruin, the only thing more lacking than the outer walls are the historical records. Only one of the walls of the gatehouse still stands. Should one visit the village without prior knowledge, it would be easy to miss that a castle even existed.

Nevertheless, the castle is said to have one rather unusual feature. Over 700 years since the unfortunate children of William de Braose breathed their last, their spirits are still said to linger, not at the site of their brutal deaths but within the confines of their former property. Believed to appear around Christmas time, local legend tells that their malnourished ghosts have been known to approach the living, begging desperately for a scrap of food to end their eternal famine.

The doomed children are not the only spirits believed to haunt the castle. Towards the end of the fifteenth century, Sir Hubert de Hurst, a former owner or tenant, reputedly discovered his wife, Maude of Ditchling, in the arms of one Sir William de Lindfield. Pulsating with rage, Hurst had Lindfield bricked up alive in the cellar. Maude, herself, was reputedly found dead the next day. In the years since, reports have claimed that Maude's tormented cries have been heard on the wind. Many visitors have also spoken of a feeling of dread when wandering the ruins. That the story is true is sadly impossible to validate. Rumours that the bricked-up lover's body was found, head in hands, I have been unable to verify. Nevertheless, as long as proof remains unforthcoming, it seems highly likely that Bramber Castle will retain its reputation as the eternal home of lost souls.

Hastings

In the brief period between William the Conqueror's landing at Pevensey Bay on 28 September 1066 and the Battle of Hastings on 14 October, his first task was to establish three castles on the south coast as a base to conduct future operations. After building his first at Pevensey, he constructed a second, 10 miles up the road, at Hastings. The Bayeux Tapestry depicts the castle as being of a motte design. The same was true of Pevensey and Dover. In 1070, with the conquest of England assured, William ordered the castle's rebuilding in stone, along with the nearby chapel of St Mary.

Throughout the Norman period, Hastings was held by the count of Eu: a French fief in the north of Normandy. When the dauphin of France, Prince Louis, launched his invasion of 1216 at the request of the rebel barons, John deliberately had the castle dismantled in a bid to thwart the rebels' cause. Three years after Louis's departure, John's son and successor, Henry III, had the castle refortified. Around six years after his wedding in 1236, he bestowed it upon his queen's uncle, Peter of Savoy, who held it until his death in 1268.

Since that time, the castle has endured a mixed history. Plagued by storms in 1287, the collapse of large segments of the sandstone cliff saw parts of the outer wall topple into the sea. Over the following centuries, more still has been lost that way. In 1339 and 1377, French raiders ransacked the nearby town, at which point the castle offered the main form of defence. Worse still followed in the aftermath of the Dissolution of the Monasteries, the consequences of which saw the castle become neglected for many years. In 1591, Thomas Pelham bought the castle and used the area predominantly for farming. By the Victorian era, the site was mostly overgrown and then further damaged when the Luftwaffe targeted the town during World War II. In 1951, it was purchased by the Hastings Corporation and opened to the public.

Threatened by the forces of nature and enemy nations throughout its 1,000-year history, the ruins of England's second Norman castle are now wild and ragged. Despite the restorations of recent times, located so close to the English Channel, it is difficult to escape the feeling that the storms of the past remain somehow trapped in the atmosphere. Legend from the 1800s recalls that local fishermen were shocked to look upon the ruins only to view the former castle as it had appeared in its medieval heyday. As expected of such a location, hauntings abound. Among the most famous is Henry II's 'turbulent priest', Thomas Becket, who was reputedly a former dean of St Mary's.

Said to join Becket on moonlit nights is the apparition of a lady in a long white dress. A prime contender for her identity could be Agnes of Faucigny, wife of Peter of Savoy, or one of the other wives of the former counts of Eu or castellans. Unfortunately, it is unclear which ladies regularly spent time at the castle. Of developing intrigue, she has often been seen walking the former tiltyard, which was reputedly the setting of mini-tournaments. That the lady in white is the wife of a doomed jouster has also been suggested.

Below ground, the former dungeons, known locally as the 'whispering dungeons', are reputedly the haunts of former prisoners. The rattling of chains and desperate groans are also said to linger as a reminder of the poor conditions in which prisoners were kept.

On the nearby West Hill, the ghost of a cloaked woman – often identified as a nun – has been seen walking. Around 7 miles from the castle lie the ruins of Battle Abbey, built by William overlooking the field of the famous battle as penance for the number of lives lost in the Norman

Conquest. Tradition states that the high altar marks the spot where Harold Godwinson fell. Like most of its type, the abbey survived unscathed until the Dissolution. At nearby St Leonards-on-Sea, the convent of the Holy Child also existed in the Victorian era and potentially fits the location of the woman's wanderings. The shape of a nun has also been seen inside the castle. She is believed to be the cause of the frightening sounds of ethereal organ music reported within the church.

A nurse in the uniform of the WWI era has been seen nearby, as has a woman carrying a child. This woman may be the same spirit as the wandering nun, albeit separate from the nun who haunts the castle itself. Local tradition records that the poor woman ended her life in the pits of despair on being deserted by her lover – a fisherman with whom she had an affair. Exactly how her life ended remains unclear, besides the belief that the child died too. She has apparently been seen walking towards the south wall of the castle, at which point both mother and baby evaporate into the darkness.

Herstmonceux

Early records confirm that William the Conqueror presented the manor at Herst to a supporter named Wilbert. By the end of the following century, a marriage between one of Wilbert's descendants, Idonea de Herst, and a Norman nobleman, Ingelram de Monceux, had led to the creation of the Herstmonceuxs.

The present castle was built on the site of an old manor house in 1441 by Sir Roger de Fiennes, a descendant of that original family. Famed in his day as the treasurer of the household of King Henry VI, like nearby Bodiam, Fiennes's construction deserves a distinction for being among the most important and unique in England.

Designed along the same lines as a typical manor house – indeed, to view Herstmonceux at a glance, it is easy to miss it is even a castle – the date of construction is of great importance concerning the development of architecture in England. Built at a time when defence against foreign invaders was no longer the necessity it once was, Herstmonceux marks a rare transition between the Bodiam-style fortress and the soon-to-arrive Tudor mansion. Similar to Bodiam, the reflection of its red walls and lofty turrets in the moat was designed to increase its sense of allure. A rare example of a castle made of bricks as opposed to stone, Herstmonceux is often regarded among the most significant brick buildings in England.

For precisely 100 years, the Fiennes family, now styled Lord Dacre, enjoyed their castle. Things changed in 1541 when Henry VIII seized the castle when Sir Thomas Fiennes's deer poaching on a nearby estate culminated with the murder of its gamekeeper. Though the family later regained the estate, Sir Thomas was stripped of his title and tried as a commoner. Found guilty, he was executed at Tyburn.

Ignored by Cromwell due to its lack of defensive qualities, the castle nevertheless entered a period of decline due to the family's rash spending patterns. By 1777 it was all but dilapidated and for a time became the home of the Royal Observatory. Bought by Alfred Bader as a present for his wife, the castle was converted into a study centre in 1994 for Queen's University, Ontario. As well as a place of education, parts are made open to the public.

Although drastically renovated and revamped over the years, various pieces of art, artefacts and bits of furniture still act as tangible reminders of the history of this former home. And, according to some familiar with its history, it is not just physical objects that serve as visual illustrations of the castle's active past. A plethora of ghosts are said to haunt Herstmonceux. Among the most bizarre is a phantom drummer, who marches the battlements. His beating drum has also been heard reverberating throughout the castle, his strikes illuminated by strange sparks.

The exact identity of this ghost has been hotly debated. It is often thought that he may be the spirit of one of the castle's former lords: Richard Fiennes. Styled Lord Dacre, Fiennes resided at Herstmonceux in the fifteenth century with his young wife, Joan. Though they enjoyed a happy marriage, Dacre was consumed by self-doubt due to his old age. Tortured by his twisted visions, it is said that to keep potential lovers away from his cherished wife, he resorted to hammering ceaselessly on a drum.

In a strangely predictable turn of fate, the young wife is said to have lost patience with her husband and locked him in a small room where he died. Although the mortal sounds of the drumming soon ceased, the spirit of Lord Dacre did not rest in peace. For the remainder of her life, the ghostly beating of that dreadful drum tormented the young murderess. It would seem ironic that her husband succeeded in keeping lovers away in death.

Regardless of the historicity behind Dacre's alleged antics, there is another candidate for the giant drummer. During the reign of Henry V – at which time the castle was still a manor house – it is said that one of the residents went to France and met a tragic end at the Battle of Agincourt. Incidentally, another spirit, this one more confidently attributed to Lord Dacre has been seen riding a horse. It has also been mooted that the stories were created as a distraction from smuggling activities.

The ghost of a young woman has also been seen wandering the ancient corridors. The lady, who is said to have starved to death, appears wearing a grey dress, her mournful sounds acting as an eternal reminder of her merciless end. In support of the story, there are accounts that a woman named Grace Naylor starved to death at the castle in 1727 after getting lost.

Grace is not the only female believed to haunt the castle. A woman in white has also been seen near the moat. Unlike the other ghosts, she was not a former resident, but a girl from a local village. According to local lore, the young girl was lured inside by Sir Roger de Fiennes. After taking advantage of her, she was then confined to one of the chambers and sought to escape by jumping into the moat. Set upon by her captor, the young woman either drowned or else was raped and murdered by the tyrannical lord. Since that time, she has been seen either walking by or swimming in the moat, desperately trying to make her way to freedom.

Completing Herstmonceux's ghostly list, the spirit of another lady reportedly haunts the grounds. Thought to be a separate entity from the ladies in white or grey, a mysterious plump woman riding a donkey has been seen. Unlike the others, she is a far calmer spirit who rides at a steady pace before vanishing as inexplicably as she appeared.

Pevensey

Besieged four times but never conquered, the battle-scarred walls of Pevensey Castle are an epic reminder of a site on which nearly 2,000 years of history has unfolded.

Before the rise of the sturdy Norman walls admired by modern-day visitors, a fortress at Pevensey can be dated to 280–340 AD and the

Roman fort of *Anderitum*. In its prime, the fort was one of the largest in Britain and served to protect England from Saxon pirates. Following the Romans' departure and intermarrying with the ancient Brits and Jutes, the *Anglo-Saxon Chronicle* records that Saxon raiders besieged a post-Roman settlement in 491 AD and slaughtered all present. Precisely what this settlement was and what became of the fort in later times is unrecorded. No further mention is made until 28 September 1066.

The date was not just a pivotal one in Pevensey's history but England's. It was on this day William the Conqueror landed at Pevensey Bay. According to legend, William stumbled as he left the boat. Worried that his men may have interpreted the fall as a bad omen, he rose to his feet and laughed it off, claiming: 'I have seized this land in both hands and I will never let it go.' Of the three castles William established in the aftermath of the Norman Conquest, his first at Pevensey was created as a beachhead. Like Hastings and Dover, it was also motte and bailey. The Normans camped there the first night before setting out on a course that culminated in victory at Hastings.

In the aftermath of William's conquest, Pevensey was granted to Robert, Count of Mortain, who built a keep inside the Roman walls. The Bayeux Tapestry appears to show the building of the original castle, which Robert updated and expanded throughout the 1070s. The wooden and Roman defences were largely successful in withstanding Robert Curthose's rebellion of 1088. Though William Rufus's forces endured a frustrating six-week endeavour, the garrison eventually surrendered due to a lack of food. Robert later made peace with Rufus, yet his son, William, Count of Mortain, was later stripped of the castle for rebelling against Henry I. Confiscated again by Stephen, the castle was later granted to Gilbert de Clare, 1st Earl of Pembroke. The subsequent switching of sides by the latter saw him captured by Stephen. Released, he rebelled against the monarch, and a second siege again ended in surrender due to a lack of supplies.

Back in royal hands, renovations in the 1190s may have led to the formation of the first stone walls at the site since Roman times. Another statement refers to a tower of Pevensey in the 1130s, yet without clarifying what material was used. Over the coming centuries, the castle would face two more sieges. Slighted deliberately by John in 1216 to prevent its use by Prince Louis of France, the castle was rebuilt during the reign of Henry III, most likely under the guidance of Peter of Savoy. It was to Pevensey that many defeated royalists fled following the Battle of Lewes in May 1264, after which Pevensey suffered its third siege. Though two local churches and the Roman wall were damaged, the castle endured for more than a year after successfully finding ways of replenishing the stocks.

At the end of the next century, the castle endured its most famous siege. Returned to the Crown on Peter of Savoy's death and owned for a time by the queen consorts, by 1399, the man appointed constable was one John Pelham. Absent fighting the cause of Henry Bolingbroke, the royalist forces of Richard II laid siege to Pevensey, at the time the residence of Pelham's loyal wife, Joan. Successful at least in keeping the marauding enemy at bay, Joan managed to smuggle out a letter:

> My dear Lord ... if it please you to know of my affairs, I am here bylaid in manner of a siege, with the counties of Sussex, Surrey and a great part of Kent, so that I may not out, nor no vitals get me without much difficulty. Wherefore my dear may it please you, by the advice of your wise council, to give remedy to the salvation of your castle, and withstand the malice of the shire ... Farewell my dear lord, the Holy Trinity keep you from your enemies, and soon send me good tidings of you. Written at Pevensey, in the Castle, on Saint Jacob day last past. By ever your own poor, J. Pelham.

Fortunately for the garrison, help arrived. Though the siege was raised, and Pelham awarded the honour of Pevensey, sadly for Lady Joan, she was later imprisoned. It is reputedly her pale ghost that has been seen wandering the battlements.

Unsurprisingly, walls that were effective in keeping people out were equally good at keeping others in. As such, the restored castle was later utilised as a royalist prison. Among the most famous inmates were James I of Scotland, who was captured on his way to France in 1405. Following him was Edward, 2nd Duke of York, imprisoned for conspiracy against Henry IV. In acknowledgement of his gaoler, Thomas Playsted, Edward bestowed £20 to him in his will. Between December 1419 and March 1420, the castle was also the residence of Henry IV's second queen, Joan of Navarre, who was imprisoned by stepson Henry V on charges of attempted regicide via witchcraft. She was later moved to Leeds Castle and released in 1422. It has also been suggested that it is her ghost as opposed to Lady Pelham that is often seen gazing from the battlements.

By the Tudor age, the castle was abandoned, and by 1573 the neglect was blatant. Orders by Elizabeth that the castle be 'utterlye raysed' was fortunately not carried out. Two cannons were placed there during the Spanish Invasion of 1588 but never fired. Various sales and purchases, including returns by the Pelhams and royals over the centuries, followed, after which the castle was given to the Ministry of Works and later English Heritage. In WWII, it enjoyed one last hurrah, playing host to a military garrison.

A key defensive structure for nearly 2,000 years, it should be considered little surprise that the two Joans are not the only ghosts reputed to haunt Pevensey. Brief sightings and sounds of large armies have been witnessed: a reminder, perhaps, of at least one of its four sieges. The ghost of a lady in white supposedly appears in a nearby field. It is not clear whether this spirit and the pale lady are the same.

Among the plethora of ghosts is that of a Roman centurion, who appears near the old walls. A phantom drummer boy, marching soldiers, and dying men all tally with what is known of the site. Witnessed nearby has also been a figure in a black cloak. Before the Dissolution, at least twenty-five monastic cells existed in Sussex. Merely 10 miles separate the castle from the ruins of Battle Abbey, whose Benedictine inhabitants were often known as the 'black monks'.

During its long history, Pevensey has seen much. Indeed, if walls could talk, no castle in England – with the possible exception of Dover or the Tower of London – could regale us with such tales. A more recent claim to fame is its use in the Rudyard Kipling classic, *Puck of Pook's Hill*, in which gold is buried there.

Doubtful though it is that real treasure lies within its towers, in his work, Kipling may just have given Pevensey a far more incredible legacy. A local of the area, the Victorian novelist's characters described the castle as 'the gateway of England'. Just a simple look at its history should be enough to confirm he was right.

Chapter 6

Kent

Dover

Situated at the most south-eastern point of England's coastline, the castle at Dover has acted as a vital defensive post since its construction. Built on Iron Age earthworks, the site was explicitly highlighted as one of crucial importance by the Roman invaders who created a lighthouse – the Pharos – on the headland. Today, the impressive structure is one of only three such creations still in existence and can be found next to the Anglo-Saxon church of St Mary-in-Castro. There is good evidence that the Saxons converted the lighthouse into the church's belfry.

In later years, the site continued to be of some importance to the Saxons before William the Conqueror put down the third of his castles there in October 1066. Records state that the Normans erected the original clay-based motte and bailey in a mere eight days – it is unclear on how broad a scale the original castle was. Successful in avoiding the chaos of the Anarchy, it was under Henry II that the castle truly began to take shape. The inner and outer baileys were both established in his time. As was the iconic keep, from the roof of which one can see the French coast on a clear day. During the period 1179–88, the king spent no less than £6,500 on its development – more than half his annual budget.

Thus, the seeds were sown for what many regard as the most impressive castle in England. With the possible exception of Windsor, it is also the largest. Located at such an important point, it stares out to sea, looking would-be invaders in the face. Ironically, invaders established it. Due to its short distance to Calais, it came to be viewed as the most important of the Cinque Ports. Like Pevensey, it has been called the Key to England.

During its history, several important things have happened at Dover Castle. Having been loyally defended by Hubert de Burgh – justiciar of

King John and Henry III and later first earl of Kent – during the siege of 1216–17 against Prince Louis of France, the castle was thoroughly added to by Henry III, who spent more than £7,000 on securing the defences. The north gate, breached during the siege, was converted into an underground defence complex. The English also made tunnels to find their way out to attack the French. To endure the age of gunpowder, Henry VIII ordered the redevelopment of parts of the castle following a personal visit.

Come the Civil War, a stroke of luck saw the castle spared. Garrisoned by a small number of Royalists, a local merchant named Richard Dawkes scaled the cliffs with a party of ten and infiltrated the Porter's Lodge to take the keys without the need to launch an assault. As military technology improved, it was the subject of massive remodelling in the eighteenth century and upgraded further during the wars against Napoleon. During this period, the castle housed more than 2,000 troops. Some of the tunnels below the castle also date from around this time. Many were used as air-raid shelters and for military planning during World War II. This area was also the HQ of Admiral Sir Bertram Ramsay, the man behind Operation Dynamo: the evacuation of Dunkirk.

Used continuously until after World War II and subjected to violent sieges, Dover is another ancient fortress with a reputation for being haunted. Throughout its 2,000-year history, tales of warmongering, murder, deceit and betrayal have been recurring features. It is the victims of such stories who are said to join the spirits of England's loyal soldiers, who locals say remain destined to defend the castle, as they did so bravely in life.

When the moon rises over the town, the apparition of a drummer boy has reputedly been seen. Accompanying his movements are the faint echoes of a drum roll that drifts across the battlements. In life, it is believed the lad was one Sean Flynn: a 15-year-old who served in the army around 1800. According to one version of events, Flynn – or possibly another drummer stationed there – was killed at Waterloo, his head ripped off by a cannonball. Another version claims that the captain handpicked him late one night to deliver some money. As he made his way to the town, two members of his own regiment brutally killed Flynn and stole the money. When his body was found, he was without a head. Since his brutal death, the ghost of the drummer has been seen and heard on many occasions. At least one psychic has claimed the boy lingered as he longed to be reunited with his devastated mother.

The spirit of a Cavalier soldier has also been seen near the keep. The figure, described as possessing long dark hair and a moustache, stands silently by the old wall before fading from sight. Similar activity is reported among the castle's oldest features, including a Roman near the Pharos and a hooded monk by the church.

Although several apparitions have been witnessed above ground, it is within the castle that paranormal activity is said to be at its greatest. Deep beneath the foundations and stretching into the white cliffs, the medieval and Napoleonic tunnels performed a vital service during the Second World War. The spirit of a seventeenth-century pikeman has been seen at the furthest end of the tunnels and even walking through a wall. Another soldier, dressed in a blue cloak, has also been witnessed walking the passageways. Perhaps most famously, the ghosts of Allied service personnel have been sighted in what was once their HQ.

Even more disturbingly, past occupants and visitors are reputed to have been alarmed by the inexplicable sensation of physical bombardment, believed to be connected with the violent attacks the castle suffered at the hands of energy siege engines. Other sounds have been heard throughout the tunnels along which heavy wooden doors once blocked what are now empty doorways. Intriguingly, the noise of slamming doors continues to resonate there.

Back in the heart of the castle, the ghost of a man has been seen in the king's bedroom. Strangely, his lower half has been seen walking through the doorway before disappearing on the other side, where no obvious exit is forthcoming. A similar story concerns a woman wearing a stunning red dress who has been seen standing by the west stairway of the keep. Although her face remains concealed, the spirit has been known to sigh and cry.

A centrepiece of English history for more than 2,000 years, no other castle incorporates the journey as completely as Dover. From Iron Age remains to WWII bunkers and mentions in *Morte d'Arthur* to tales of headless drummers, Dover has it all. As complete and perfect a physical castle as one can find, it has become the very definition of quintessential English, Norman and Plantagenet. Nor does its capacity to surprise show signs of diminishing. A quick search of Google or YouTube can delight many a ghost hunter. A strange clip caught on camera in 2011 shows a peculiar blurred shape move past one of the exits. Of even greater intrigue, no sooner had the shape departed when a security guard appears, clearly tracking the movement. Precisely what caused it remains unclear. The footage seems to have caught a genuine mystery.

Hever

Erected as a country house around 1270, the wealthy Bullen family upgraded Hever into a castle around 1460. Located in the village of the same name – approximately 30 miles from London – the castle remained in the same family until 1539 when a series of unfortunate events saw it pass to new owners. Before this, two decisions would ensure the family's rise and future infamy. The first was of the early Bullens to change the spelling of the family name. The second, of their descendant Thomas, 1st Earl of Wiltshire to marry the Duke of Norfolk's daughter, Lady Elizabeth Howard. Of their many children, one was named Anne. Not Bullen. But Boleyn.

At times referred to as a castle in miniature, modern-day visitors are often taken aback by the cosiness of the setting. The dining hall is only 40 feet long and set up for small gatherings instead of lavish banquets. By contrast, the Italian-style gardens and Hampton Court-like maze are famed attractions. In the estate's fine gardens, Anne first met Henry VIII after her return from France. The castle still contains one of Henry's locks: something taken on his travels and fitted to the doors to ensure his security. Around 1526, the king began an affair with Anne's sister, Mary. It was also after the king that Mary's second child, officially the son of husband William Carey, was named.

Henry found Anne a far tougher nut to crack. When Henry's divorce from Catherine of Aragon was finalised, the scene was set for Anne, now marchioness of Pembroke, to take the empty consort's throne. When Henry and Anne married – possibly for a second time – in January 1533, Anne was already pregnant with the future Elizabeth I. Three more attempts ended in tragedy, after which the king's patience wavered. With this, the wheels were set in motion for the famously sad climax of Anne's existence. She was executed on Tower Green after being found guilty of a range of trumped-up charges. According to legend, her lips continued to mutter for several seconds after her beheading by a specialist swordsman, brought in at her own request – she having such a little neck. Bizarrely, the authorities failed to have a coffin on-site and required the improvisation of an arrow chest. When it was opened years later, her remains were allegedly found with her head tucked underneath her arm.

Anne's downfall would have dire consequences for Hever's owners. On her father's death in 1539, after retiring to Hever in disgrace, Henry requisitioned the property for his fourth wife, Anne of Cleves. As time passed, the property fell into disrepair and, at one point, was used as a farmhouse. Only in 1903, after the purchase by William Waldorf Astor, did its return to prominence begin to take shape.

Though Hever itself is not thought to contain any significant mysteries, the castle is one of at least four that Anne is supposed to haunt. Her ubiquitous spirit reportedly roams the building and grounds, particularly the lovely bridge that crosses the river, aptly named Eden. That Anne's bereaved soul should return to the garden seems a fitting epilogue, not least as her rise to glory had deprived her of the bliss she had perhaps at times taken for granted.

Leeds

Standing on a series of naturally formed islands in the centre of a tranquil lake, pale-stoned Leeds has been described as a 'lady's dream castle'. Located 5 miles south-east of Maidstone, where the River Len flows through a small village after which the castle is named, Leeds is another of those incredible fairy-tale fortresses whose great walls and miniature turrets on days when the lake is calm presents the illusion of being lost in time.

Impossible though it is to guess from its present appearance, the site dates back to 857 and a Saxon leader named Leed. The original wooden structure was created on two islands in the middle of the river that ultimately formed the lake. A stone castle dates to 1119 and the Norman warlord Robert de Crevecoeur. Throughout the next century, Leeds remained in the same family; among their number, Hamo de Crevecoeur served as Lord of the Cinque Ports. In 1278, the castle entered royal hands when William of Leybourne was unable to pay off his debts. Something of a rarity in English history, Eleanor of Castile, the queen consort of Edward I, bought Leeds, establishing its reputation as the 'castle of the medieval queens'. Due to Edward and Eleanor's love for the place, a series of improvements followed. Among them were the barbican and a gloriette in the garden with royal apartments. The lake may have been converted into its present form at this time.

Constructed more as a home than a defensive fortress, in 1321, Leeds experienced its only siege. Edward II orchestrated the attack when Margaret de Clare, the wife of constable Bartholomew of Badlesmere, refused Queen Isabella entry. Consequently, not least due to Margaret's order for her archers to open fire, killing six of the royal party, she was held in the Tower of London. Between 1327 and 1330 – from Edward II's abdication to Edward III's uprising against his mother and regent, Roger Mortimer – Isabella used Leeds frequently. Later that century, Anne of Bohemia spent the winter of 1381 there before her marriage to Richard II, who entertained the French chronicler Jean Froissart within its walls in 1395. Richard was also reputedly imprisoned at Leeds before being relocated to Pontefract – see Pontefract Castle – yet this is unconfirmed.

Continuing Leeds's tradition as the castle of the royal wives, Henry VIII granted it to Catherine of Aragon, having transformed the castle for her in 1519. Fortunately, Leeds escaped action in the Civil War due to the parliamentary leanings of its owner, Sir Cheney Culpeper, who used it as an arsenal and prison. On the restoration, Charles II granted Cheney's relative John, 1st Lord Culpeper, 5,000,000 acres in Virginia in gratitude for helping him flee. Thus began a long-term connection between the family and the state of Virginia. A commemorative sundial is kept at the castle that tells the time in Belvoir, Virginia; a sister device exists in Belvoir. Instrumental in establishing the connection was a marriage between a Culpeper daughter and the Fairfax family. Among their number, General Thomas Fairfax had been so influential in winning Cromwell the war.

In later years, the castle served as a private residence and hospital in WWII before the final owner, Lady Baillie, left the castle to the Leeds Castle Foundation. A flamboyant socialite, who hosted the type of hootenannies made famous in the Great Gatsby, it is thanks to her that the foundation cares for the castle and welcomes the public. As well as being chosen for television and filming, its use has extended to matters of diplomacy. On 17 July 1978, the castle hosted foreign ministers from Egypt and Israel, as well as a US secretary of state. In September 2004, it also hosted peace talks between the UK and Northern Ireland.

Like many former homes, Leeds has its fair share of reputed hauntings. Most prominent is the Black Shuck, which is associated with death among the owner's family. On another occasion, a woman investigating the phantom hound's disappearance through a wall marginally avoided tragedy when rubble fell moments later.

The origin of the dog is open to conjecture. According to local lore, its presence lies with the depressing tale of Eleanor of Gloucester, initially mistress and later second wife of Humphrey, Duke of Gloucester. Eleanor was found guilty of witchcraft and necromancy in 1431, most notably burning a likeness of Henry VI. As punishment, she was imprisoned at the castle for life, and her ghost is said to glide the corridors. Either intertwined or separate from the Black Shuck, the castle is also reputedly the haunt of two other dogs: one white and another black. Incidentally, Lady Baillie is believed to have kept such dogs as pets.

A ghostly lady brushing her hair has been seen in both the grounds and the queen's room, which was also reportedly subject to a time slip. Joan of Navarre is known to have frequented the room during her imprisonment – see also Pevensey Castle – also for witchcraft. She was released on Henry V's orders in 1422. Longstanding conjecture still blames her for Hal's untimely death just six weeks later. She would survive another 15 years before being laid to rest alongside Henry IV in the east section of Canterbury Cathedral.

Rochester

Few castles in England have played a more influential role in medieval history than mighty Rochester. Originally a motte and bailey located where the River Medway meets ancient Watling Street – one of the earliest and most important trade routes in the country – the castle was given by William the Conqueror to his half-brother, Odo, Bishop of Bayeux, upon whom William bestowed the earldom of Kent. During those early years, Odo was arguably the second most important figure in England.

Influential in augmenting Norman rule in the south, the castle was besieged by William Rufus during the Robert Curthose rebellion of 1088 after Odo pledged his support to Curthose and made Rochester his HQ. After defeating the garrison, Rufus abandoned the original castle and charged Gundulf of Caen, subsequently bishop of Rochester, to build a replacement in stone. Among his other claims to fame were Rochester Cathedral, Colchester Castle and, most famously, the Tower of London.

It was thanks to the tireless work of Gundulf that the modern castle visitors know and love today began to take shape. In 1127, Henry I granted the fortress in perpetuity to the archbishop of Canterbury. Under the guidance of Archbishop William de Corbeil, the magnificent keep was erected within Gundulf's walls. Standing 115 feet in height, it was the tallest tower in England and one of the earliest. Available evidence indicates that Rochester was based on the mighty French castle of Loches.

En route between London and Dover – and London and Canterbury – Rochester was of significant strategic importance throughout the medieval era and became a frequent target of uprising. After the siege of 1088, the castle suffered two more full sieges, one of which is quite rightly regarded among the greatest on English soil.

That event occurred in 1215 when King John laid siege to the traditionally royal castle after reneging on Magna Carta. The barons had made Rochester a key base after capturing it from Stephen Langton, the archbishop of Canterbury. Exactly how that occurred is unclear. The chronicler Ralph of Coggeshall implies that John had demanded Stephen return the castle, which he refused. Aware of this, the constable, Reginald de Cornhill, changed sides and held it for the barons. Writing to his justiciar, Hubert de Burgh, John pointed a stern finger at Langton, who temporarily departed the country.

Intent on recapturing Rochester, John began his siege. The exact size of the garrison is unclear, though the chroniclers place the number at 95-140 knights plus those of lower rank. During the siege, the famous chronicler of St Albans, Roger of Wendover, tells of how a crossbowman had John in his sights and asked his commander, William d'Aubigny, for permission to fire. On mulling the matter over, d'Aubigny stated that ending the life of a king was for God to decide. Undoubtedly on William's mind was the fate of John's elder brother, Richard the Lionheart, who had succumbed to a crossbow attack in 1199.

Throughout the seven-week siege, the hearts and minds of the garrison were tested to the utmost. Watching devices like siege engines being assembled before them was undoubtedly hugely morale-sapping – not least as supplies became limited. About 700 knights rode out from London to relieve the rebels, but on reaching Dartford, their nerves failed them. The destruction of the bridge by royalist forces may have influenced their decision. The Barnwell Annalist lamented: 'Our age has not known a siege so hard pressed nor so strongly resisted.' So trying did conditions get, he also noted that the garrison was forced to resort to eating the flesh of their horses.

Try as the brave Rochester garrison might, by cunning and dogged persistence, John finally got his reward. The key was the burrowing of a mine, which was eventually used to undermine the walls. The precise location of John's mine is still a mystery. Recent research has offered persuasive evidence that it ran more or less alongside the Victorian wall, though it is difficult to know the exact beginning and end. The sounds of mining were undoubtedly a source of additional torment to the defenders. Yet this would have been nothing compared to the silence that confirmed the firing of the mine was imminent. A letter sent by John to Hubert on 25 November ordered the justiciar send post-haste forty bacon pigs, least good for eating, for the firing of the mine. The blast caused at least one corner of the keep to collapse, forcing the garrison to take shelter deeper inside. The Barnwell Annalist reported that 'for such was the structure of the stronghold that a very strong wall separated the half that had fallen from the other'.

On taking the castle, John wisely spared the majority, all of who had fought bravely and were willing to come to peace. So unexpected was John's success, Barnwell also stated that few now put their faith in castles. Colchester, Framlingham and Hedingham all fell soon after. As fate had it, John's endeavours did little good. Significantly damaged in the siege, the castle was recaptured by the barons, under the leadership of Prince Louis, and in 1217 restored to royal ownership.

Significant work needed to be done on both castle and town walls at a high cost. In 1264, the walls were tested again when civil war broke out between Henry III and Simon de Montfort, 6th Earl of Leicester. The constable at the time was Roger de Leybourne, who operated alongside John de Warenne, Earl of Surrey. Opposing them was the baronial heavyweight, Gilbert de Clare, Earl of Hertford and Gloucester. After the royalist garrison razed the suburbs, and the king's hall within the castle itself, the combined forces of de Clare and Simon de Montfort attacked from the city. Within their arsenal was a fire ship, either as a cover or to destroy the bridge. They entered the town on Good Friday, 18 April 1264, and raided the cathedral. Though hostilities ceased on Easter Sunday, the castle's outer defences fell, and the royals stood firm until 26 April when a relief force led by Prince Edward was reported to be en route.

It was during this time an event is said to have occurred that gave rise to arguably Rochester Castle's greatest legend. Engaged to the royalist Sir Ralph de Capo was Lady Blanche de Warenne, Surrey's daughter, both of whom were stationed at the castle. The engagement was viewed as a slight on Gilbert de Clare, who had previously desired Blanche for himself. During the siege, Montfort retreated when Henry III's forces followed him, at which point Capo opened the gates and laid chase. In the events that followed, Gilbert noticed Lady Blanche alone on the battlements. Wearing an identical surcoat to Capo, he duped his way into the castle and initially fooled Blanche. As Blanche was seized, Capo noticed his love was in trouble and fired an arrow at Gilbert's torso.

It was here that fate, alas, struck a cruel twist. Unaware that his enemy wore a breastplate beneath his surcoat, the arrow deflected away and pierced Blanche's breast. According to legend, that very night, Blanche's ghost appeared inside the castle. Since then, she has been seen many times, usually close to where she succumbed to the arrow. An epilogue of the story tells that a furious Capo pursued Gilbert through the streets and aboard his escape vessel. Sadly for Capo, his foot got tangled, and he was brutally slaughtered. Though the story is plausible, there is an undeniable sense of Victorian melodrama about it. The earliest this author can date the story is 1829.

In the century following the aborted action of 1264, Rochester's woes proved less severe. In 1314, the castle served as the temporary prison of Elizabeth de Burgh, queen consort of Robert the Bruce, after which the continuous reuse of the materials, poor management and severe gales left it in a sorry state. A partial ruin until the later years of Edward III, redevelopment began and continued during the reign of his grandson and successor, Richard II. During the Peasants' Revolt of 1381, the stone castle was besieged for the final time, the interior plundered, and at least one prisoner released.

From the reign of Henry IV onwards, Rochester's history has been less eventful. Part of the dower of Catherine of Valois, widow of Henry V, little of note appears to have occurred in the following centuries. Visiting the castle in the 1600s, Samuel Pepys bemoaned its condition. Its use in the Civil War was limited, not least as its owner, Sir Anthony Weldon, supported the Roundheads. When the Royalists took the castle in 1648, they did so peacefully.

One of many picturesque ruins that inspired a painting by Turner, another to take a keen interest was Rochester local Charles Dickens. Among his writings, Dickens penned references to the 'glorious pile – frowning wall – tottering arches – dark nooks – crumbling stones' that had survived since the days of Gundulf. Rochester appeared in no less than two of Dickens's classic works, *The Pickwick Papers* and *The Mystery of Edwin Drood*. Far more bizarrely, his ghost is reputed to stalk the old burial ground close to the moat every Christmas Eve. Though Dickens was famously laid to rest in Westminster Abbey's Poet's Corner, local legend tells that it was in the shadow of Rochester's mighty bastion the great novelist wished to rest in peace.

Immortalised in war, literature and art, the imposing remains of Rochester Castle act as a fine testament to England's violent past. Local legend also tells that many others join the ghosts of Blanche and Mr Dickens. Strange mists are reputed to appear from nowhere. A lady in green, perhaps also Blanche, has been seen coming down the stairway. A white-haired man has also been seen. More concerning eyewitness accounts tell of a tall, dark figure who often appears in the chapel. Reports of this entity have included violent threats, not least his telling one visitor to 'Get out'. Exactly who this evil force is and why he feels the need to intimidate is unclear. Perhaps even now, responsibility for the castle's survival still weighs heavily on those who defended it so bravely.

Scotney

Nestled in the River Bewl valley, Scotney is another of England's fine residences. A picturesque country house with well-manicured National Trust gardens in the modern-day, within the estate lies a medieval castle or fortified manor. The ruins, set upon an island in the centre of a lake, are often designated the 'old castle' to separate it from the far newer building constructed under the guidance of Anthony Salvin between 1835 and 1843.

The origins of the moated medieval residence can be dated to around 1378 and one Roger Ashburnham. During the Elizabethan era, its owners, the staunchly Catholic Darrell family, used the property to hide the Jesuit priest Richard Blount. The house was the subject of a search by the Catholic pursuivants during the Christmas festivities of 1598. When the lady of the house noticed Blount's belt sticking out as he occupied the hidey-hole, her loudening voice made the pursuivants suspicious. As if by divine intervention, their attempts to batter the outer wall were halted by a thunderstorm. As the soldiers dined that night, a servant successfully distracted them with a warning that their horses were in the process of being stolen. During their brief absence, Blount swam across the moat to safety.

When the castle began its slide into decline in the 1600s, William Darrell started reusing the stone for the east range. The family continued to hold the estate until 1778, when it was sold to Edward Hussey, whose grandson and namesake built the new castle. His descendants maintained it until 1970, at which point it entered public ownership.

Before Hussey's time occurred arguably the castle's most legendary story. In 1720, owner Arthur Darrell died abroad. His body was returned and buried in the churchyard of nearby Lamberhurst. During the burial, a strange figure in a dark cloak was spotted among the mourners and overheard to whisper, 'That is me they think they are burying.'

Although those in attendance conducted a thorough search, the man in black was never found. Was he a ghost? A conman? Or had Arthur Darrell still been alive at this time and watched another man being laid to rest in his place? Rumour has since abounded that Arthur faked his death as his sisters had continuously sued for control of the estate. In his later years, he reputedly made a living as a smuggler. Central to the story are claims that Darrell used Scotney's grounds to set up his operation and even murdered an excise officer and flung his body in the moat. Since that time, the murdered man's ghost has reportedly been seen heading towards the old castle only to vanish on knocking on the door.

Strange as it sounds, the story is plausible. Smuggling depended on utmost secrecy. The possibility that Darrell shipped home the body of another man from overseas can also not be ruled out. Yet plausibility and proof are two very different things. As far as history is concerned, Arthur Darrell was buried in 1720. The stranger in the graveyard has never been seen since. If he even existed at all.

Chapter 7

Surrey, Berkshire and Oxfordshire

Farnham

The ruins of Farnham serve as a reminder of the power once possessed by the see of Winchester. Constructed in 1138 by Henry of Blois, grandson of William the Conqueror, brother of King Stephen, and a bishop himself, Henry's fortress lasted a mere seventeen years before becoming a victim of Henry II's attempts to erase the scars of the Anarchy. Under the king's guidance, a stone replacement followed during the late twelfth and early thirteenth centuries.

Throughout its history, the castle has remained a permanent asset of the bishops. In the early 1400s, it was the domain of John of Gaunt's son, Cardinal Henry Beaufort, who presided over Joan of Arc's trial in 1431. The nearby and relatively modern Catholic Church of St Joan of Arc was named in her honour. During the latter part of the seventeenth century, Bishop George Morley set to work on adding to the castle, which was slighted in 1648. In the Second World War, Farnham operated as a Camouflage Development and Training Centre before focusing on intercultural training and serving as a conference centre.

Renowned for its imposing keep and rural location, Farnham is a castle steeped in atmosphere. When viewed from a distance as evening turns to dusk, the skeletal ruins cause strange shadows over the town below. Eyewitness accounts also tell of a hazy form inhabiting the ruins. Strangely the sound of bells has been known to reverberate, although the tower has not possessed any for years.

Unsurprisingly, given the atmosphere, the castle has a reputation for being haunted. A procession of phantom monks has been seen walking through the moat before disappearing. That the castle was associated with the monks of St Swithun's is, of course, well known. In the great hall, a ghostly monk or reverend has been seen on the stairway, which is also reputedly the haunt of Bishop Morley. The seventeenth-century bishop has also been witnessed in other parts of the castle – and world.

Joining them is said to be the sad ghost of a girl who was ordered to dance until she dropped. The pitter-pattering of feet and audible gasps have all been experienced in the great hall, on which a sombre atmosphere is said to descend. Footsteps and children's voices have also been heard in other parts of the castle, while poltergeist activity and even full apparitions have been noted. Stories abound that a soldier was shot in the face in the cellar: a location where modern-day visitors occasionally recall pain in their head or face.

Completing Farnham's list of ghostly tales is that of a spirit who appears close to the keep. After appearing initially as a hazy form, the strange apparition proceeds to transfigure as a full-bodied woman dressed in a pale gown and a full cord girdle. Descriptions of her attire may infer she is of the twelfth century; however, no recognition has been suggested. Only that on being stared upon, she permeates the power to frighten one to death with her frown.

Donnington

Donnington Castle was the brainchild of Sir Richard Abberbury the Elder, chamberlain to Anne of Bohemia, queen consort of Richard II. Though work on the castle officially began in 1386 to guard against a French invasion, Abberbury's ancestors had acquired the manor almost a century earlier. In 1398, the family sold the castle to Thomas Chaucer, son of the legendary Geoffrey: himself a relative through marriage of John of Gaunt, the third son of Edward III. After remaining under royal control throughout the Tudor period, Elizabeth I's granting of the castle to Lady Russell marks her out among the first women to hold the title in English history.

Like many, it was in the Civil War, the castle met its destiny. In 1644, Parliamentarian general John Middleton arrived with 3,000 troops and demanded the garrison's surrender. The Royalist leader Sir John Boys was himself a relative newcomer, having taken control after Charles I usurped the castle from John Packer following the First Battle of Newbury. The inconclusive result of the Second Battle of Newbury on 27 October 1644 led to further assault from Sir William Waller. However, fortunately for the garrison, the assistance of a Royalist force commanded by Prince Rupert helped stem the tide.

For more than nineteen months, neither the loss of three towers nor severe damage to the curtain walls forced them to surrender. After using the winter months to reinforce their defences, the garrison held firm until April 1646 when Charles I ultimately permitted Boys to negotiate with the Roundheads. Though Parliament ordered the castle's slighting, the magnificent gatehouse retains its seat of prominence on its original spur overlooking the old road that connected Bath to London. The site is now under the care of English Heritage and open to visitors.

In the years since its legendary last stand, the castle has acquired a reputation for being haunted. Several ghosts are said to roam the ruins, including one on both floors of the gatehouse. So natural is his appearance, he has often been mistaken for a guide. A white dog is also said to run down the hill towards the woodlands. A phantom guard also reportedly appears around the gatehouse, in addition to a lady in green, believed to be one Lady Hoby, who lived there in the reign of James I.

Far more bizarre are reports of occasional time slips. Among the most notable concerns the ghostly re-enactment between a Royalist patrol and Parliamentarians, as well as a violent skirmish in which a Royalist soldier has a woman in a headlock.

Windsor

Beloved worldwide as the quintessential royal residence, for almost 1,000 years, the castle at Windsor has overlooked the River Thames and surrounding countryside. The view of the south façade, which incorporates the famous round tower and twin-towered gatehouse from along the 'Long Walk', is one of Britain's most iconic. Like the similar view along the Mall to its sister residence, Buckingham Palace, few sights lend more to the magic and majesty associated with the British monarchy. Even in the modern-day, for young and old alike, the romantic aura that surrounds Windsor remains powerful. It has often been said that no country in the world carries out such pomp and circumstance quite like the British.

Begun by William the Conqueror in the 1070s to help augment his rule over England's Home Counties, Windsor started life as a motte and bailey with three wards added around a central mound. The castle was later expanded and upgraded in stone and became a royal palace in the reign of Henry I. Upgraded further by his grandson, Henry II, the castle withstood a fierce siege during the First Barons' War. Before this, it was in Windsor's dungeons that John imprisoned Maud de Braose, wife of William de Braose, and their son, also William – see also Corfe Castle. On John's death, his son and successor, Henry III, spent huge sums on repairs. Throughout Henry's reign, a luxurious palace was built within the walls, including state apartments for himself and his queen. Henry's great-grandson Edward III would enhance this further. After revamping and developing the palace, Edward created what has been described as 'the most expensive secular building project of the entire Middle Ages in England'.

Edward's work survived the Tudor era and formed the basis of several key improvements. The most special of these occurred during the reigns of Henry VIII and Elizabeth I, whose additions helped upgrade the fine royal palace into a setting of diplomatic entertainment. Enjoyed by James I as a hunting lodge and by Charles I to house his impressive art collection, in the Civil War, its purpose changed to that of a military headquarters and prison. On the restoration, Charles II rebuilt large parts of the castle in league with the Baroque architect Hugh May. A period of neglect preceded further renovation by Georges III and IV, which brought the exterior more or less to its present state. It is now the preferred weekend retreat of HM Elizabeth II and holds claim to being the oldest and largest inhabited castle in Europe.

The centrepiece of English history for almost 1,000 years, it is no surprise that Windsor has amassed a host of legends. A recent article suggested as many as twenty-five ghosts are reputed to haunt the castle, many of which possess royal pedigree. Among the most prominent is the king who took six wives. Over the years, Henry VIII's ghost has been spotted and heard wandering the cloisters and corridors many times. Eyewitness accounts refer to his appearance as reminiscent of his later years, oversized and plagued by his famous ulcerated leg that had developed courtesy of a jousting accident. Joining her former husband is Anne Boleyn, who has been seen peering through the window of the

Dean's Cloister. Past accounts tell of her looking drawn and withered – a stark contrast to her headlessness at the Tower of London.

Haunting the royal library is the ghost of their daughter, the future Elizabeth I. Often preceded by the sound of heeled shoes on the bare floorboards, Elizabeth has also appeared near the Dean's Cloister, close to where her mother has been seen. A child of only 2 ½ when Henry VIII had Anne beheaded, Elizabeth was deprived of a loving relationship with her mother. Even in the brief periods in which they were alive, circumstances often separated the pair. That the two may have crossed paths on their ethereal wanderings is a comforting thought. In contrast to her mother's somewhat haggard appearance, Elizabeth has reportedly been seen in an attractive black gown.

Shortly before Christmas 1648, King Charles I was brought to Windsor in preparation for his trial after being kept on the Isle of Wight – see Carisbrooke Castle. Immediately after his beheading on 30 January 1649, his body was returned to Windsor for burial in St George's Chapel in the same vault as Henry VIII and Jane Seymour. Legend speaks that as the coffin, draped in black, was brought towards the castle, the previously blue sky became unfathomably darker, a precursor to a blizzard. The story also tells that the black pall over the coffin had miraculously turned white as a sign of Charles's innocence. Since that time, Charles's ghost has also been seen haunting both the library and a canon's house in the castle precincts.

Joining the Tudor royals in their nocturnal wanderings is said to be the tormented spirit of George III. Famously Britain's longest-serving king – having ruled 1760–1820 – the 'mad' king has been seen peering mournfully through a window in the library. George III was confined mainly to Windsor in his latter years and enjoyed taking and returning the salute of his guards every afternoon. As his body remained in state, guards passing the king's window were shocked to see him standing there. On making the order to salute the king, the ghostly monarch returned their salute one last time.

Run-ins with the extraordinary are by no means limited to the royals. In April 1906, a sentry was shocked when a group of men appeared to be walking towards him. When his challenge went unanswered, his charge with a bayonet saw him attacking thin air. A search of the grounds achieved nothing. As a consequence, the sentry was confined to the barracks for three days for neglect of duty.

Beloved in the day for its incredible views, the Long Walk is an area some prefer to avoid at night. While on patrol in 1927, an 18-year-old guardsman reportedly became so overcome with grief that he shot himself. In the weeks that followed, one Sergeant Leake took the watch and was shocked when the sound of footsteps preceded the apparition of his late colleague. When the relief arrived moments later, the apparition vanished. In the hours that followed, practically all present admitted that they had seen the ghost in recent weeks.

Many other areas of the castle are also associated with the paranormal. The Deanery is said to be the haunt of a boy who utters 'I don't want to go riding today'. The Prison Room in the Norman Tower has been the subject of appearances from a phantom cavalier. Ghostly footsteps have also been heard in the Deanery and on the stairs in the Curfew Tower.

Another strange happening occurred in 1873. A night-time visitor was intrigued by what appeared to be a new artwork close to St George's Chapel. Noting three standing figures all in black and a fourth crouched down, about to be struck with a sword, he asked the nearest sentry, who was unfamiliar with the piece. On returning to examine it, the figures had disappeared.

Among the earliest ghosts to haunt the castle is that of William of Wykeham, bishop of Winchester and chancellor of England. Also founder of Winchester College and New College, Oxford, William was appointed chief architect by Edward III and has been seen casting a critical eye over his work.

A far more alluring spectre said to haunt the grounds is that of Herne the Hunter. Exactly who Herne was has become the source of conjecture. Regarded by some as an ancient spirit of Windsor Forest, Herne was also said to have been a hunter for Richard II after bravely saving the monarch from a cornered stag. Legend relates that the wounded Herne was healed through a combination of witchcraft and being told to wear the stag's antlers. Herne's new standing was met with jealousy among his colleagues, leading to their framing him for theft. Shamed, he hanged himself on 'Herne's Oak' and has since become something of a free spirit of the forest. Shakespeare included the legend in his 1597 play, *The Merry Wives of Windsor*. Sadly, there is no written evidence prior to Shakespeare's play, and what is believed to have been the original tree was felled in 1796.

Another put forward as the tree in question was blown down in 1863. Queen Victoria approved of the legend and had another planted on the spot. However, this was removed in 1906. Another story equates Herne with yeomen Richard Horne, who was caught poaching there during the reign of Henry VIII. Legend states that the appearance of Herne is a prelude to bad luck. In 1962, a group of youths reputedly found a hunting horn, a blow on which summoned Herne on a black horse. On seeing the ghost, the group ran for their lives.

Of the many spirits believed to frequent the castle, Queen Victoria is surely among the most interesting. An elegant statue of Victoria stands outside the palace, put up in honour of her golden jubilee in 1887. Victoria is conjectured to have been intrigued by the craze of spiritualism and proceeded to hold séances within the castle – many of which were conducted to contact her beloved Albert. The prince himself is reported to have died in the Blue Room. Rumours that her notes on the events were discovered and burnt by the dean of Windsor after her death for fear of public outcry cannot at present be substantiated. Following her death, an event that took place during the brief reign of her great-grandson, Edward VIII, is said to have proved highly offensive to her spirit. Enamoured in life with a particular spruce tree, the king made the controversial decision to remove it. As a consequence, many minor misfortunes are said to have befallen the workmen. At least one is reported as having witnessed Victoria's ghost waving her arms wildly in anger.

In more recent years, other fascinating tales have come to light. Evidence suggests that the Crown jewels were relocated to a vault beneath the castle in World War II. During the war, Windsor's specially built shelters were often used as a refuge from the Luftwaffe. In 1992, the castle was famously subjected to a dreadful fire. The resulting damage led to extensive restoration work costing approximately £36.5 million. For Elizabeth II, the damage was another lowlight of her *'annus horribilis'*.

Oxford

Although the *Domesday Book* makes no mention of Oxford Castle, the *Abingdon Chronicle* places the construction of the first castle around 1071–73. Built by Robert D'Oyly the elder, another important 'companion' of

William the Conqueror, the fortress appears to have been a large motte and bailey surrounded by a moat fed from a stream that ran off the Thames. After withstanding a siege during the Anarchy and again in the First Barons' War, the original timber earthworks were upgraded in stone.

Later in the reign of Henry III, the king converted the castle into a prison for unruly university clerks. This purpose continued in the fourteenth century, along with county administration. After suffering large-scale destruction from a Roundhead siege by Colonel Ingoldsby in 1646 and then deliberate destruction in 1652, what remained continued to be used as the local prison. A newer gaol, later renamed HM Prison Oxford, was built on the same site in 1785. In 1996, the prison closed, and the site was converted into a hotel, restaurant and visitor attraction.

Several ghosts are said to haunt the castle. The spirit that plagues the mound is believed to be one Mary Blandy, who was executed for patricide in 1752. Her tale is a strange one. Blandy, raised a mild-mannered lady, was found guilty of murdering her father using arsenic, which she claimed was intended as a mind control potion to make him approve of her intended love. The affair was the subject of much press attention, which continued in the following century.

In addition to Blandy, other shadowy figures and white mists have reputedly been witnessed throughout the site, as well as the resonations of peculiar footsteps, bangs and voices. A paranormal investigation of the crypt in the 1970s apparently got so out of hand that they needed a priest to perform an exorcism. Since then, the unexplained activity has quietened.

Chapter 8

Essex, Cambridgeshire, Suffolk and Norfolk

Colchester

Below ground in parts of Colchester, a strange layer of reddish/brown ash juxtaposed with remnants of Roman pottery is one of the few reminders of a grand rebellion that took place against the Roman invaders in 60 AD. Also found in London and St Albans, the strange substance has been dubbed Boudica's layer in honour of a mysterious first-century tribal leader. In British folklore, she is more commonly known as Boudicea, the literal Celtic definition of which was Victory.

When Emperor Claudius ordered the invasion of England in 43 AD, Boudica's husband, Prasutagus, was one of several minor kings who agreed to acknowledge Claudius as a 'client king'. On his death in 60 AD, he left half of his estate to the Romans – now ruled by Nero. The other half he granted to his widow and their two teenage daughters. A short time later, the local Roman administrator declared Prasutagus's remaining lands a slave province and swiftly conquered it. On taking Boudica captive, the queen of the Iceni tribe was publicly flogged, and her daughters violently raped.

Over the following months, the fires of revenge were lit. An alliance of disgruntled local tribes unleashed their fury on the areas unguarded when the main armies left for Anglesey. At the head of a force of around 120,000, Boudica put the enemy settlements to the torch and descended on the Roman capital of *Camulodunum*: the precursor to Colchester. A daylong siege saw the residents retreat to the mighty Temple of Claudius. Sadly, within its walls, they were also put to the torch. The rebellion continued for some time, ultimately culminating in an epic battle in which Boudica may have perished. Other sources suggest she committed suicide to avoid capture or died of illness.

For the citizens of *Camulodunum*, the transition was just beginning. Following the Norman invasion, a castle was built on the foundations of the old Roman temple under the guardianship of one Eudo Dapifer, who became the castle's steward. By 1100, the keep was completed. According to the available evidence, the architect was none other than Gundulf of Caen, Bishop of Rochester – see also Rochester Castle. A far more modern legend places Gundulf, Colchester and the Tower of London as central to the works of the novelist and Anglo-Saxon expert J.R.R. Tolkien who based a wizard on him as well as his Two Towers.

The keep at Colchester has much in common with its London cousin. Measuring 152 feet by 112, it is approximately one and a half times the size of the White Tower and broader than it is tall. The keep is not only the largest in Britain but the largest to survive in Europe. Now only two storeys, it was once far larger and would have been still had the Georgian renovations not been misguided. The Roman temple itself had been the biggest in Britain.

Since its creation, the castle has endured a fascinating history. A charter created by Henry I in 1101 designated it a royal castle. From this time onwards, both castle and town were granted to Dapifer until he died in 1120. Over the next 150 years, kings Henry I, II and III all visited the castle. In the case of the latter, the years 1214–17 were especially important. In 1214, the constable was William de Lanvalai, one of the rebel barons engaged in conflict against John. After failing to win William over, John replaced him with a Flemish mercenary, Stephen Harengood, who improved the defences. Magna Carta, however, stipulated the castle's return to de Lanvalai. After laying siege to Rochester, John subsequently took his armies to Colchester under Savari de Mauléon. Despite the help of the French, the siege that lasted from January to March ended with John granting the garrison safe passage to London. In early 1217, the royalists surrendered it to Prince Louis as part of a truce between the would-be usurper and the minority government of Henry III. It returned to Henry later that year as part of the Treaty of Lambeth on Louis's surrender.

During its time as a royal castle, Colchester had many functions and owners. Among the most interesting was its use as a county prison for the self-proclaimed Witchfinder General Matthew Hopkins's infamous interrogations. In 1648, Royalists Sir Charles Lucas and Sir George Lisle were both executed at the rear of the castle. An obelisk marks the point where, legend says, grass no longer grows.

Another who met his maker was the controversial religious philosopher James Parnell, who was imprisoned in 1656 for blasphemy. Convinced that the truth of God lay not in the way of the traditional preacher, Parnell travelled among the minor religious sects, who conducted their meetings in secret to avoid persecution. Parnell walked well over 100 miles to visit Quaker founder George Fox at his prison in Carlisle. On meeting Fox, Parnell left the meeting a full-on Quaker and soon began on the path of the hotheaded zealot. In July 1655, he arrived at Coggeshall in Essex as a local vicar was preparing an anti-Quaker prayer. On attending the service, he was arrested for his passionate arguments against the prayer and imprisoned in Colchester Castle. When he appeared at his trial, a lenient jury convicted him only of writing a pamphlet, for which they imposed a £40 fine. Parnell's admittance of the charge but refusal to pay the fine saw him returned to the dungeons.

Life in prison, alas, would not be easy. Worse still, Parnell's gaoler, one Nicholas Roberts, made it his mission to break his spirit. Rather than endure typical cell life, Roberts kept him in a deep oubliette-style hole and forced him to climb a rope for his rations. Injuries from at least one mishap and a refusal to accept medical attention hastened his decline. He died a martyr no later than 4 May 1656 and was buried in an unmarked grave in the castle grounds.

Since his sad demise, Parnell's spirit has reputedly been seen haunting the lower dungeons. He has been described as a small, thin, somewhat gaunt man who walks with a limp: an accurate description of Parnell, especially towards his end. Joining him in his ethereal journeys are said to be the spirits of Roman and Royalist soldiers, the former of whom have been seen close to the old temple walls. Local legend tells that a daring local spent the night in the dungeons as a wager. Whether engaged by the tormented spirit of the martyred Quaker or merely psyched out by his imagination, the man refused to return to the castle.

Hadleigh

Began by Hubert de Burgh, later first earl of Kent, sometime between 1215 and 1229 to guard the Thames Estuary, construction at Hadleigh was something of a stop-start project. On being granted the 'honour' of Rayleigh Castle in Essex by King John around the time of his appointment as justiciar of England, Hubert decided against continuing work on the masonry and timber castle. Instead, he set to work on building a new one on a mound of soft London clay to the south of the town of Hadleigh. Just as things were taking shape, Henry III confiscated the castle as a punishment for Hubert's failure to plan appropriately for the king's desired expedition to France to reclaim the ancestral lands of Henry II.

While Hubert endured a turbulent few years, in which the king stripped him of his earldom, sacked him as justiciar and imprisoned him before finally making peace and allowing him a quiet retirement, progress at Hadleigh was gradual. The park was in place by 1235, growing to some 142 acres by the end of the century. At this time, the castle was probably of octagonal design, reminiscent of nearby Orford in Suffolk. Henry's son and successor, Edward I, visited twice: mostly for hunting purposes. Though his second queen, Margaret, complained about the standards, his son Edward II paid it far greater attention. Edward III upgraded the castle significantly for the dual purpose of defence and fine lodgings close to London.

Throughout this period, it was customary for Hadleigh to be granted a tenant for life, following which it would revert to the Crown. Among them was Edmund of Langley, Duke of York and Humphrey of Lancaster, Duke of Gloucester, before several consorts, including Edward IV's queen, Elizabeth Wydville, and three wives of Henry VIII: Catherine of Aragon, Anne of Cleves and Catherine Parr. On Henry VIII's death, Edward VI sold it to the controversial lawyer Lord Richard Rich on condition the raw materials be reused elsewhere, which occurred up to a point. Thanks to the stones' removal and subsidence due to a combination of the weather and its location on London clay, the castle fell into ruin. Throughout this time, the castle parks also helped furnish the navy.

Forlorn, neglected, yet undeniably picturesque, what remained has become a firm favourite among artists. A visit in 1814 by John Constable inspired an oil painting. Later that century, the castle became famed for other activities: not least illicit trading. Local legend has long told that nineteenth-century smugglers used hidden chambers to hide their wares and scared people off with coloured lights. Tradition also associates Dick Turpin with the ruins, yet this isn't easy to prove.

Undoubtedly, the smugglers' behaviour can explain many of Hadleigh's famous ghost stories. Indeed, the farce has something of a primitive Scooby-Doo feel about it. Nevertheless, stories of strange lights continue to plague the area. Other tales of local fame include a ghostly woman in white. Seemingly of connection to this lady are the strange accounts of an unfortunate local milkmaid named Sally, who saw the apparition one morning and was told to return to the castle at midnight. Petrified, the milkmaid stayed away, only to be confronted by the ghost and struck so hard she nearly dislocated her neck.

Other versions of the ghostly tale speak of her dancing with visitors until they drop down dead. This story also seems to connect with another of the castle's legends: that of a man in black who offers to buy souls in exchange for a song. Joining the Devil in his unholy bargaining is a black dog who has been seen stalking the ruins. The apparition of a lady in grey, a boy in shorts and a semi-transparent white horse are just some of the other alleged connections with the site.

Of the strange colourings, among the most prominent are a series of blue lights seen near the castle. In addition to the smugglers, the origin has been linked with local man James 'Cunning' Murrell. Regarded as a white witch, Murrell, the seventh son of a seventh son, found work in the local community as a cobbler, doctor, chemist, fortune-teller and curse lifter. Local stories tell of him owning a plethora of strange objects, including a mirror for looking into the future, a telescope and a charm that could detect lying. Murrell moved to Hadleigh sometime after 1810 after being apprenticed as a chemist in London and often collected herbs from the castle ruins at night.

While a reputation for experimentation may partly explain his association with the blue lights, since he died in 1860, Murrell's ghost has been said to haunt the ruins. Local lore also claims that his box of magic was buried in the garden of his cottage. No evidence of anything being found has ever reached the public domain.

Woodcroft

Established in the late thirteenth century, moated Woodcroft, near Peterborough, has enjoyed a relatively quiet history. The one exception came during the English Civil War when the castle became a Royalist stronghold. Most famous of its occupiers was the Royalist clergyman Dr Michael Hudson, who commanded the garrison.

A graduate of Queen's College, Oxford and chaplain to Charles I, when the war began, Hudson was appointed head of reconnaissance – or scoutmaster – to the northern army, after which he escorted the king to Newark in 1646. When the war was over, Hudson was arrested at Sandwich in Kent for attempting to flee to France. For a time, he was imprisoned in London House, the home of the bishop of London. On 18 November, he escaped, during which he is alleged to have smuggled letters from the king to Major-General Rowland Laugharne: one of his commanders in Wales. In January 1647, he was captured again on reaching Hull and imprisoned in the Tower of London. He escaped a year later after outfoxing his guards by placing a basket of apples on his head.

Back in the fold and commissioned a colonel, Hudson took up residence at Woodcroft and later that year engaged in combat on the roof when an armed body of Roundheads infiltrated the castle. He was thrown from the battlements but managed to cling to a gargoyle, from which an enemy severed his fingers. On being captured on falling into the moat, he was offered a final choice, to be killed in the water or on land. On choosing land, he was whipped over his head by a musketeer. Another Roundhead removed his tongue as a souvenir.

Since his death, Hudson's ghost has been seen, usually in the moat, as he frantically repeats his attempt to escape. He was laid to rest in Denton, Northamptonshire. An application for reinterment at Uffington was either not granted or did not go ahead. Regardless of how he met his end, Hudson's story should serve as a shining light of the virtues of intellect, loyalty and courage. As was said by his biographer, Augustus Charles Bickley, who wrote for the Dictionary of National Biography in 1895, 'His boldness, generosity, and almost fanatical loyalty are undoubted.'

Bungay

The ivy-clad remains of the twelfth-century castle in the town of Bungay act as a strangely appropriate allegory of the faded glories of a once-powerful family. Erected by the Norman warlord Roger Bigod around Henry I's coronation in 1100, the site on which Bungay was constructed takes advantage of a natural curve on the River Waveney. The castle was an important feature during the occupancy of Roger's son, Hugh Bigod, one of many whose allegiance during the Anarchy swayed according to the ebb and flow of the political tide. Hugh raised an army against Stephen in 1136, culminating in the royals besieging him at Norwich. Stephen later made peace with Hugh and awarded him the earldom of Norfolk.

Early in the reign of Henry II, Hugh's loyalty was again tested, leading to his being disinherited. When the king changed his mind in 1164, Hugh set to work on the magnificent keep, which took around ten years to build. On taking up his sword for Henry the Young King in the revolt of 1173–74, Hugh was forced to surrender to Henry II after trying to capture the royal castle at Haughley. Hugh died in Palestine or Syria on crusade.

In 1294 the castle was returned to the family. Under the ownership of Roger Bigod, 5th Earl of Norfolk, the imposing gatehouse was added, which survives to this day. After falling out of favour with Edward I, the castle reverted to royal control and later fell into ruin. In 1483 the Yorkist royals granted it to the Howard family, the Bigods' successors as magnates of Norfolk. It remained the dukes' property until being taken over by a local trust in the twentieth century.

Once the home of powerful warlords, Bungay is reputedly the haunt of its most feared former owner. Courageous and charismatic in life, the spirit of Hugh is said to stalk the castle, not as he appeared in life, but in the guise of a demon hound or Black Shuck. Known locally as 'Bigod the Bold' or 'Bigod the Restless', the phantom hound is said to keep watch over the ruins, his hairy paws stomping the grassy verges and casting ominous shadows on the weathered walls when the moon shines brightly. What should become of anyone brave – or foolish – enough to wander the craggy remains at night is perhaps better left untested. Such is Bigod's reputation as a capable leader and crusader, the legend continues to be feared to this day.

Orford

Since the dawn of time, people of every civilisation have been fascinated by the mysteries of the sea. According to the ancient Greeks, many creatures were said to inhabit vast kingdoms beneath the waves, their architecture and culture comparable to those on the surface during the golden age of Antiquity. Some of the great fables of the time told of the siren people: a bizarre mix of human and fish, who inhabited the waters under the guardianship of Poseidon. Even in the Middle Ages, many sailors feared contact with a siren. Terrible stories told of ancient seafarers plunging to their deaths on being possessed by strange hypnotic singing.

The people of England have always enjoyed a unique relationship with the sea. An island state, the economy of many coastal towns and villages developed on their ability to fish and trade. As the centuries passed, the amassing of one of the greatest navies in the world only intensified the sea's importance. Even in the present day, maritime folklore remains a central part of local culture and identity, despite the seeming likelihood that their existence transcends the pale of reality.

On the east coast of Suffolk, a unique memorial within the walls of Orford Castle commemorates a weird tale that is reported as having occurred during the reign of Henry II. The hexagonal castle is itself something of a rarity in England. Henry personally appears to have been influential in its design and construction: having ordered work to begin around 1165 to quell any threat of rebellion from the Bigod family – see Bungay Castle. Two years after work began, the fortress is said to have played host to one of the greatest mysteries to ever emerge from the sea. The nearby abbey's chronicler, Ralph of Coggeshall, penned the following account in 1200:

> At the time of Henry II, when the knight Bartholomew of Glanville kept the castle at Orford, men fishing in the sea caught in their nets a wild creature. He was handed over to the castellan for inspection. He was naked and was like a human being in all his limbs. He had a long shaggy beard, and his chest was covered with hair.
>
> The said knight had him kept in custody for a long time, day and night, lest he went back to the sea. He eagerly ate whatever was brought to him but if it was raw he pressed it between his hands until

all the juice was expelled. He would not talk, or rather could not, even when tortured and hung up by his feet. Brought into church, he showed no signs of reverence or belief. He sought his bed at sunset and always remained there until sunrise.

The sight of this hairy, human-like creature thrilled Bartholomew. Indeed, over the coming weeks, the being became something of a local tourist attraction. Besides eating, his main love, unsurprisingly, was swimming, which he was allowed to do under close guidance. For several hours, he would return to the sea, watched by crowds on the shore, as he dived between the nets before returning to the surface.

Precisely who or what this mysterious character was has remained unclear for almost 900 years. Accounts from the time described him as a naked 'wild' man, with no interest in anything on land except ringing out fish and eating it raw. Since that time, many have argued that his characteristics matched the ancient traditions of the merman. Due to his strange appearance, the locals feared that God had cursed them with a creature famed as the bringer of storms and sinker of ships. As was further reported by Coggeshall:

> He was allowed to go into the sea, strongly guarded with three lines of nets, but he dived under the nets and came up again and again. Eventually he came back of his own free will. But later on he escaped and was never seen again. As to whether he was a mortal man, or some fish pretending to be human shape, or was an evil spirit hiding in the body of a drowned man, as can be read in the life of blessed Ouen, it is not possible to be precise; the more so because so many wonderful things of this kind are told by many to whom they have happened.

In addition to the temporary residence of the wild man, the castle is associated with at least one ghost. Within the ruins, the spirit of a sailor is said to dwell. Tradition recalls that he walked with a limp and dressed in the clothes of centuries past.

Enthralling though tales of the ghostly sailor may be, it is the mystery of the so-called 'wild man' that has ensured Orford's lasting fame. Over the years, sightings of similar creatures have been witnessed throughout the country. Among the most famous must be the mermaid of Zennor in Cornwall. Accordingly, a choir singer of some talent was seduced by a beautiful stranger at church and disappeared without a trace. Whether the stories are based on actual events, tall tales of sailors or cases of mistaken identity, the jury remains out. Depressingly, the characteristics Coggeshall describe have much in common with a grey seal. Yet surely it beggars belief that something so obvious could be kept in the castle for two months and not be recognised even in the twelfth century.

Though his brief time in the limelight ended centuries ago, the wild man of Orford remains an integral part of the local culture. No less than twenty baptismal fonts have been decorated with an engraving of the sea creature. Whether he ever existed or his spirit returns to the castle before disappearing once more, one thing is for sure: until firm proof comes to light, the story's appeal is unlikely to fade. Man, fish, manatee or seal, the wild man seems destined to remain a mystery of the sea.

Burgh

The village of Burgh Castle is steeped in history. Lying on the east bank of the Waveney, just under 4 miles west of Great Yarmouth and within the Norfolk Broads National Park, it has at times come under the boundaries of Suffolk and Norfolk and was the former as recently as 1974.

Far deeper into its history, the village was the setting of a third-century Roman fort. The most likely candidate for the ruins was recorded in one contemporary document as *Gariannonum*: one of a string of seaports along the so-called Saxon shore. Like many, its primary role was to combat Saxon pirating raids. In the sixteenth century, the famed antiquary William Camden became possibly the first person to identify the site with 'Cnobheresburg', reputed to have been the first Irish monastery in England. The monastery was founded around 630 by Saint Fursey as part of the Hiberno-Scottish mission recorded by the venerable Bede.

Few castles mentioned in this book share Burgh's ancient pedigree. Following the Norman Conquest, a motte was constructed in the southwest corner with the imposing flint Roman walls acting as a bailey. The site appears to have led a relatively uneventful existence until the motte was removed in 1770 and the area levelled. The ditch was filled in 1839, and the site opened to the public, under the care of the Norfolk Archaeological Trust and English Heritage.

Though the castle's existence in the post-conquest era was somewhat subdued, the pre-Norman site is rich in legend. One particular tale is believed to date from 418 AD, by which time the Danes had replaced the Romans. Hearing that a large band of Saxons had been spotted wandering the area, their leader, Gonard, invited the Saxon chief, Siberg, to a meeting and immediately imprisoned him. Before his departure, the Saxon warlord informed his men to wait three days and to commence their attack on the fourth if he had not safely returned.

Sure enough, four days later, there remained no sign. On attacking the fort, the Saxons initially struggled to combat the rampaging Danes and were countered when two of the fort's gates opened to reveal swarms of Danish warriors. Either in preparation for such an attack or to mark his victory, Gonard erected sharp wooden posts around the fortress. On these, an estimated 4,000 Saxons were impaled.

A few days later, a victorious Gonard had a vision of two angels doing battle. In his dream, the white angel clasped the black angel by the throat, after which they fell to earth and melted on impact. Concerned the dream was a portent of doom, Gonard sent for the still imprisoned Siberg and demanded he interpret the vision. After initially saying nothing, Siberg pointed to the horizon. To his horror, Gonard noticed a large force, championed by Siberg's brother, Cerdag. Siberg took advantage of Gonard's shock and smashed the Dane in his skull with his battle axe.

Hoping to confer with the Danish occupiers, Cerdag sent a messenger with a white flag to the fort. Shortly after entering, the messenger was thrown from the battlements. In the resulting melee, the Saxons emerged victorious; however, Cerdag discovered Siberg mortally wounded.

In the centuries since, several hauntings are said to have plagued the old fort. On 27 April, the anniversary of the first battle, reruns are said to have been witnessed. On 3 July, the second anniversary, a figure wrapped in a white flag has also been seen being hurled from the ramparts and rolling towards the beach. Beyond the sand, a ghostly fleet reputedly sails, while the ubiquitous Black Shuck also reportedly stalks the ruins. According to many folklorists, Black Shucks are often seen at sites that have witnessed evil or bloodshed.

Further to the pre-Norman mayhem, local lore tells that the former local Baron Rudolph Scarfe haunts the site. A mischievous spirit, if not a dangerous one, the thirteenth-century mercenary was excommunicated from his homeland and picked up a wage as a soldier of fortune at the castle. Scarfe's ghost has also been reported nearby, including Great Yarmouth. He has even been recorded in two places at once and in a variety of different shapes. Scarfe reputedly takes pleasure in tricking and teasing his victims and has also been equated with the Black Shuck. One researcher has even claimed that he saw a human figure morph into a werewolf before running off into the night.

Castle Rising

Situated in the heart of the Norfolk countryside, the strong keep of Castle Rising remains one of the most remarkable defensive structures ever built. Standing tall behind the ruined bridge and gatehouse, the impressive fortifications are a fitting legacy to William d'Aubigny II, 1st Earl of Arundel, who began the work around 1140 to celebrate his marriage to Henry I's widow, Adeliza of Louvain.

William further enhanced the defences around 1173 to protect it from the forces of Henry the Young King, who revolted against his father, Henry II. Inherited by his descendants until being acquired by the Montalt family in 1243, Emma, the wife of Robert de Montalt, sold it in 1331 to Edward II's widow, Isabella, for £400. Following the queen's death in 1358, the castle formed part of the duchy of Cornwall, the first beneficiary of which was Isabella's grandson, Edward the Black Prince. Though the century ended with the castle in good condition, gradual neglect saw it fall into disrepair throughout the fifteenth century. Despite Henry VIII's sale of the castle to Thomas Howard, 3rd Duke of Norfolk in 1544, the fortress appears to have been abandoned after the execution of Howard's grandson, 4th Duke of Norfolk in 1572.

A luxury residence for more than 400 years, a typical eighteenth-century passerby would have seen little more than a windswept ruin. Exposed to the elements, its condition deteriorated further, leaving only the well-built keep intact. Thanks to Fulke Greville Howard and his wife, Mary, the castle entered a phase of loving restoration in the nineteenth century. A combination of English Heritage and the management of its current owner, a Howard descendant, has ensured its future.

This once fine home may have lain empty since the days of plotting to liberate Mary, Queen of Scots, but even now, it is said that the castle is not completely deserted. Bizarre sounds have reportedly been heard within the keep at night. Others have complained of feelings of unease. Though no scientific reason has been found as to why one should feel such anxiety, local legend has long claimed that the spirit of the castle's most famous owner still dwells within its walls. Dubbed the 'she-wolf of France' from 1757 onwards, Queen Isabella has sadly long been viewed as something of a reviled character in England due to her role in her husband's abdication.

Precisely what happened to Edward II has never been fully explained – see Berkeley Castle. On the king's dethronement, his fourteen-year-old son, Edward III, began his minority under the regency of Isabella and Roger Mortimer, 1st Earl of March. Just three years later, the young king organised a coup of his guardians – see Nottingham Castle. While Mortimer was returned to the Tower and put to death at Tyburn, Isabella appears to have endured long periods of semi-isolation at Castle Rising. In contrast to the evidence that she was a regular host and a doting grandmother, especially to the Black Prince, unsubstantiated tradition tells that her restless spirit remains trapped within the fortified walls. Hysterical cries and manic cackles are said to reverberate around the keep, while footsteps have also been heard throughout the upper floor despite being empty. Though her apparition has never been seen, a lingering feeling of unease is also commonly reported.

Further to Isabella's alleged haunting of the castle, it has been claimed that a secret tunnel was built for her beneath the castle, connecting it to Red Mount Chapel at nearby King's Lynn. So far, no trace of the tunnel has ever been found – not that one should have been necessary. The conjecture that she was banned from showing her face in public would seem to contradict her later appearances at court. An even more bizarre legend claims that the 'she-wolf' haunts the castle in the guise of a white wolf as penance for her husband's treatment. Some locals allege that the beast with blood-red eyes has been seen, drool dripping from its fangs and a howl that could scare half to death. The apparitions of monks are also reputed to have been seen at the castle and nearby.

Though many years have passed since Castle Rising was a substantial family home, even now, there is no denying that the imposing Norman keep still has all the hallmarks of a castle impenetrable to attack. Whether Isabella was actively involved in her husband's murder or disappearance is impossible to prove. Nor whether her time in Norfolk was entirely voluntary. Yet, as far as local legend is concerned, there is a certain irony that the abandoned walls now seem destined to imprison the spirits of its past, after a history of defending them.

Framlingham

Built in 1148 at the height of the Anarchy, the original motte and bailey at Framlingham was swiftly destroyed by Henry II in the aftermath of Henry the Young King's revolt of 1173–74. Later that century, the powerful Roger Bigod, Earl of Norfolk, constructed a stone castle on the site, which was conquered in 1216 by King John following a two-day siege.

Bigod's design was a strange one: having a curtain wall of thirteen mural towers but no keep. In the reign of Edward I, his descendants upgraded the fairy-tale walls into a fine country residence, around which the parkland set the foundation for the beautiful gardens described in later centuries. By this time, the castle was primarily used as a hunting lodge and formed the heart of the vast estates of, firstly, the Mowbrays and their successors as dukes of Norfolk, the Howards. It was during their tenures the two artificial lakes were created, and the castle extended in brick. The result was one of the most impregnable looking fortresses the country had ever seen.

Come 1636, the Howards' financial difficulties saw the estate fall into disrepair. No longer able to provide the luxury accommodation for which it had become famed, the Howards gifted the castle to Pembroke College, Cambridge, who erected a poorhouse on the site. The facility was closed in 1839, after which the estate was used as a military drill hall and county court. It was used in WWII for defensive purposes after entering public hands in 1913.

Famed in some quarters as an iconic English country estate, Framlingham was not without its darker side. By the end of the thirteenth century, a prison had also been erected, primarily to hold poachers. In the fifteenth century, it also held religious dissenters, most notably the Lollards.

Scenes of uprising were also common. In 1297, Roger Bigod, 5th Earl of Norfolk, led a popular movement against Edward I and enjoyed considerable success before going bankrupt. Consequently, Framlingham passed to the Crown on his death. In 1381, the castle was again associated with uprising: this time the Peasants' Revolt during the tenure of William de Ufford, 2nd Earl of Suffolk. In 1485, John Howard's loyalty to the Yorkists saw his son, Thomas, 2nd Duke of Norfolk, stripped of the castle and placed within the Tower. It would return to him in 1513 after fighting for Henry VIII at Flodden.

The fortuitous death of Henry VIII in 1547, the day before he was due to sign Thomas, 3rd Duke of Norfolk's death warrant, quite literally saved the duke's bacon. The castle, however, passed on Edward VI's orders to Princess Mary. It was at Framlingham Mary amassed her forces before marching on London to bring an end to Lady Jane Grey's strange nine-day reign. Among Mary's early moves was to free Norfolk, who retired to Kenninghall. When his grandson, Thomas, 4th Duke of Norfolk, was executed in 1572 for conspiring with Mary, Queen of Scots, the castle reverted to the Crown until James I granted the much-declined residence to Thomas Howard, 1st Earl of Suffolk.

A shadow of its former glories since Mary's departure, the workhouse is all that survives of its interior, which is now home to a museum. While much has changed since its heyday, Framlingham is reportedly haunted by many spirits of its past. Disembodied faces have been seen. Somewhat disconcertingly, ghostly footsteps, cries of anguish and children talking have also reportedly been heard, mainly across the courtyard. Staff and visitors alike have often spoken of an eerie presence at the castle, as though the sounds could have come from a recording. As Marc Morris pointed out in his book, *Castles and Kings*: 'If you want to imagine yourself in the guise of a medieval warrior ... there are few better places to visit than Framlingham.'

Norwich

A motte and bailey castle at Norwich was already in existence in 1075 when the earl of Norfolk, Ralph de Gael, led a popular uprising against William the Conqueror. Due to the castle being under the earl's control, a siege was required to ensure Norfolk's defeat, which came when William offered the garrison peaceful terms.

As expected of a pre-1086 creation, Norwich was one of the forty-eight castles mentioned in the *Domesday Book*. Records indicate that the castle was built on an existing Saxon settlement and required the destruction of between 17 and 113 houses to complete. Later archaeological studies have confirmed the bailey was even built atop a Saxon cemetery. The stone keep, which survives today, was added 1095–1110, around which time further reinforcements included the deepening of the ditch around the motte. Stone upgrades followed from 1130 onwards, following which it appears to have avoided conflict in the Anarchy. Hugh Bigod, 1st Earl of Norfolk, briefly captured it during the revolt of Henry the Young King with the help of Flemish mercenaries; however, it was back in Henry II's hands by 1175. In 1216, it was taken by Prince Louis in the First Barons' War.

Before this time, the castle became something of a haven for the Jews of Norwich. As was typical of the time, the Jewish community was set up close to the castle. From 1220 onwards, the castle was also used as a prison for debtors and felons and remained so until around 1887. Seven years later, the museum of Norwich was opened on the site and is now a popular tourist site.

A place of toil and incarceration, Norwich is another castle reputedly haunted by the horrors of its past. The apparitions of people in Victorian clothing have allegedly been witnessed. Prominent among them, a woman in a black dress has been reported since the early 1800s. In 1820, three young men awaiting transportation encountered such a bizarre experience that it merited a mention in the gaol's journal. What exactly they saw was never revealed in detail. Whatever it was, it does not appear to have been repeated.

St Michael's Mount, Cornwall.

Tintagel Castle and Merlin's Cave, Cornwall.

The gatehouse and outer curtain wall of Berry Pomeroy Castle, Devon. (*Mike Davis*)

Unless otherwise specified, all images are from the author's collection or presently in the public domain.

Powderham Castle, Devon.

Corfe Castle, Dorset. (*Mike Davis*)

Lulworth Castle, Dorset. (*Samuel Hieronymus Grimm, 1790*)

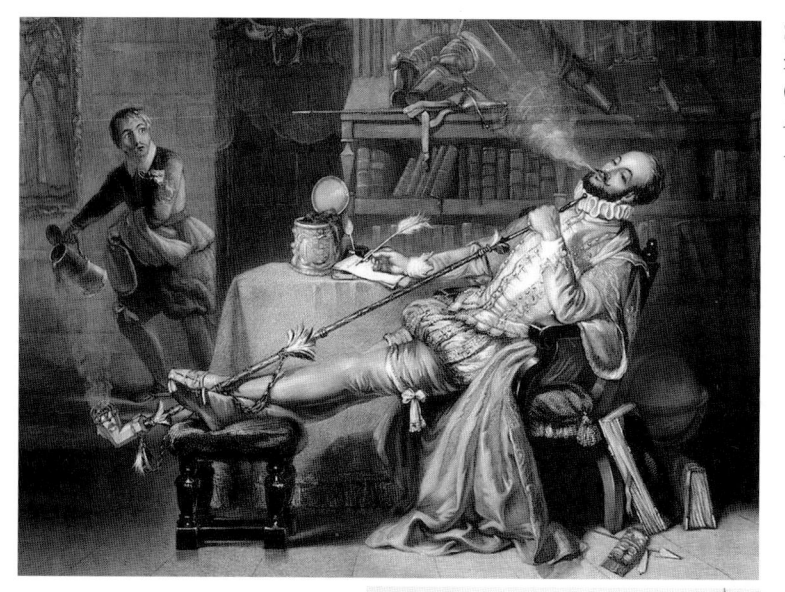

Sir Walter Raleigh's first pipe in England. (*Frederick William Fairholt's*, Tobacco, *1859*)

Dunster Castle, Somerset. (*Mike Davis*)

The gatehouse of Farleigh Hungerford Castle, Somerset. (*James Mackenzie* – The Castles of England, *1896*)

Nunney Castle, Somerset.

Taunton Castle, Somerset.

Edward II receiving the crown. (*The Chronicle of England* (*folio 10*) British Library MS 20 A, ii)

Old Wardour Castle, Wiltshire.

Henry II, Richard I, John and Henry III.
(*Matthew Paris*, Historia Anglorum)

The gatehouse of Carisbrooke Castle, the Isle of Wight.

Porchester Castle, Hampshire.

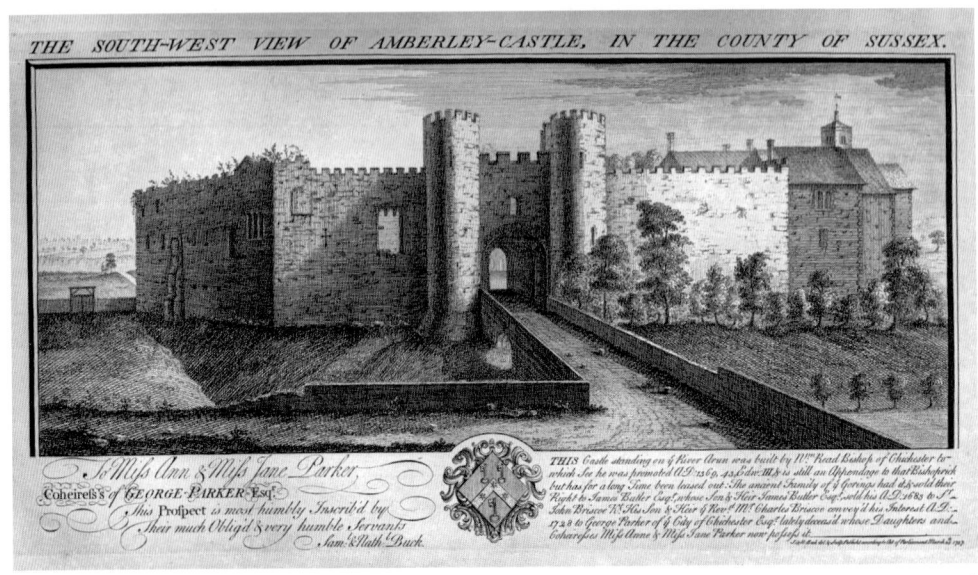

The south-west view of Amberley Castle, Sussex. (*18th century engraving by Samuel and Nathaniel Buck*)

Arundel Castle, Sussex, prior to 19th-century renovations. (*A series of picturesque views of seats of the noblemen and gentlemen of Great Britain and Ireland, 1840*)

Bodiam Castle, Sussex.

Construction of the first castle at Hastings, Sussex. (*As depicted in the* Bayeux Tapestry)

The remaining wall of Bramber Castle, Sussex.

Herstmonceux Castle, Sussex.

Pevensey Castle, Sussex. (*Mike Davis*)

Dover Castle, Kent. (*Mike Davis*)

Anne Boleyn. (*Wenceslaus Hollar, circa 1530s*)

Hever Castle, Kent.

Leeds Castle, Kent.

Rochester Castle from across the Medway. (*Engraving by G. F. Sargent, 1836*)

Edward III. (*The Garter book, 1435, British Library*)

The two castles at Scotney, Kent. The older castle appears in the foreground.

Donnington Castle, Berkshire. (*William Byrne, 1778*)

The Military Knights of Windsor attending chapel in the lower bailey of Windsor Castle, Berkshire. (*Joseph Nash, 1840*)

Colchester Castle, Essex.

Orford Castle, Suffolk.

Castle Rising, Norfolk.

The outer curtain walls of Framlingham Castle, Suffolk. (*Mike Davis*)

Kenilworth Castle, Warwickshire. (*Mike Davis*)

Tamworth Castle. (*Sketch by J. C. Buckler, 1849*)

Mary, Queen of Scots. (The Life of Mary, Queen of Scots Drawn from the State Papers with Subsidiary Memoirs, *by George Calmers, 1822*)

Charles Dickens in New York. (*Jeremiah Gurney, circa 1867–8*)

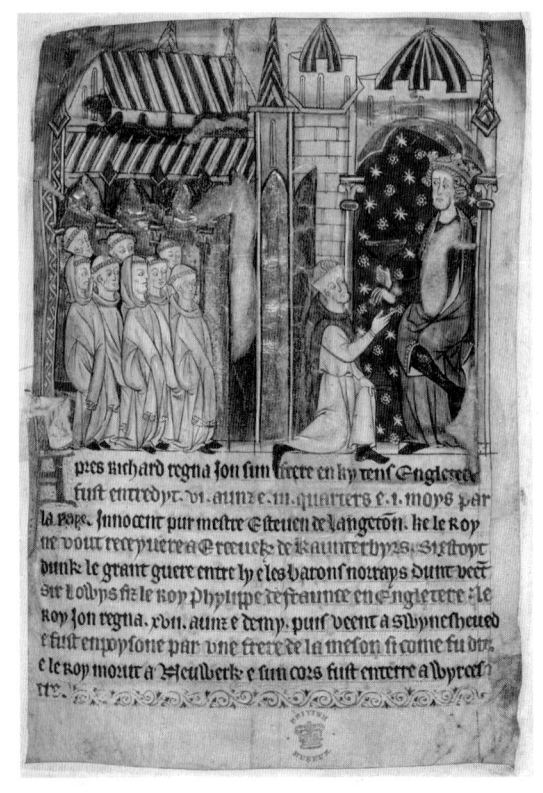

The alleged poisoning of John at Swineshead Abbey in October 1216. (*Cotton MS Vitellius A XIII, British Library*)

Belvoir Castle, Leicestershire.

Newark Castle, Nottinghamshire.

The gatehouse of Nottingham Castle, Nottinghamshire. (*Mike Davis*)

Bolsover Castle, Derbyshire.

The Fair of Lincoln in 1217. (*Matthew Paris*, Chronica Majora)

Tattershall Castle, Lincolnshire.

Bolton Castle, Yorkshire.

Clifford's Tower, (York Castle), Yorkshire.

Conisbrough Castle, Yorkshire.

Richard III. (*Caroline A. Halsted's* Richard III, *1844; from the original portrait, artist unknown, circa late 1500s*)

Pontefract Castle, Yorkshire in the 17th century. (*Alexander Keirincx, circa 1640*)

Richmond Castle, Yorkshire. (*Watercolour painting by S. Howitt, 1802*)

Ripley Castle, Yorkshire. (*Reverend Francis Orpen Morris, 1880*)

Skipton Castle, Yorkshire. (*Artist unknown, circa 1890s*)

The gateway at Lancaster Castle, Lancashire. (*Artist unknown, circa 1900*)

Muncaster Castle, Cumbria. (*Morris's Country Seats, 1880*)

Barnard Castle, County Durham. (*Artist unknown, circa 1900s*)

James VI, King of Scotland 1567-1625, and I of England 1603-25. (*Philip Sidney's* A History of the Gunpowder Plot, *1905; from a print circa 1621*)

The keep at Newcastle Castle, Tyne and Wear.

Hylton Castle, Tyne and Wear.

The ruins of Tynemouth Castle and Priory, Northumberland, including the lighthouse. (*Oil on canvas by John Wilson Carmichael, pre-1867*)

Alnwick Castle. (*Mike Davis*)

Bamburgh Castle. (*Mike Davis*)

Chillingham Castle. (*Mike Davis*)

Woodland outside Chillingham. Some believe there to be faces in the leaves, as well as a ghostly nun-like figure

Dunstanburgh Castle. (*Mike Davis*)

Warkworth Castle. (*Mike Davis*)

Chapter 9

Warwickshire, the West Midlands and Staffordshire

Kenilworth

Few castles hold a candle to the mighty Kenilworth. Began in the 1120s by Geoffrey de Clinton, the lord chamberlain and treasurer to Henry I, work appears to have occurred around the keep, construction of which may have been in stone from the offset. Progress continued under his son and namesake on Geoffrey's being acquitted of treason around 1130. His great legacy was the church of St Michael and All Angels in Buckinghamshire, often regarded as one of the finest in England. Having survived the Anarchy, the castle was garrisoned by forces loyal to Henry II and enlarged significantly by King John. Massive defences at the cost of £1,115 included the building of the Mortimer and Lunn towers and the damming of local streams to create an artificial lake or mere.

John's lavish spending had been for the specific purpose of keeping out outsiders. If just one criticism can be made of John regarding his additions at Kenilworth, it is that he did too good a job. A clause of Magna Carta required him to submit the castle to baronial authority, which equated to the surrender of an important military site. In 1244, six years after the marriage of Eleanor, younger sister of Henry III and widow of William Marshal the Younger, to Simon de Montfort, 6th Earl of Leicester, the king granted Kenilworth to the princess and her controversial new husband.

It was from here that Simon conducted operations. After rebelling against Henry in 1263, Simon defeated him at the Battle of Lewes a year later. One of the likely terms of the, now lost, Mise of Lewes, drawn up in the aftermath, led to Prince Edward – later Edward I – being handed over and held prisoner at Kenilworth, reportedly in poor circumstances.

After escaping while on a supervised hunt, Edward gathered the king's forces and Simon was killed during the barons' defeat at the Battle of Evesham on 4 August 1265. In the aftermath of the baronial collapse, most of Simon's supporters took refuge within the castle. The six-month siege that followed is officially the longest in English history. The eventual surrender that followed in December 1266 was also an important milestone as it led to the Dictum of Kenilworth that allowed both sides to come to peace.

Since surviving the onslaught, Kenilworth has enjoyed an equally fascinating journey. Granted by Henry III to his second son, Edmund 'Crouchback', Earl of Lancaster – also de Montfort's successor as earl of Leicester – Edmund enjoyed holding tournaments there, including a memorable one in 1279 inspired by the legends of Camelot. Passed on in 1298 to his son, Thomas, Earl of Lancaster, Lancaster's marriage to Alice de Lacy made him the wealthiest nobleman in the kingdom.

Significantly improved with a new great hall and several other defences, Kenilworth's importance only increased. It was inside the great hall on 21 January 1327 that the recently captured Edward II officially resigned as king of England. It was also at Kenilworth where Henry V was mocked by the French with a gift of tennis balls – a move that the local canon of St Mary's, John Strecche, claimed led to the Agincourt campaign and later inspired Shakespeare. In between these events, Edward II's queen, Isabella, used Kenilworth as a favoured base. Later that century, Henry, Earl of Lancaster, his son, Henry of Grosmont, Duke of Lancaster, and Grosmont's successor, the powerful duke of Lancaster, John of Gaunt – son of Edward III, also uncle and regent of Richard II and father of the later Henry IV – followed in King John's footsteps by spending big and creating a palace within the walls. Thanks to this, the castle served as a pivotal base for the Lancastrians in the Wars of the Roses.

The final jewels in Kenilworth's crown followed in the sixteenth century. A chief supporter of Edward VI and the brains – or lack of them – behind the scheme to put Lady Jane Grey on the throne, John Dudley, 1st Duke of Northumberland, was rewarded with Kenilworth in 1553. During his brief ownership, Dudley built the new stables before his execution for treason against Mary Tudor. Ten years later, Kenilworth was restored to the family when Elizabeth I granted the castle to Dudley's son and her long time favourite, Robert Dudley, Earl of Leicester. The Tudor additions took Gaunt's palace to the next level and appear to have been in place for her fourth and final reception in 1575: an event that inspired Sir Walter Scott's *Kenilworth. A Romance*. Previous visits had already occurred in 1566, 1568 and 1572. The castle was lovingly maintained during the reigns of James I and Charles I, the latter of whom bought the castle as a present for Queen Henrietta Maria.

A famous royal visit in 1624, during which Ben Jonson performed *The Masque of Owls at Kenilworth*, would, however, be something of a swansong. Successful in withstanding the armies of Henry III and Edward IV, the one thing no castle could conquer were cannonballs. Held by parliament after Charles's garrison vacated the property after the Battle of Edgehill, security concerns prompted the decision to have the castle slighted in 1649. The man responsible, Colonel Joseph Hawkesworth, ironically acquired the property for himself and converted the gatehouse into a residence. Use of the surrounding area as farmland continued after his eviction during the Restoration.

A beloved tourist attraction during the day, at night, a strange feeling of melancholy envelops the ruins. Among the supposed ghosts is a man in black who was said to have lost a swordfight. The ghost of a young boy has also been seen, as has a small girl who has been known to shock passers-by by inquiring of the whereabouts of her father. The apparition of an elderly woman has been seen in the gatehouse. Horses have also been seen close to their former stable block. Far more bizarrely, the castle is also reputedly the haunt of a clutch of chickens.

Developed over six centuries, even as a ruin, Kenilworth never fails to delight. As long as it stands, the words of the architectural historian Anthony Emery will remain valid. Kenilworth is 'the finest surviving example of a semi-royal palace of the later Middle Ages, significant for its scale, form and quality of workmanship'.

Warwick

A short distance from the ruins of Kenilworth stands the mighty Warwick Castle. Few castles in England can claim the fame of Warwick. Indeed, only a handful of such buildings are more recognisable.

Evidence suggests that some form of fortification has existed at Warwick since the reign of Alfred the Great. Initially constructed to guard the Fosse Way by Alfred's daughter, Æthelflæd, a stone fortress was then created on the site following the appointment of the first earl of Warwick, Henry de Beaumont, in 1088. A temporary wooden structure likely preceded the main building work. The *Domesday Book* confirms that the castle was constructed shortly after the Norman Invasion at the expense of four local houses.

Although little remains of the early stonework, and none of the Saxon burh or early Norman motte and bailey, a sense of timelessness still encompasses the castle. For modern-day visitors, a tour of its elegant rooms and strong walls in the middle of the historic town can almost be compared to stepping back in time. Just a simple look at the iconic towers from the grassy interior or from across the Avon is to view the stunning Canaletto landscapes that hang from the walls of modern art galleries. Similarly, the view from the elegant battlements or gothic windows superbly captures the unspoilt great hall where Piers Gaveston was put on trial. Slightly out of keeping with the English Heritage sites, whose windswept ruins bear the scars of civil war, a visitor can almost be tricked into believing they have strolled into a theme park rather than a former palace or military fortress. No truer is it than in the case of Warwick that looks can be deceiving.

A survivor of the early carnage that ensued in the Midlands following the Norman Conquest, Warwick developed mostly unscathed during the Anarchy. Things would change for the worse in 1153 when the cunning Henry of Anjou – a year later Henry II – tricked Gundreda de Warenne, the wife of Roger de Beaumont, 2nd Earl of Warwick, into opening the castle gates by falsely reporting the death of her husband. According to one contemporary text, Warwick, ironically, died on hearing the news.

During Henry's reign, the castle was returned to the de Beaumonts to acknowledge their support of his mother, Matilda. After this, considerable work was done, most notably construction of a stone keep to replace the motte and bailey. During the revolt of 1173–74, the new earl remained loyal to Henry and used the castle for provisions. In 1264, Warwick was the victim of a surprise attack from the forces of Simon de Montfort, who was based at nearby Kenilworth. The owner, William Maudit, 8th Earl of Warwick, and his wife were taken to Kenilworth and ransomed. On Maudit's death in 1268, his title and castle passed to nephew William de Beauchamp, henceforth the ninth earl. The fifteenth-century chronicler John Rous also claimed de Montfort slighted part of the castle.

Over the coming two centuries, further work was carried out. Most of what survives dates to the Beauchamp Family's peak of power in the fourteenth century. During the tenure of the tenth earl, Guy de Beauchamp, Piers Gaveston was captured and held there. Along with Thomas, 2nd Earl of Lancaster, Guy directly accused Gaveston of stealing royal treasure. The nearby Gaveston's Cross was erected in his honour. Under the eleventh earl, Thomas de Beauchamp, further additions were made, including the gatehouse, barbican, and the iconic Caesar's and Guy's Towers. A dungeon lies beneath Guy's Tower that legend tells held French prisoners of the Battle of Poitiers in 1356.

The Beauchamp line, alas, came to an end in 1449. Replacing them, Warwick became the chief seat of Richard Neville, 16th Earl of Warwick, infamously 'The Kingmaker'. It was within these walls that Neville held Edward IV – the king he had made – his temporary prisoner. On Neville's death in the fog of Barnet field, the castle passed to George, Duke of Clarence, younger brother of Edward IV, and husband of Warwick's daughter, Isabel. After Clarence's death at the Tower in 1478, Richard, Duke of Gloucester – later Richard III – oversaw two new gun towers: the Bear and Clarence. Sir Thomas More recorded that it was at Warwick Richard conspired to murder the princes in the Tower.

In the Tudor age, Warwick suffered mixed fortunes. On visiting the castle during the reign of Henry VIII, John Leland wrote that

> the dungeon now in ruin standeth in the west-north-west part of the castle. There is also a tower west-north-west, and through it a postern-gate of iron. All the principal lodgings of the castle with the hall and chapel lie on the south side of the castle, and here the king doth much cost in making foundations in the rocks to sustain that side of the castle, for great pieces fell out of the rocks that sustain it.

After Leland's visit, Edward VI granted Warwick to John Dudley, later first duke of Northumberland. Edward's sister, Mary, subsequently executed him for his role in the accession of Lady Jane Grey. So ineffective had Dudley's ownership been, when Elizabeth I visited for four nights in 1572, a timber assembly was required for her lodgings. Fortunately for all concerned, granting of the castle to Sir Fulke Greville by James I in 1604 ensured its future. A fine poet and playwright, Greville also had a good head for business and an eye for detail. Indeed, such qualities would earn him a promotion in 1614 to chancellor of the Exchequer.

No sooner than Greville arrived, the castle was plunged into further chaos. While converting it into a country house, some of the Gunpowder Plotters raided the stables. A Royalist siege in 1642 failed to breach the walls, and the Parliamentarian garrison saw out the war without much harm. The author, Sir Richard Bulstrode, wrote: 'Our endeavours for taking it were to little purpose, for we had only two small pieces of cannon which were brought from Compton House ... to which they could do no hurt, but only frightened them within the castle, who shot into the street, and killed several of our men.'

Frightened they may have been, Warwick's conversion from military fortification to fine country estate ensured that it avoided slighting. Useful in holding Royalist prisoners captured after Edgehill, the process was repeated in 1651 after the future Charles II's defeat at Worcester. Modernisation of the interior continued, which ensured that the castle was in a fit state for a visit in 1695 by William III. In the following century, Capability Brown created the gardens that made Warwick famous. In the 1870s, the castle played host to the renowned architect Anthony Salvin, who oversaw developments that grace the modern visitor today.

Incredibly, Warwick's fascinating history remained far from complete. Born in 1861, Daisy Greville was a renowned socialite and countess of Warwick. An activist – and even champagne socialist – in her later days, Daisy caused a scandal for her lengthy affair with the prince of Wales, later Edward VII. She later published her memoirs, which catalogued their romance, and was the subject of the famous ballad, 'Daisy, Daisy'. Following in her footsteps was the seventh and final earl, Charles Greville. Before the castle's sale in 1978, Greville became the first British peer to act in a Hollywood film. His exploits earned him the amusing nicknames, 'the duke of Hollywood', and 'Warwick the Filmmaker'.

A true survivor of England's blood-soaked history, within the medieval walls of Warwick Castle, many former inhabitants reputedly continue to dwell. Undoubtedly the most famous surrounds that commonly known as the 'Ghost Tower'. Officially termed the Watergate Tower, many of the stories concern a former owner who met a violent end.

Many rightly regard Sir Fulke Greville as the castle's saviour. Sadly for Warwick's most iconic lord, in 1628, following an argument with his most trusted servant, Greville was brutally stabbed in the chest. The reason, somehow predictably, concerned finances. In this case, exclusion from his master's will. With the baron bleeding before his eyes, the mortified servant slit his own throat and died instantly. Sir Fulke, unlike the servant, did not die immediately. Instead, he was forced to live out his remaining weeks at his residence in Holborn with a severe infection from his wounds. On his death, he was brought back to Warwick for burial.

More than three centuries have passed since the unfortunate incident, but it is said that the presence of the castle's former owner still lingers. Cries of torment have been heard resonating throughout the tower. Legend also claims that his ghost emerges from his portrait and wanders the 'Ghost Tower'.

It is not only human spirits that are said to haunt the castle. A large slobbering black dog was once said to plague the grounds. Regarded as an omen of doom, this particular haunting is said to have arisen courtesy of one Moll Bloxham, who was caught stealing from the stores during the Middle Ages. Following a series of indignant torture, it was said she put a terrible curse on the castle in retribution for her ill-treatment.

According to local tradition, the woman soon disappeared and was never seen again. However, around this time, a black dog with blood-red eyes began plaguing the castle grounds in the dead of night. Several attempts were made to kill the beast, but the hound continued to terrorise the community. That this dog harboured the woman's spirit appears to have originated from Bloxham's vow to haunt the castle after her brutal torment. Furthermore, it was not until after her disappearance that the dog appeared. Intriguingly, a kennel is still housed within the castle grounds despite the apparent breaking of the curse following the luring of the beast from the highest tower into the River Avon.

Over the years, many other apparitions have been seen at Warwick. Sightings of a ghostly lady are a common claim. Soldiers, usually from the Civil War, have also been seen patrolling the battlements. The ghosts of children and servants were so frightening for one cleaner, she resigned her post and refused to return. One incredibly evil spirit is said to haunt the dungeons, of which many have complained of the atmosphere to the point they refuse to enter.

A product of continuous evolution, to call Warwick a castle is itself something of a simplification. A place of defence, a stately home, a prison, community, and menagerie, few sites better represent the ongoing transition that any castle must endure. As Sir Walter Scott summed up only too well, Warwick Castle is 'the fairest monument of ancient chivalrous splendour which yet remained uninjured by time'.

Dudley

William Camden recorded an old legend that Dudley Castle was so named in honour of the endeavours of a Saxon lord named Dud or Dodo, who established a burh on the original site. Though no proof of this has been found, Dudley's origins can safely be dated to 1070–71 when William the Conqueror constructed a Norman motte and bailey atop a limestone crag. The castle was clearly in working condition when the *Domesday Book* was compiled. Like most of its type, the timber defences were developed and refortified over the coming two centuries, giving birth to the emphatic stone castle that now exists alongside Dudley Zoo.

The modern zoo is not Dudley's only eccentricity. The corner of the lecture room reveals one particular oddity: two pieces of a large fourteenth-century stone coffin – or coffins. The disturbing eyewitness report of a cleaner once claimed that a glance in the ravaged tomb's direction revealed the sight of riding boots next to it. The ruined stonework was retrieved from Dudley Priory, which was the resting place of the lords of Dudley before the Dissolution. Among their number was the de Somery family, who tradition tells were particularly unruly in their attempts to expand the castle, at times resorting to extortion.

When the de Somerys died out, the castle passed by marriage to the Suttons. After this, it became the property of the controversial John Dudley, 1st Duke of Northumberland. When Dudley fell from grace for his role in Lady Jane Grey's accession, the castle returned to the Suttons and entered a period of decline. Garrisoned by the Royalists in the Civil War, Dudley was besieged by the Parliamentarians in 1644. A second siege led by the prominent Roundhead Sir William Brereton saw it surrender on 13 May 1646.

As per usual with former Royalist strongholds, parliament ordered its slighting. Sadly, this would not be the end of the castle's hardship. On 24 July 1750, a raging fire burned for three days unabated, thus condemning Dudley to a legacy as a romantic ruin. The exact cause of the fire remains unclear; however, a supply of gunpowder appears to have been stored there. The site was incorporated into the zoological gardens in 1937 and is now a beloved tourist attraction.

Owned by men of a dubious ilk, besieged by Roundheads and gutted by fire, the castle is reputedly the haunt of many spirits. Further to a gruesome reputation surrounding the crypt, tradition tells that an elderly lady hanged herself from the ramparts after unruly youths killed her cat.

Most famous of Dudley's apparitions is the 'grey' lady, Dorothy Beaumont. Forced to endure her baby's death during childbirth, the grieving mother succumbed shortly after. The double tragedy is believed to have occurred during the siege of 1646, which may indicate that stress was a likely contributor. Her deathbed request for her daughter to be buried alongside her was sadly not respected. Nor did her husband attend the funeral. The Grey Lady Tavern in the grounds is named in her honour.

Dudley's final spirit is also said to date from the Civil War. A Roundhead drummer on a mission to offer terms of surrender was killed by a musket ball fired by a Royalist on the battlements. Legend says that it is bad luck to hear him.

Tamworth

Constructed on the site of a Saxon burh built in 913 by Æthelflæd, the daughter of Alfred the Great, the well-preserved castle in the town of Tamworth stands dominantly on an ancient mound overlooking the rivers Tame and Anker. In the eighth century, the Saxon king of Mercia, Offa, built a far earlier palace on the site that succumbed to the Viking invasion of 874, leaving the town 'for nearly forty years a mass of blackened ruins'. Equally ineffective though Æthelflæd's burh proved during the Viking invasions of 943, the abandoned site remained highly regarded due to its proximity to the two rivers. Work on the present castle began under William the Conqueror's steward, Robert le Despenser, after receiving the land in gratitude for his role in the Norman Conquest.

The castle thrived under his successors, the chief of whom was Robert de Marmion, later husband of le Despenser's niece, Matilda. The ancient keep and curtain walls remain remarkably unchanged since that time. Though numerous expansions and alteration have helped develop the castle, pure luck also ensured its survival. The failure to carry out an order by King John in 1215 to raze it due to the desertion of Robert de Marmion, 3rd Baron Marmion of Tamworth, saw the family regain it on John's death. In 1643, a two-day siege and a lack of counter-resistance ensured the avoidance of a parliament-ordered slighting. Thanks to this and the fine condition of the earlier work, the castle has developed a reputation as one of the best-preserved of its type in England.

Thousands of tourists visit the castle each year, of which stories of royal visitors enthral many. Since the arrival of Henry I, no less than five monarchs have graced it with their presence, notably: Henry II, Henry III, Edward II, Edward III and James I, along with Charles I while still a prince. Equally famed for its beauty in the nineteenth century, the nearby castle mill was the setting of a masterpiece by Turner. A visit by Sir Walter Scott also inspired an inclusion in his 1808 poem, *Marmion: A Tale of Flodden Field*.

According to legend, living royalty are not the only guests for which Tamworth is famous. The battlements of the medieval fortress are said to be haunted by a lady in white. In life, the girl was captured by the castle laird Sir Tarquin and locked up in one of the towers. Although she developed a fondness for the evil lord, the young girl was soon rescued by the aptly named Sir Lancelot du Lac. When Lancelot killed Sir Tarquin, the wretched young woman was said to have thrown herself from the battlements in grief for her captor.

Although many centuries have passed since her imprisonment, it is said that her spirit continues to linger. She has been seen, not in the tower, but walking the battlements where she took her life. Legend also tells that her mournful cries have been heard long into the cold nights.

Joining the lady in white is a far different woman. Shortly before the Normans occupied the castle, the local convent of Polesworth Abbey existed nearby. Believed to have been set up by a nun named Saint Eadgyth – more commonly Editha – in the ninth century, the convent thrived until its demise at Robert de Marmion's hands. At their lowest ebb, the nuns prayed to Editha for protection against the unruly villain.

Subsequent events have ensured the legend's notoriety. According to one version, the ghostly nun appeared one night at Marmion's bedside and struck him with her crozier. Another version recounts that, in 1139, years after the event, Marmion held a grand feast in which many nobles attended. With the gathering in full swing, the spirit of the angry nun grabbed him by the throat and threatened that unless the nuns were to return to their convent, he would die a terrible and untimely death. Unwilling to tempt fate, Marmion restored the nunnery a short time later.

More than 1,000 years have passed since her death, yet the spirit of St Editha is still said to return to the castle from time to time. Local lore places the legendary meeting as having occurred in the middle room of the Norman Tower, also known today as the 'Ghost Room'. During the first part of the twentieth century, a photograph was taken of the stairway. Although the stairs were empty at the time, the ghostly vision of a figure in the habit of a nun can be seen on the negative.

In more modern times, accounts of paranormal activity in the castle have shown little signs of abating. One such encounter involved a staff member seeing to an exhibition titled 'The Tamworth Story', only to be caught off guard by the feeling of grit thrown in her face. An even more bizarre story concerns an alarm malfunction on 24 February 1999. Strange reports tell of a dragging sound and the engineer being waved at by a lady at an upstairs window. Exactly who was responsible remains a mystery. No trace of a break-in was ever found.

Tutbury

According to tradition, the medieval castle at Tutbury lies on the ancient remains of an earlier Saxon settlement. Like nearby Tamworth, the lords of Mercia are known to have inhabited the area and named it after the god Thor.

Situated in the large village of the same name on the banks of the River Dove, the castle is now a well-preserved ruin. Begun as a Norman stronghold around 1071, it fell into disrepair when the owner, William Ferrers – the descendant of early owner, Henry de Ferrers – participated in Henry the Young King's rebellion against Henry II in 1174. In 1264, Tutbury was nearly destroyed by Prince Edward, later Edward I. Two years later, Henry III confiscated the castle as a punishment for the rebellion of Robert de Ferrers, 6th Earl of Derby. In 1269, Henry III granted Tutbury to his second son, Edmund 'Crouchback', 1st Earl of Lancaster, who oversaw significant renovations the following year. Another inheritor of the Lancaster inheritance, John of Gaunt, 1st Duke of Lancaster, upgraded the castle further, which helped ensure its status as one of England's most important. During Gaunt's tenure, the castle was often the residence of his wife, Constance. According to legend, Robin Hood and Maid Marian were married at the castle.

Come the late 1500s, Tutbury's condition began to deteriorate. Further to the sieges of 1174 and 1264, the Roundheads targeted the castle around 1643 due to its Royalist garrison. The siege ended in 1646, leaving the castle uninhabitable. Fortunately for modern-day history lovers, destruction work was never completed. Although the castle has remained uninhabited since, ongoing renovation work since the restoration of the monarchy has helped keep what remains intact. In 1780, a folly was also constructed on the motte and is now known as Julius's Tower.

It is somewhat ironic considering the castle's past that the crumbling shell of the south tower is one of the few parts to have remained mostly unchanged. A magnificent example of Norman stonework, the tower is not only a rare survivor of the era but also acts as a tangible reminder of the confinement of the castle's most infamous guest. Mother of James VI of Scotland and I of England, Mary, Queen of Scots, incurred the wrath of her cousin, Elizabeth I, for her continuous attempts to usurp the throne of England. Although her eighteen-year imprisonment included several different prisons, it was within the damp fortified walls of Tutbury she regarded her captivity to have begun. According to many visitors and employees, her restless spirit still resides at this, her most loathsome of all prisons.

Mary's reasons for disliking Tutbury are no mystery. Isolated at the top of a steep hill, the castle is particularly exposed to the elements. Of equal dislike to her were the fumes of the marsh below. Plagued by declining health due to the cold and damp and tormented by a picturesque view of freedom over the surrounding town, Mary endured a wretched existence confined to two chambers of the south tower. In total, she suffered on no less than four separate occasions within the walls of Tutbury, during which she plotted unashamedly against Elizabeth. After being initially imprisoned on being caught up on the fringes of several plots, including the Norfolk and Ridolfi Plots of 1568–72, Mary's end came when the Babington Plot was foiled in 1586. A series of coded letters passed between several Catholic conspirators, including Anthony Babington, found their way into the possession of top Elizabethan spymaster Sir Francis Walsingham. As a result, Mary was executed on 8 February 1587 – see also Fotheringhay Castle.

Famously Mary's prison, his mother's former presence there did little to detract James I of England from staying at the castle. Indeed, James visited several times between 1619 and 1624. In August of the latter, he knighted Henry Rainsford and Edward Vernon there. That the king ever witnessed his mother's ghost is unrecorded. Nevertheless, since her execution, tradition has claimed that the spirit of the infamous queen often returns to Tutbury. Dressed in pure white silk, resembling the style of the Tudor era, her ghost has been seen atop the south tower where she spent many troubled hours. She has also been seen, usually between 10:15-11:00 pm, looking through one of the windows of the great hall that overlooks the modern car park. Eyewitnesses have described her as sad and lonely, as she seems destined to watch others depart.

Whether Mary is also the identity of another lady is the subject of an ongoing mystery. Usually witnessed as a cloudy mist originating around the north tower, the 'Lady in White' is reputedly a frequent presence in photographs. Local historians have conjectured this spirit may well be the mistress of the house who had an affair. On arriving for her forbidden rendezvous, she was shocked to find the steward had murdered her lover. Overcome with grief on seeing his bloody sword and her lover dead, she impaled herself.

Joining the unfortunate duo is a figure in black who has reputedly been seen peering out through one of the windows of the great hall. Dressed in the armour of the Middle Ages, the ghost of a man has also been witnessed. Known as 'the keeper', the enigmatic figure has appeared, stepping out from the John of Gaunt Gateway, shouting the barely audible commands of 'Get thee hence!' to unsuspecting tourists.

Another ghost who haunts the great hall is that of a sad little boy. Dressed in a white shirt, the boy reportedly sits on the stairs as if waiting for someone to arrive. Thought to be the spirit of a peasant, the ghost dubbed 'the Frenchman' has been seen wearing shabby clothes of centuries past. This outgoing spectre has a reputation for reaching out to female visitors in his native tongue, as though intent on ending many years of loneliness.

Completing the list of hauntings is a little girl named 'Ellie'. Often regarded as the castle's most playful spirit, the perpetual 5-year-old has been seen and felt in many parts of the castle. Another to appear dressed in white, with equally pale hair, the naughty child has been seen laughing and smiling. She is also thought to be responsible for inexplicable accounts from guests who have had their hands touched, rings moved, or strange sensations felt on their arms. Particularly active in the King's bedroom, the apparition is also the most reported of the castle's resident ghosts, regularly convincing sceptics that the past and the present are very closely linked.

Chapter 10

Northamptonshire and Leicestershire

Barnwell

Constructed in 1132, the destiny of this traditional motte and bailey castle established in the northern part of the village of Barnwell had much in common with its contemporaries. After avoiding instant destruction in the Anarchy, the castle was rebuilt in stone by the powerful Berengar le Moine around 1266. As Moine failed to obtain a licence to crenellate, it passed in 1276 to Ramsey Abbey. When the Dissolution of the Monasteries saw the end of the local priory, Henry VIII granted the manor to the Montagu family. In the English Civil War, the staunch Royalist Sir Edward Montagu used it as an arsenal. Though it avoided the type of siege and slighting experienced by many other castles, when the war was over, Montagu built Barnwell Manor close by. In time, the manor became home of the duke of Gloucester, while the castle and priory were left to the elements.

Abandoned for more than 350 years, little now remains of the castle. At times, a Union Jack can be seen flying above the imposing gatehouse, whose twin-towers are thickly coated in moss. Due to its location on land still owned by the duchy of Gloucester, the castle is one of the few in this book that isn't open to the public. Indeed, a brief glimpse from the nearby road is all that is accessible without prior appointment.

Worthy of inclusion, however, are a few strange legends that date from the castle's early days. A story from the thirteenth century relates that one Marie le Moine was bricked up shortly after the castle's construction. A similar account concerns Berengar's brother, Wintner. The limited evidence makes it difficult to clarify whether these tales have become merged and misunderstood or whether two separate individuals were bricked up, perhaps together. It is reputedly Marie's ghost that has been seen haunting the ruins.

The medieval priory was also once located in the grounds. The monastery was famously the home of the Barnwell Annalist, whose chronicling of the reign of King John was particularly important. Local lore tells that someone murdered a monk on the site; however, his identity appears unrecorded. Local stories also speak of a historian named Tom Lichfield who attempted a séance in 1948 and made contact with the abbot of nearby Ramsey Abbey, who told of the site being used to mete out justice and execution in the fourteenth century. He also spoke of a hidden chest which concealed the remnants of a 'ruined life'. What caused the ruin of this life is unknown. Yet locals say that should a strange breeze blow through the estate on an otherwise still day, the entity of the monk is close at hand, destined to forever walk the grounds scaring people with the cracking of his whip.

Fotheringhay

Nothing now survives of medieval Fotheringhay. The original castle, constructed around 1100 as a motte and bailey close to the modern village of the same name, was most likely property of Simon de Senlis, Earl of Northampton, before passing to David of Scotland. The prince was married in 1113 to Northampton's widow, Maud of Huntingdon, whose parents had been granted the area by William the Conqueror. When David was crowned king of Scotland eleven years later, the castle passed to his subsequent heirs before being confiscated by King John around 1212. John's decision to seize Fotheringhay and many others proved deeply unpopular with his barons and added to the increased friction that culminated in Magna Carta. As a consequence of David, Earl of Huntingdon's rebellion, John gave the castle to William Marshal, 2nd Earl of Pembroke. William returned the castle to John's son, Henry III, in 1220.

According to the Barnwell Annalist, Henry presented it to Hubert de Burgh in 1221 on the justiciar's marriage to Margaret, sister of Alexander II of Scotland. However, an unexpected complication arose when the hot-headed William de Forz, 3rd Earl of Aumale, briefly captured Fotheringhay and installed a garrison after plundering the nearby countryside. Evidence suggests that either Henry III did not honour Margaret's dowry, or he deprived Hubert de Burgh of the award in 1232 when he sacked him as justiciar and stripped him of the earldom of Kent. Subsequently, the castle remained in royal hands until the reign of Edward II.

Besides the brief period in the Second Barons' War when Robert de Ferrers, 6th Earl of Derby, took the castle, Fotheringhay's status was relatively secure. Granted to John of Brittany, the castle passed from his widowed niece back to the Crown, at which point Edward III gave it to his fourth son, Edmund Langley, Duke of York. John Leland recorded that Langley spent vast amounts on the Norman castle, and left it to his eldest son, Edward, who died at Agincourt.

As Edward had died without issue, Fotheringhay passed to his nephew, Richard, 3rd Duke of York, who regarded it as a favoured residence. Others who viewed it fondly were York's wife, Cecily, and Elizabeth Wydville, queen consort of Edward IV. Here, York's son Richard, later duke of Gloucester and Richard III of England, was born. In June 1482, the conspiring Alexander Stewart, Duke of Albany, came to Fotheringhay to confirm the Treaty of Fotheringhay with Edward IV to usurp James III as king of Scotland.

As the Wars of the Roses fared poorly for the House of York, the castle remained in Lancastrian hands. Henry VIII allocated the castle to Catherine of Aragon. Despite spending vast sums improving it, she took up residence at Kimbolton Castle. A prison during the reigns of Elizabeth I, James I and Charles I, the castle fell further into decline and was later demolished.

In the modern-day, to walk Fotheringhay's motte and former bailey has more in common with a stroll through an Iron Age hill fort than a once favoured royal residence. Among the greenery grows a rare thistle. Though its origin is unclear, the former habitation of the princes of Scotland seems a logical guess. Yet local legend offers a different reason for the flower. As indicated by the name Queen Mary's Tears, it may be associated with its most famous resident.

Historians will always regard 16 May 1568 as a decisive date in the history of England and Scotland. On this day, the recently dethroned queen of Scotland, Mary Stuart, arrived in England. Initially hoping for her cousin's help in regaining her throne, instead, she began a long period of imprisonment that ended at Fotheringhay. Brought to the castle – at the time, a state prison – for her trial, Mary, draped in black velvet, was tried in the great hall on 14 October 1586 and convicted of treason on 25 October.

After waiting throughout the winter for her cousin to put her signature on the death warrant, Elizabeth finally relented on 1 February. William Cecil's orchestration of movements behind the queen's back saw the execution was conducted post haste. At 8:00 am on 8 February 1587, after a night in the chapel, Mary appeared before a crowd of 300 and climbed the specially erected scaffold. There, within the same location where she had conducted her legal defence, she removed her gown and revealed a scarlet petticoat – famed as the colour of martyrdom. Maimed by the initial blow of the axe, prompting her to cry weakly, 'Sweet Jesus', with a second, Mary succumbed to her fate. Eyewitness reports decry a comical nature, in which the executioner held the Scottish queen's head aloft, only to discover she had been wearing a wig. Upon its separation from the wig, a small Skye terrier concealed among Mary's clothing leapt free to cause mayhem among the authorities. Sadly, the poor blood-soaked animal sank into a pit of melancholy and died a short time later. Mary was initially buried in Peterborough Cathedral before being relocated to Westminster Abbey in 1612.

The castle itself may no longer stand, but the materials were mostly reused. The grand staircase on which Mary descended and the great hall windows were acquired by the landlord of the Talbot Hotel in the nearby market town of Oundle. In keeping with the so-called 'stone tape theory', it has long been said that Mary's ghost has been seen peering out the window.

While her ubiquitous spirit wanders various residences, local legend claims that the sprouting of the lovely thistle in summertime marks the castle's solitary reminder of the executed queen. In so doing, one could argue Mary's final words to her ladies in waiting came true after all. 'Cause rather to joy than to mourn, for now shalt thou see Mary Stuart's troubles receive their long-expected end.'

Rockingham

The iconic double-fronted gatehouse is a rare reminder of Rockingham's former prestige. Added during the final three years of Henry III's reign, the twin D-tower structure is one of the most imposing of its type in England. Indeed, one of the finest medieval defensive fortresses ever made.

The reasons behind its construction may well have been connected to a memory that had undoubtedly lingered in the king's mind since 1220. That summer, William de Forz, 3rd Earl of Aumale refused to surrender the castle following the papal demand that all castellans of the royal castles should submit them. The eight-day siege that stood between the king and its recovery proved one of the major distractions of the year and a significant waste of treasury funds.

Unlike many of his forebears, including his father John, Henry III was indifferent to hunting and hence less interested in Rockingham's perks. Lying in the heart of the now diminished Rockingham Forest, the castle was a favoured hunting lodge of many Norman and Plantagenet kings: the last of whom to visit was Edward III.

Like many in the Norman era, the castle was erected as a motte and bailey on a site that had been used since the Iron Age. The location was viewed as an important one due to its unrestricted views across the Welland Valley. Less than three decades passed before William's eldest son and namesake, William Rufus, decided to upgrade the timber fortifications with a stone keep and outer curtain wall. For the next four centuries, Rockingham served as a royal castle until Henry VIII granted the lease to Edward Watson in the 1500s. Watson's grandson later acquired the freehold, and the castle remains operated by their descendants.

A castle in disrepair at the time of the Watsons' arrival, the once-beloved royal hunting lodge soon became a much-loved noble one. As work progressed, a new Tudor house equipped with stunning gardens replaced parts of the dilapidated site. Ever loyal to the royals, the family maintained a small Royalist garrison in the early years of the Civil War, and several skirmishes with their Roundhead foes followed. In 1643, Parliamentarian troops led by Henry Grey, 1st Earl of Stamford, breached the castle, and three years later, parliament ordered its slighting. Only in the following centuries would the newer building become fit for permanent residence.

Further restoration had been undertaken when the legendary writer Charles Dickens first graced its walls. A good friend of owners Richard and Lavinia Watson, Dickens was a regular visitor to the castle and was recorded as having spent several days there in November 1849. During his time at Rockingham, Dickens is recorded as having entertained his hosts by acting out scenes from *Nicholas Nickleby*. It is also believed that this very castle set the stage for Chesney Wold in *Bleak House*.

Deprived the castle may be of a resident ghost, there is a wonderful legend that during his stay at Rockingham, Dickens came face to face with the spirit of Lady Dedlock when taking a stroll behind the 400-year-old yew hedge. That this should indeed have happened would seem especially remarkable, as Dedlock was a character from his own novel.

Regardless of the exact veracity of the claim, past biographers and commentators have paid testament to Dickens's ability to fantasise about real-life conversations with his creations. It is an intriguing thought that such was his imagination, a character that would gain literary fame quite literally jumped off the page and inspired his writing.

Belvoir

Situated among picturesque hillside that overlooks the Vale of Belvoir near Grantham, the original castle is thought to date back to the Norman settlers. After serving as a royal manor until 1257, it passed to the de Ros family, who were granted a licence to crenellate. The legitimate line died out in 1508.

Gutted by fire during the Wars of the Roses, the new owners, the Manners family, rebuilt the castle between 1528 and 1555 using stone from the nearby Belvoir Priory and Croxton Abbey, which were gutted during the Dissolution. During the Civil War, the castle experienced further mishaps when the Manners used it as a Royalist stronghold. Charles I himself is recorded as having spent a night there on his way to Lincolnshire. When the Roundheads destroyed the second castle, a third was begun in 1654 and completed in 1668.

For the next century, Belvoir prospered. In 1799, the owners of the time, recently elevated from earls of Rutland to dukes, started a significant upgrading. Sadly, the work would meet with travesty in October 1816, when a third fire tragically hit the gothic-revival. Lost along with the new building were masterpieces by Sir Joshua Reynolds, Sir Anthony van Dyck, Titian and Sir Peter Paul Rubens. The present building was completed by 1832 and is the fourth castle to have stood on the site.

Now home to the eleventh duke of Rutland, as it was for his predecessors – and the earls before them – the nineteenth-century castle retains the ambience of former days. The neo-gothic architecture presents an impressive example of the medieval style associated with the earlier castles. The inclusion of several fine articles and pieces of art has also been carefully selected to reflect the castle's earlier history.

Surrounded by approximately 15,000 acres of land and fine gardens, the castle is celebrated as one of Britain's finest stately homes. A popular site for weddings, many are surprised to learn that the elegant castle hides a somewhat darker history. The ghost of a highwayman has reportedly been seen near the rally track, usually in January. So real has the apparition seemed, many passing motorists at night are reported to have stopped in confusion.

A far more significant shadow is cast by an act of reputed evil from the early seventeenth century. Hailing from nearby Bottesford, Joan Flower was employed at the castle with her daughters Margaret and Philippa. Even in the local village, the Flowers were not a well-liked family. Described as possessed of scruffy hair, dark piercing eyes and a lack of devotion to Christianity, Joan was shunned as a witch by her neighbours. As time wore on, stories evolved of her regularly consorting with spirits of the dead and placing curses on those who she disliked. The countess took particular note of the idle gossip. When Margaret was reportedly caught stealing from the castle stores, the countess sacked the young woman.

Though countess Cecilia was initially delighted to be rid of what she considered an evil presence, according to local legend, she was soon forced to incur the wrath of the so-called witches of Belvoir. About a year or so after Joan's dismissal, the countess and the earl fell victim to a terrible illness that left them close to death. Although they both eventually recovered, during which both suffered 'serious convulsions' and one if not both were left barren or sterile, sadly, the mystery virus also appears to have plagued the couple's children. Their daughter Katherine suffered and recovered. The prognosis, however, was less encouraging for sons Henry and Francis, both of whom were titled, Lord Roos. In 1613 and 1620, the pair suffered dreadfully before passing away.

Unsurprisingly, locals accused the three women of being behind the mysterious illness, and in 1618 they were arrested on suspicion of murder. In the chaotic trial that replicated a similar one of July 1616, stories came to light that Joan had resorted to devil worship in the aftermath of her dismissal. The defendant herself also reputedly admitted to several heinous crimes before later recanting.

Subjected to the barbarity of an angry crowd, Joan Flower asked to undergo trial by ordeal. The exact origin of this method is unknown, although it is believed to date to Saxon times. Asking for bread, Joan stoutly claimed that the food would never go through her if she were guilty. Local legend tells that after a mere mouthful and the mumbling of words inaudible to most present, she choked to death.

Precisely what happened is another of those events in which local legend dominates. According to most local historians, Joan died in prison, more likely succumbing to the challenging conditions. Her guilt, nevertheless, supposedly proven, the fate of her daughters was in no doubt. On 11 March 1618, the authorities hanged the wretched sisters at Lincoln Castle. In the centuries since, the story of the Belvoir witches has become part of the area's folklore. Indeed, the witch trials are often re-enacted at the castle by actors in period costume. Another legend tells that Philippa drugged the guards and escaped.

So what exactly became of the two Roos brothers? That the pair died young is beyond doubt. Visitors can find the earl's tombstone in the nearby church of St Mary the Virgin. The remains of Cecilia and the earl's first wife, Frances, lie on either side. His deceased sons reside at the foot of the tombs, their monuments holding skulls as a symbol of their untimely deaths. An inscription on the tomb recalls the story that the two sons both tragically died in infancy of wicked 'practise and sorcerye'.

Chapter 11

Nottinghamshire, Derbyshire and Lincolnshire

Newark

A howling gale battered the streets of Newark on 18 October 1216. Houses collapsed, bridges were damaged, and several people were injured as the storm of seemingly biblical proportions unleashed its fury on the bustling market town.

That those within the sturdy walls of the nearby castle feared the onslaught quite so much is a matter for speculation. The fortress was begun around 1135 as a typical Norman motte and bailey after Henry I granted Alexander, Bishop of Lincoln, permission to construct a castle. The bishops upgraded the original timber construction in stone towards the end of the century. Alexander also oversaw the addition of a mint, which was a significant boon for the local economy.

Such was the storm's ferocity, it must be considered a stroke of good fortune that the upgrades had already been made. Far less welcome were the circumstances that preceded the storm. Affected by dysentery, fatigue and enemy forces, King John arrived at Newark Castle on the back of a stressful crossing from Norfolk, before which he had worsened his failing condition by gorging on unhealthy food, peaches and sweet cider. The abbot of Croxton, renowned for his medical skills, was asked to treat the king on his arrival. Realising that it was futile, he performed the last rites and spent the night at prayer. As the chroniclers recorded, there was a sense that Newark had been the setting of a necessary evil. For on that fateful night, the devil had come for John's soul.

Visiting Newark in the modern-day, there is something undeniably imposing about the fortress. The jagged walls, comprised of medieval stone and nineteenth-century brick, are an alluring assortment that creates an ominous silhouette in grim conditions. Property of the bishops for much of its history, the castle passed to the Crown following the Dissolution. It was occupied by a Royalist garrison in the Civil War and rendered useless by the Parliamentarians in 1648. In the 1840s, Anthony Salvin oversaw its renovation before further restoration occurred in 1889 when the corporation of Newark bought the castle. It is open to the public and contains a heritage centre.

Eight hundred years may have passed since that fateful night when King John breathed his last, yet according to local legend, Newark's dark past continues to haunt it. Tradition tells that a ranger was found hanged in the king's bedroom around 1900. Since that time, his spirit has been seen there. Chanting and banging has been witnessed in the dungeon. An oppressive feeling has also been felt in the oubliette, in which an apparition was sighted.

Absent John's ghost appears to be, it is in the story of his death that the castle has achieved its greatest fame. As was reported in the chronicles, John died from a combination of dysentery and fatigue brought about by his unhealthy lifestyle. Yet, according to the *Brut Chronicle*, John's decline was more deliberate. Local legend has built on the account and given rise to the theory that John was murdered due to fears that he intended to raise the price of bread. A second contributing factor was his apparent lust for the abbot of Swineshead's sister, a chaste nun, during his stay there four days earlier. Regarded as a move of severe consequence – not least due to the abbey owning a mill – a monk of the order, Brother Simon, was cast in the role of assassin. The chronicler claims that he made the ultimate sacrifice by tasting John's refreshments, the king's usual taster having been lost in the chaos of the royal train's disaster in the Wash tidal estuary a day earlier. Local tradition also states that the monk was buried in one of the abbey's walls and remains there to this day.

Is it possible that John's death was premeditated? True, the king's decline *appears* to have been previously unforthcoming. Likewise, regicide may not have been without motive. That said, the lack of contemporary evidence for the tale and confirmed manner of John's gorging on sweet foods seems satisfactory explanation without foul play. The rumour that William Shakespeare chanced upon the chronicle and used it for his play, *King John*, based loosely on the king's life, seems likely. In keeping with the legend, Shakespeare depicts the monk as John's poisoner.

Potentially of greater credibility is the account that John, doubting his chances of reaching heaven, ordered on his deathbed that he be adorned in the habit of a monk in an attempt to con St Peter as he manned the pearly gates. When the clerics opened the tomb at Worcester in 1797, according to a written account by an engraver named Valentine Green, there was little evidence that his skull was blackened, as would have been typical in a man subjected to poisoning. A cowl typically used to adorn a monk was, however, reputedly present. That this was a gesture of respect by the abbot of Croxton, who also oversaw the salting and burial of John's entrails, is possible. Similarly, accounts from the chroniclers that John was the target of pilferers on his death may have enticed the abbot to clothe the late king in the monk's gown. Alternatively, it could just be that at least part of the legend may have been correct.

Nottingham

Little now remains of the once-mighty royal castle located in the centre of Nottingham. Constructed as a motte and bailey around 1067–78 on a natural outcrop with 130-foot-high cliffs to the south and west, the castle was blessed with a uniquely commanding position that made it difficult to siege.

Few castles in England can match Nottingham in terms of complexity: a feat owed almost entirely to its natural position. The timber fortifications were upgraded in stone from 1150 onwards, as the city gradually evolved as a Norman powerbase. An upper bailey sat at the highest point of what was adoringly labelled 'castle rock', with a middle bailey to the north in which Henry II added royal apartments. A far larger outer bailey was also situated to the east.

Following Henry II's developments, Nottingham enjoyed a special relationship with the Plantagenet royals. Occupying an important strategic point on the Trent and situated in the centre of England close to three of the most extensive royal forests – Barnsdale, Sherwood and Rockingham – the castle ticked the essential boxes. For such reasons, Prince John set up his HQ at Nottingham while brother Richard the Lionheart was away fighting in the Third Crusade. During Richard's imprisonment at the pleasure of Duke Leopold of Austria, many of

John's supporters gathered at Nottingham. A year later, the castle was the setting of a momentous battle between the pair. Richard's forces, aided by the type of siege machines he had used in the Holy Land, and the support of the prominent lords, David, Earl of Huntingdon and Ranulf de Blondevilles, Earl of Chester, John was forced to surrender in just a few days. In later years, these events became merged with the legend of Robin Hood, whose exploits with his Merry Men were set among Sherwood and Barnsdale.

Doubtful though it is that a historical Robin Hood was a contemporary of John or Richard, Nottingham itself had much to recommend it. The famous Ye Olde Trip to Jerusalem, which lays claim to being one of the oldest pubs in England, is located within 400 feet of the castle and traces its origins to 1189. Two other local inns claim heritage to the 1200s. On 19 October 1330, it was from tunnels dug into the rock that the 17-year-old Edward III, assisted by Sir William Montagu and a handful of other loyal companions, staged a coup d'état against his regents, Roger Mortimer, 1st Earl of March and Queen Isabella – see also Berkeley Castle. In the aftermath of Edward's success, Mortimer was forced to endure a further period in the Tower of London before suffering execution. Isabella, meanwhile, was confined to retirement – see Castle Rising.

After the overthrow, Edward III enjoyed a close affinity with Nottingham. A regular visitor, at which times he often held parliaments, the castle's prominent defences made it a logical choice to hold important prisoners. David II of Scotland was held there in 1346, some thirty years before the speaker of the House of Commons, Peter de la Mere, experienced something similar as a consequence of his 'unwarrantable liberties with the name of Alice Perrers, mistress of the king'. In 1365, Edward III strengthened the castle with a new tower west of the middle bailey and prison under the High Tower. Richard II used the castle at least twice for state councils. The queen consort of Henry IV, Joan of Navarre, also used the castle as her primary residence before and after her husband's death. After a lapse following her death in 1437, regular maintenance occurred during the Wars of the Roses. It was at Nottingham in 1461 where Edward IV was proclaimed king. Around that time, the construction of a new tower and royal apartments began, described by John Leland as 'the most beautifulest part and gallant building for lodging'.

True to Leland's description, Nottingham was maintained as a royal castle throughout the reigns of Henry VII and VIII, albeit with declining fortunes during the latter. The castle was dropped as a royal residence around the end of the reign of Elizabeth I. Charles saw the increasingly neglected castle as an important strategic site and, in August 1642, used it as a rallying point for his armies. Soon after his departure, the castle became occupied by the Parliamentarians and was improved.

In 1651, what remained was destroyed on the orders of John Hutchison, leaving only Henry III's 'good stone gateway with two towers'. The duke of Newcastle, Henry Cavendish, built the 'ducal' mansion house on the site 1674–79, which rioters burned down in 1831 in protest of the 4th duke's opposition to the reform act. By that time, the duke had lost interest in the area, which the slum dwellers lamented as 'the worst in the Empire outside India'. Derelict until 1875, the mansion was rebuilt to house the first municipal art gallery outside London, which continues to welcome visitors.

An imposing structure even in the modern-day, Nottingham Castle is still very much the heartbeat of a city where the present meets the past and where history meets legend. A famous statue of Robin Hood stands proudly in the fortress's shadow, joined by others of the merry outlaws and wall plaques acting out scenes from the ballads. Below the castle and accessible via a passageway, a dark cave named Mortimer's Hole is reputedly the place from where Edward III staged his attack and Mortimer was held. Legend tells that Mortimer's ghost continues to haunt the area, mostly playing out the circumstances of his capture. The tormented cries that have supposedly been heard are believed to denote the regents' overthrow. Local legend tells that the caves were carved by Sir Lancelot.

Perhaps the most disturbing of Nottingham's hauntings and legends concerns an event from 1212. Complicated relations between John and the Welsh, notably his son-in-law Llywelyn ap Iorwerth, Prince of Gwynedd, who had married John's illegitimate daughter, Joan of Wales, led to John taking twenty-eight sons of Welsh nobility hostage, including Llywelyn's first-born, Gruffudd. In what can only be described as the epitome of John's cruelty, he hanged all twenty-eight hostages – bar Gruffudd – from the ramparts. Local legend claims that their spirits still linger at the castle in connection with that horrific event.

Bolsover

Standing proudly over the Derbyshire town of the same name, the elegant walls of Bolsover Castle are a stunning legacy of the grand ambition of Sir Charles Cavendish.

Like many of England's great fortresses, the story of Bolsover is very much one of two castles. In the modern-day, the seventeenth-century walls rise imposingly over surrounding woodland. However, five centuries earlier, the image would have been very different. The original fortress was constructed by the Peveril family, whose number had been supporters of William the Conqueror. On the death of William Peveril the Younger sometime after 1155, it passed to the newly crowned Henry II, who spent £116 on Bolsover and nearby Peveril to combat the revolt of his son, Henry the Young King. On John's accession, the title 'Lord of the Peaks' was granted to William de Ferrers, Earl of Derby; however, both castles remained royal property. During the First Barons' War of 1216, John gave Ferrers permission to take possession; bizarrely, the refusal of castellan Brian de Lisle to yield required Ferrers to resort to force. This led to a minor civil war among the Royalists, while the rest of the country was plagued by actual civil war between Royalist and baronial rebel. The situation remained unresolved until de Lisle finally surrendered in 1217.

The castle again returned to royal control around 1223 after the nobles loyal to Henry III finally agreed to honour the papal mandate that all royal castles should be surrendered. Over the coming two decades, Henry spent £33 on repairs and £181 on four more towers along with a new barn and kitchen. During the reign of Edward I, the castle was granted to local tenants for farming purposes and gradually fell into disrepair. This trend continued until the Crown sold Bolsover to George Talbot, 6th Earl of Shrewsbury, in 1553. On George's death, Gilbert, the seventh earl, sold the castle to Cavendish: his stepbrother and brother-in-law.

Cavendish had the earlier castle demolished and drew up ambitious plans for a new one with renowned designer Robert Smythson. As work was ongoing when the two men passed away, it fell to Cavendish's sons, William and John, to finish it. The 'Little Castle' was completed in 1621, and work remained on schedule until it was taken quickly by the Roundheads and slighted. When the war was over, William Cavendish, made 1st Duke of Newcastle in 1665, returned to re-establish the fortress, reportedly in good condition on his death in 1676. A century later, however, it was described as ruinous. Around that time, the castle fell into the hands of the dukes of Portland, who kept it as a family retreat. It was used as a vicarage until it passed to the Ministry of Works in 1946.

Property of illustrious families and a centre point of local politics for more than nine centuries, it is hardly surprising that Bolsover has a reputation for being haunted. Indeed, in 2017, staff voted it the spookiest in the care of English Heritage. In so doing, it beat off some stiff competition, many of which are included in this book. Unexplained lights and noises have been witnessed in various parts. Smells and even physical assaults have also been reported, while things on display have been known to move.

Several ghosts are said to haunt the castle. A woman in a bustle dress has been seen on many occasions. The same is true of a ghost of a child. A man in a Tudor ruff has reputedly been seen along with a woman wearing a scarf in rooms below the castle. Most chillingly of all, the tower kitchen is reportedly the haunt of a woman placing a small child into the fireplace. Exactly who this woman was and why she has been seen doing so is unrecorded. Sadly, the tale suggests murder or cover-up.

Further to the alleged hauntings of the castle, the area is also the subject of a brilliant legend. The devil himself appeared one day in Bolsover and demanded of a local blacksmith a pair of metal shoes to cover his cloven hooves. The blacksmith got to work and – whether deliberately or not – banged a nail into the soft part of the foot. Caught off guard by the hellish pain, the devil set off like a flash, accidentally crooking Chesterfield's famous spire in the process.

Peveril

Rising high above the village of Castleton in the heart of Derbyshire's Peak District, the ruined eleventh-century fortress of Peveril Castle offers some of the most picturesque views in the country. Also known as Peak Castle due to its lofty location on a limestone outcrop, a visit on a clear day is worth the effort for the sights alone. From the mighty Hope

Valley to the dry limestone Cave Dale, here the surrounding landscape is visible at its finest.

Established as the *caput* of the feudal barony of William Peveril, on which the honour of Peveril was formed, the castle dates to shortly after the Norman Conquest. William is conjectured to have been an illegitimate son of William the Conqueror – himself a bastard. Though there is no proof of this, Peveril was a vital supporter of the king.

Mentioned in the *Domesday Book*, the castle appears to have been set in stone from the offset. Along with nearby Bolsover, it remained in the family until the death of William Peveril the Younger around 1155, when Henry II confiscated them. William had already fallen out with Henry for supporting Stephen during the Anarchy. This, in turn, would lead to his capture in the First Battle of Lincoln in 1141. Henry suspended Peveril on suspicion of attempting to poison Ranulf de Gernon, 4th Earl of Chester. He was also accused of 'plundering and treachery', which led to Henry's decision to keep the property for himself.

Over the coming decade, Henry visited the castle at least three times, including his hosting of Malcolm IV of Scotland in 1157. As with Bolsover, Peveril was garrisoned during the revolt of 1173–74 and gained by William de Ferrers, Earl of Derby in the First Barons' War. In contrast to Bolsover, there is no evidence that Ferrers damaged the castle after Brian de Lisle refused him entry. In 1223, Peveril and Bolsover were both surrendered to the king in compliance with the papal mandate that the royal castles should be returned. Efforts were also made to refurbish it for Henry III's visit in 1235. Henry later granted it to his son, Prince Edward – later Edward I. In 1264, Simon de Montfort, 6th Earl of Leicester, pressured the king into giving him possession after it had previously been inhabited by William de Ferrers's son, Robert 6th Earl of Derby. It returned to the Crown after de Montfort's death and formed part of the dowry of Edward's first queen, Eleanor of Castile.

By the late thirteenth and early fourteenth century, building work at Peveril reached its zenith. Edward III granted the castle and barony to his powerful son, John of Gaunt; however, the duke of Lancaster merely reused the materials. For nearby Pontefract, this would be a significant bonus, yet for Peveril, it was the beginning of the end. By 1609, it was described as 'very ruinous and serveth for no use' and subsequently abandoned.

Still officially the property of the duchy of Lancaster, the head of whose number still sits upon the throne, the castle is managed by English Heritage and welcomes thousands of visitors every year. Due to its picturesque nature, the area remains popular with hikers and artists. Tradition tells that, on Easter morning, the sun would 'dance for joy at his rising', prompting many locals to climb up to the castle to watch the sunrise. It was a visit to Peveril that inspired Sir Walter Scott's *Peveril of the Peak*. The novel, set in 1678, was Scott's longest. Few accounts describe the castle ruins in such magnificent detail.

Immortalised by a legendary writer, local tradition claims that over the centuries, the castle has developed a few tales of its own. Strange lights, usually blueish, have been witnessed close up and from a distance. Peculiar sounds have also been heard. Like many English castles, a black dog reputedly stalks the ruins, its eyes an eerie red in the darkness. The ghost of a medieval knight has also been reported within the keep while his horse waits below. Bizarrely, the apparition of an old lady and another horse has been seen there. Little is known about the origins of these stories. Logically, one could connect the knight to the castle's former garrison, if not Sir William Peveril himself. Though the castle was part of Eleanor of Castile's dowry, a personal connection is less clear.

Completing Peveril's tales of mystery, a strange soothing, yet sad arrangement of melodic overtones have been heard: most likely that of a woman singing. The mournful singing seems an appropriate soundtrack for the lonely setting. It is almost as though the voice laments the once-great fortress's lack of purpose, which is now destined to remain lost in time.

Lincoln

Lincoln is a rare castle in England. Along with Lewes – within whose walls the future Edward I slept the night before the 1264 Battle of Lewes – the castle is one of only two built with two mottes. When William the Conqueror reached Lincoln in 1068, he discovered a vibrant Viking trading centre with a population of around 7,000. Due to its location at a strategic crossroads and with the old Roman walls already offering a solid foundation, Lincoln proved the perfect place for William to augment his command of the north.

The castle was one of two Lincolnshire ones to be mentioned in the *Domesday Book*. Like many of William's fortresses, it required removing unoccupied residences first – sources claim as many as 166. The original keep was likely of timber construction, a stone upgrade of which may have been in place when Matilda's supporters occupied the castle at the first Battle of Lincoln on 2 February 1141. Though a siege from Stephen's forces caught them off guard, a counter-attack led by Matilda's half-brother, Robert, Earl of Gloucester, yielded a victory and Stephen's imprisonment. Sadly for Matilda, she was unable to complete her conquest of England and never crowned queen. A new keep, the fifteen-sided Lucy Tower, was constructed soon after on the larger of the two mottes and named in honour of the countess of Chester, mother of the earl of Chester, who had earlier been granted permission to fortify.

Stephen's siege would not be the only major challenge the castle was forced to withstand. On 20 May 1217, Lincoln witnessed its second major battle, often known as The Fair of Lincoln. After several months of ongoing siege by the baronial forces against the brave castellan, Nicola de la Haye, the royalist garrison was relieved by troops led by William Marshal, 1st Earl of Pembroke, Peter des Roches, Bishop of Winchester, and the Norman heavyweight Falkes de Breauté. After entering the city from the north, thus avoiding the need to climb its famously steep hill, a plan, cleverly orchestrated by des Roches, allowed Marshal's forces to take the poorly defended north gate while Falkes created a useful diversion. On taking the fight to the streets of the lower town, Prince Louis of France's forces, led by the count of Perche, declined the option to either surrender or take to the fields and went down fighting.

Some sources suggest only three royalists lost their lives that day, compared to several hundred baronial. Some of the rebels fled for London, while others drowned trying to escape by river. The royalists, meanwhile, sacked the city for its loyalty to the rebels. The victory would prove a decisive one in the direction of the war and ultimately secure Henry III his throne. Among the moves made by his regency later that year was the third issue of Magna Carta. A copy of the original document remains on show at the castle.

In the aftermath of the battle, Henry's government carried out several necessary renovations. A new barbican was built on the west and east gates. The observatory tower, added to the original fourteenth-century square tower in the Victorian era, is located on the other motte. As for its future purpose, the walls that had proved excellent at keeping people out, unsurprisingly, proved equally suitable for keeping felons in.

Exactly when Lincoln's role as a prison began is unclear. Back in 1375, one Agatha Lovell – reputedly complicit in the murder of her master, Sir William de Cantilupe – escaped justice after bribing her gaolers. From 1787, the castle was officially the city's prison. In 1823, a courthouse was added that remains in use. The prison closed in 1878 when a new site was selected outside the city. The Lincolnshire archives took their place, and in more recent times, it was used for the filming of *Downton Abbey*.

Still beloved for its well preserved Norman walls and a copy of Magna Carta, this former prison and place of war reputedly contains a few darker memories. Unexplained lights and noises have been experienced among the former cells, not limited to the jangling of keys and the slamming of doors. Until around 1872, prisoners were publicly executed from the Mural Tower, which overlooks the upper town. The Victorian chapel is also somewhat mournful in ambience. The pews are strange, almost coffin-like, and put in as a reminder of one's mortality. Many visitors claim to have been disturbed by a presence and lights there.

Of the more alluring stories, the ghost of a lady carrying a babe in arms has reportedly been seen walking down the stairs of what was once the women's prison. The same is true of a lady in black in Cobb Hall who appears to walk in the direction of the old gallows. Shadows have also been reported in the observatory.

Among the saddest of Lincoln's stories is that of a loyal dog. Local lore has long told that the hound kept a vigil around the castle following his owner's hanging. Precisely who the criminal was and why he was executed is unknown. Nevertheless, it is a nice thought that even in death, man's best friend continues to bestow the type of loyalty often lost among the living.

Tattershall

The great tower is all that remains of the fifteenth century home of Ralph, 3rd Lord Cromwell, who served as lord treasurer to Henry VI 1433–43. What existed on the site before Cromwell's ostentatious construction of 1430–50 is a mystery. It is also possible that the original fortress, built by Robert de Tattershall in 1231, was more of a fortified manor than a typical thirteenth-century castle. Cromwell's rebuild was carried out in brick: an expensive and fashionable move at the time. Indeed, the castle has been described as 'the finest piece of medieval brickwork in England'.

Since Cromwell died in 1456, the 130-foot brick tower, equipped with an abundance of beautiful tapestries and gothic fireplaces and surrounded by a picturesque moat, has enjoyed mixed fortunes. Confiscated by the Crown from Cromwell's niece, Joan Bourchier, following her husband's downfall during the Wars of the Roses, Tattershall was acquired by the prominent Elizabethan Sir Henry Sidney in 1560 and later sold to the earl of Lincoln. The tower remained in the earls' hands until 1693, during which the cellar may have served as a Civil War prison. Under its subsequent owners, the Fortesques, it fell into disrepair.

By 1910, Tattershall's glories seemed destined to be a thing of the past. Though the tapestries had either disintegrated or been removed, the three iconic fireplaces remained intact. However, the tower's future was threatened when a buyer from America had the pieces stripped out. Fortunately, Lord Curzon of Kedleston purchased the building and ensured its survival. After a considerable search, the fireplaces were discovered in London and returned.

From 1911 to the onset of the First World War, the castle benefitted from a series of costly restorations. On Lord Curzon's death in 1925, he left it to the National Trust. His lasting legacy – besides serving as viceroy of India, leader of the House of Lords and nearly prime minister – was his commitment to preservation. His contributions saw such things enacted in British Law in 1913 in the form of the Ancient Monuments Consolidation and Amendment Act.

Although Curzon and many of the lovely tapestries have now gone, stories persist that the 66-foot wide, four-storey great tower remains inhabited by at least one past resident. While in the day, the view from the battlements is one of the most splendid in the locality: a rare chance to take in the distant countryside and grounds where gatherings of peacocks dwell, as the light turns low, a strange white shape has been seen drifting across the battlements. The ghost's identity remains another of the great castle mysteries. It is commonly assumed that this white shape is the same lady dressed in white, adorning a Norman headdress, who has been seen roaming the interior, and responsible for the strange poltergeist activity reported inside one of the turrets. Tradition states that the lady gazes out from the ramparts as she waits in vain for the return of her lost love.

Chapter 12

Yorkshire

Bolton

In common with beautiful Leeds Castle, the biggest surprise for many on hearing of Bolton is that the castle is not located in the significant town of the same name. Indeed, this impressive fourteenth-century castle is not in Lancashire but across the Pennines in the village of Castle Bolton in the Wensleydale area of Yorkshire. Often used as a location for filming, credits include the 1952 film *Ivanhoe*, the 1998 film *Elizabeth*, and the TV series *Heartbeat* and *All Creatures Great and Small*.

The castle was built to a quadrangular design during the reign of Richard II by the prominent Ricardian courtier, Richard, 1st Baron Scrope. In common with Castle Corfe and Castle Rising in the sense that the local village grew around the castle and took its name from it, Bolton is also rare for having remained with the Scrope family throughout its history.

Arguably the castle's most remarkable claims to fame concern the family's adherence to Catholicism. In the aftermath of the Pilgrimage of Grace in 1536, the then owner, John, 8th Baron Scrope, incurred Henry VIII's wrath for offering sanctuary to the abbot of Jervaulx, Adam Sedbar. While Sedbar was sadly discovered and executed, Scrope narrowly made it to Skipton. In retribution, the king ordered Bolton Castle be razed; however, fortunately, the damage was repairable, and Scrope returned to parliament a few years later.

During the reign of Henry's Protestant daughter, Elizabeth I, Bolton was again a location of destiny. After suffering defeat in the Battle of Langside in 1568, Mary, Queen of Scots successfully fled to England and was imprisoned in Carlisle under Henry, 9th Baron Scrope. Due to Carlisle Castle's poor condition, in July, Mary was moved to Bolton and imprisoned there six months before being relocated to Tutbury.

According to tradition, Mary successfully mounted an escape from Bolton, losing her 'shawl' on the way to Leyburn. It was from this that the local cliff edge was dubbed 'The Shawl'. Like Carlisle, Bolton was far from ideal for a prisoner of Mary's status and required tapestries and other furnishings to be brought in. While there, she was kept under the watchful eye of Sir Francis Knollys, who granted Mary use of Scrope's quarters in the south-west tower. Due to her vast entourage, only half could be accommodated at the castle, meaning others had to find suitable lodgings nearby.

As was common practice with royal prisoners, Mary was allowed individual freedoms, including going hunting. She also learnt English there, after previously having spoken French, Latin and her native Scots. Before leaving for Tutbury in January, she is alleged to have met up with local Catholics, which may have led to her brief escape.

Unsurprisingly given the castle's imposing nature, those who bore witness were rarely unimpressed by Bolton. An account by Sir Francis Knollys described the walls as 'The highest walls of any house he had seen.' John Leland also wrote of 'An Astronomical Clock' in the courtyard and of the practice of conveying smoke through tunnels from the hearth in the main hall. Damage in the Civil War, followed by the usual parliamentary slighting, was also not enough to bring the fortress to its knees. After the death of Emanuel Scrope, 1st Earl of Sunderland, in 1630, the castle passed through his illegitimate daughters, whose descendants now run it as a tourist attraction.

Beloved by visitors and a feature on the big screen, Bolton retains the aura of a castle where history is very much alive. A further link can possibly be found in the form of its most famous inhabitant. It has long been theorised that the lady in a dark cloak that has been seen roaming the corridors and grounds is none other than Mary Stuart. Witnessed in the modern day, she is usually mistaken for a visitor who doesn't reappear. Eyewitness accounts are also recorded in old books located at the castle, by those who believed they had witnessed the ghost of Mary, Queen of Scots.

Clifford's Tower (York Castle)

A series of anti-Semitic riots brought shame upon the city of York in 1190. The Purging of the Jews, led by Richard de Malebisse – a local severely in debt to prominent moneylender Aaron of Lincoln – with the assistance of a friar of forgotten identity, remains a tragic chapter in the city's history, itself not without a reputation for violence.

The catalyst for the chaos appears to have been three-fold. Further to the general anti-Jewish feelings of the population and the false rumour that the crusader king, Richard the Lionheart, had ordered attacks, Malebisse used a chance house fire as the opportunity to stir up trouble. As usual in England, the Jewish population, who were granted special privileges from the Crown, tended to live among themselves close to the main fortress. When the violence intensified, their leader, Josce of York, led his people to refuge inside the castle. When the mob breached the walls, they massacred those who hadn't been driven to commit mass suicide or killed in the fire designed to burn the corpses. Estimates place the death count at 150.

Before the Norman Conquest, York was the Viking capital of England. Known in the native tongue as Jórvík, the city was seen as an important one by William on his first Northern expedition and ordered a castle to be built in 1068. As usual, the first castle to be erected was a timber motte and bailey, which was constructed between the rivers Ouse and Foss at the expense of several hundred houses. Contemporary accounts suggest its building took a mere eight days, after which the new Norman overlords used it to defend against a local uprising. It is possible that the castle and its sister fortress, Baile Hill, were damaged during the Viking attacks of 1069 that culminated in the Normans razing the city. As well as significant damage occurring to York Minster, both castles fell to the Viking raiders. A year later, the dreaded 'Harrowing of the North' restored Norman rule.

By the compiling of the *Domesday Book*, York Castle was a much-extended fortress surrounded by a large moat and artificial lake fed by the River Foss. While Baile Hill was abandoned – only the motte remains visible – the original castle developed in importance. Henry II visited four times and hosted William the Lion of Scotland in 1175. Following the horrors of 1190, the keep was rebuilt – again in wood. After Richard the Lionheart's death, John used the keep for his quarters during his regular visits to the north. Around this time, the castle was first used to house prisoners, including those from John's Irish campaign.

John's eldest son, Henry III, continued such practices. On one fateful visit in Christmas 1228, the wooden keep was destroyed by a violent storm. When Henry visited in 1244, at which time rumours of a Scottish invasion were rife, the king ordered it be rebuilt in white limestone. Costing around £2,600, the substantial new castle included a two-storey keep arranged in a quatrefoil plan.

Within this 'King's Tower', many of the city's detainees were held, conditions of which were described as 'appalling'. Similar could also be said of security measures. Of particular note, twenty-eight are recorded as having mounted a mass breakout in 1298. In 1308, the tower was used with varying success to hold the outlawed Knights Templar, while Edward II also used it to incarcerate rebel barons. After Roger de Clifford's rebellion of 1322 culminated in the Battle of Boroughbridge, Clifford was brought to the keep and executed. It has been falsely speculated that it was in his honour the keep was renamed Clifford's Tower.

For York Castle, the fourteenth century onwards saw a decline in its fortunes. While royal visitors tended to take up lodgings in the Franciscan friary, the castle was used primarily for local administration as well as remaining a prison. Richard III began work to remove parts in disrepair, yet his death at Bosworth put paid to any replacements. On his visit in the sixteenth century, Leland reported that the castle was in significant need of repair, besides the water defences. The authorities shut the castle mint down in 1553, and the former Templar mills were given to local charities. By this time, only the gaol and executions remained of the castle's early purposes. Among the most notable executions was that of Robert Aske after being returned to York from the Tower of London in chains following his involvement in the Pilgrimage of Grace. Later that century, the equally Catholic 'pearl of York' Margaret Clitherow served three terms there. During the last, she gave birth to her son.

By the seventeenth century, York's time as a royal castle had passed. In 1614, King James I sold it to the Cliffords, who improved it for the Royalist cause and reopened the mint. On 23 April 1644, Ferdinando Fairfax, father of General Thomas Fairfax, commenced a siege that, within six weeks, involved combined Roundhead and Scottish forces of more than 30,000. Efforts by Prince Rupert in June to counteract the siege were initially successful; however, his troops encountered defeat at Marston Moor. On 14 July, the garrison surrendered and left the city with their heads held high. After the garrison honoured Cromwell's visit of 1650 with a gun salute, the garrison-controlled tower was officially separated from the prisoner-filled bailey. Repairs were made following the restoration when the previous owners, the Cliffords, were again granted control. Stone from the dissolved St Mary's Abbey also contributed new buildings close to Clifford's Tower.

Famous among the inmates at this time was Quaker founder George Fox, who would have experienced first-hand conditions that had reached new levels of infamy. When the renowned prison reformer John Howard came to York later that century, things were generally improving, yet conditions in the felons' prison remained poor. One especially sad story from 1739 tells that nine prisoners suffocated in one night. That same year former inmate Dick Turpin was executed nearby.

Fortunately, the days of brutal execution were now becoming a thing of the past. The tradition from the 1500s that felons be hung from the top of the tower was replaced from 1813 onwards with the new 'short drop' method, which allowed executions of fourteen at a time. The tower remained the county prison until 1900 when the final inmates were moved to Wakefield. Among the last prisoners held there was 23-year-old local thug Mary Fitzpatrick, who faced trial for the murder of James Richardson, who was discovered lying in water, minus his watch and chain.

Only the tower now remains of the once-great York Castle. Such was its poor condition in the Elizabethan age, the then keeper, Robert Redhead, achieved local infamy for selling certain parts for profit. Plans to pull Clifford's Tower down in 1596 were met with uproar. However, within a century, its image had changed. Now loathed locally as the 'minced pie', on St George's Day 1684, an explosion destroyed the interior. Whether the damage was accidental, brought about by the patriotic celebrations, or deliberate remains unclear. It was down to this explosion that the limestone walls turned pink. The phenomenon remains a strange one. Ever since its rebuilding in stone in the reign of Henry III, it has been said that the walls of Clifford's Tower bleed. An explanation has been made that iron oxide flows in the rain, yet, strangely, the quarried stone did not contain any.

Further to the stories of the walls bleeding, another strange account tells of a modern-day woman who, under hypnosis, recounted the past life of her family hiding beneath St Mary's Church in 1190. Sadly, the rioters discovered them in the crypt and murdered them. Most associated with the city dismissed the story: not least as St Mary's had no vault. Yet, in 1975, a chamber was discovered in the spot the woman had described.

Conisbrough

Started as a motte and bailey in the eleventh century by the powerful William de Warenne, Earl of Surrey, the stunning walls of Conisbrough Castle offer a fine illustration of the evolution of Norman architecture. William the Conqueror granted Warenne several estates in Yorkshire, Norfolk, Suffolk, Essex and Sussex, including the manor of Conisbrough, which had previously been the property of Harold Godwinson. Later in the following century, one Hamelin Plantagenet, a bastard half-brother of Henry II, acquired the castle through marriage to the original Warenne's great-granddaughter, Isabel, and began the process of rebuilding it in stone.

Aided by his son, William, 5th earl of Surrey, several additions were made. Among the crowning achievements was the magnificent keep, which rose to a height of 92 feet. Most of these features were in place when King John visited in 1201. The castle remained in the family till the fourteenth century, interrupted by periods of repossession by the Crown.

One of the most significant challenges occurred in 1316 when the owner, John de Warenne, 7th Earl of Surrey, attempted to divorce his wife. Frustrated at the lack of progress, John blamed Thomas, Earl of Lancaster, and foolishly kidnapped his wife and held her at Conisbrough. Thomas later seized the castle, which was granted to him by Edward II. The decision was reversed, however, when Thomas rebelled against Edward in 1322. Edward visited Conisbrough after Lancaster's execution and spent around 40 marks on repairs before it was returned to de Warenne after the king's overthrow in 1327. Later that century, Edward III granted the castle to his son, Edmund of Langley, 1st Duke of York, who held it until his death in 1402. It was then used by his son Edward until he was killed at Agincourt, and later the property of Richard, Duke of York and the future Edward IV.

Somewhat inevitably, the combination of imposing walls and steep hillside later came back to haunt Conisbrough. Plagued by subsidence, including a 'specular landslide', Henry VIII gave the castle to the Carey family. Due to its dire state, it avoided further mishaps in the Civil War and was bought by the duke of Leeds in 1737. Such was the beauty of the area and allure of the architecture, a passing glimpse in 1811 helped inspire Sir Walter Scott to write *Ivanhoe*, published eight years later. Like many ruins, it is now under the care of English Heritage.

A home of nobility and royalty, Conisbrough Castle remains a sight to behold. Though the landscape may have changed, helped in part by the fires of industry, the stunning architecture – especially of the keep – makes it an iconic reminder of the country's past. A popular tourist attraction in daylight hours, when night falls, a different atmosphere is said to descend. The flickering of ghostly candles has been reported where the chapel once stood. Strange noises have also been heard in various parts.

Prominent among the spirits said to reside at Conisbrough is that of a monk. Descriptions of the holy man in a grey habit suggests that he may have been of the Tironensian order, who had priories in Lincolnshire and Northumberland, as well as the south of England. Joining the phantom monk is a lady in either a white dress or a grey one. Over the centuries, she has been seen many times atop the keep. Tradition tells that she fell to her death; whether by suicide or foul play remains a mystery.

Further to the ghost stories, during road-widening excavations in 1955, the grave of a mysterious knight was uncovered in the churchyard of St Peter's. Despite a lion rampant appearing on his shield, his identity remains unknown. Legend claims that a secret tunnel connects the castle to the church. Though some proof has emerged that some form of underground passage exists, perhaps for refuse, evidence for something long enough to connect both buildings is still to be found.

Helmsley

Situated in the small market town of the same name in the North York Moors, the ruins of Helmsley are both rugged and atmospheric. The castle was established in the 1120s by Walter l'Espec on land that William the Conqueror had granted to his half-brother, Robert, Count of Mortain. The original design of double ditches around a rectangular bailey differed from the typical motte and bailey establishments. Equally different was the owner's desire for religious reform. It was on the castle's land that Walter helped found the first Cistercian abbey in the north at Rievaulx and the Augustinian priory at Kirkham.

Childless at his death in 1153, Walter's castle passed to his sister and into the family of Peter de Ros, to whom she was married. In 1186, his relative Robert, son of Everard de Ros, began converting the timber structure to stone, strengthening of which continued over the next 150 years. It may well have been for the five-day visit of Edward III in 1334 that the family enlarged the east tower. The castle remained in the same family's hands until they sold it to Richard, Duke of Gloucester – the future Richard III – the year his brother, Clarence, was killed at the Tower of London. After Richard's death at Bosworth, Henry VII restored the castle to the de Ros family.

During the Tudor age, Helmsley enjoyed a new lease of life. A sumptuous mansion was built inside the walls in place of the old hall. Other additions included the conversion of the barbican into a luxury residence. As Edmund de Ros had died childless in 1508, the castle passed to the Manners family, who were made earls of Rutland – see also Belvoir Castle. In 1632, it passed to Katherine, widow of George Villiers, 1st Duke of Buckingham. As Buckingham had died in 1628, his controversial son and heir inherited the castle. His dubious lifestyle earned him a deserved reputation as a renowned scoundrel: indeed, it was from the second duke's antics that gave rise to the rhyme, *Georgie Porgie*.

Buckingham had already been deprived of his estates when his future father-in-law, General Thomas Fairfax, laid siege to the castle in 1644. After the Royalist garrison held out for three months, the Parliamentarians slighted it. Gone the east tower, gate and much of the walls, fortuitously, the mansion remained unharmed. Since the restoration, the castle passed through various owners, one of whom, Thomas Duncombe, had a new mansion built to overlook the fortress, which was left a picturesque ruin and sketched by Turner. The old castle still forms the heart of the estate and later entered the care of English Heritage despite remaining under private ownership.

Uninhabited for more than 300 years, many strange things reportedly still happen at Helmsley. A ghostly cavalier has been seen stalking the battlements. Joining him is a lady in green. Over the years, she has been known to wander both inside and outside the castle, her dress rustling in a timeless breeze. A couple in Edwardian garb have also been seen walking the walls near the old gardens.

Perhaps the most prominent legend is that strange pixie-like creatures appear throughout the estate. Despite fitting the profile of something from a fairy tale, such creatures have been reported for centuries. Be they tricks of the light, real-life animals or insects, the power of suggestion or something as yet unexplained, the strange beings are still witnessed in the estate, as well as the wider countryside.

Knaresborough

Overlooking the calm waters of the River Nidd in a pleasant market town close to Harrogate, Knaresborough is a castle steeped in legend. Begun around 1100 and developed by Henry I, the castle was reputedly the place of refuge sought by Hugh de Moreville, the leader of the quartet of knights who famously rid Henry II of the 'turbulent priest' Thomas Becket.

After conspiring to murder the archbishop of Canterbury on 29 December 1170, the king reportedly advised de Morville, Reginald FitzUrse, William de Tracy and Richard le Breton to flee to Scotland. In so doing, they used Knaresborough as an interim sanctuary. De Morville, de Breton and de Tracy were all responsible for building the church at Alkborough in Lincolnshire as a form of penance. Until 1690, a stone that formed part of the chancel recorded as much. The church's creation failed to appease Pope Alexander III, who had the quartet excommunicated on Maundy Thursday, 1171. On being granted an audience in Rome, they were all ordered to fight for fourteen years as Templars.

While the sinful knights passed into infamy, Knaresborough's development continued. Highly regarded by King John, who took control of the castle in 1205, £1,290 was subsequently spent on improvements. Another £2,000 went on rebuilding work during the first twelve years of the fourteenth century. Following on from work commissioned by Edward I, Edward II proceeded to complete his father's early initiatives, most strikingly with the addition of the keep. Around the time of the castle's completion, Edward II gifted it to his controversial favourite,

Piers Gaveston, 1st Earl of Cornwall. The king used the castle as his lodgings while Gaveston was besieged at nearby Scarborough.

Four years after Edward II's dethronement and death, the young Edward III granted Knaresborough to his new queen, Philippa of Hainault. From that time onwards, the castle was upgraded to a royal residence, and the queen enjoyed spending her summers there. Their third son, John of Gaunt, also had a close affinity with the castle and took possession of it in 1372. On Gaunt's death, it became the property of his third wife, Katherine Swynford. For the next three centuries, Knaresborough enjoyed a relatively trouble-free history before being taken by the Roundheads in 1644 and slighted four years later. It is from the original stonework that many contemporary buildings in the town centre were built.

Now under public ownership and open to all-comers, Knaresborough continues to fascinate and delight. Stories have long abounded that the ghosts of two men haunt the castle, the most dominant of whom has been seen leaning over the second spirit, which lies flat out on the ground. Though their apparitions have been described as misty, the right arm of the standing entity is reported as being outstretched. That the haunting is a replay of a brawl from long ago has been mooted.

Since 2000, the castle has been the home of ravens, one of which was gifted by the Tower of London. An outstanding YouTube video also shows another bird at the castle, an African pied crow named Mourdour, seemingly asking, 'Y'all right love?' in a Yorkshire accent. In answer to the reader's inevitable question, yes, ravens and crows can mimic human speech, similarly to parrots. Regardless of whether the footage is genuine, there is no doubt that the brilliant Mourdour is Knaresborough's most incredible living legend!

Middleham

Often called the Windsor of the North, Middleham is another castle abounded in infamy. Constructed by Robert FitzRandolph, 3rd Lord Middleham, before 1190 close to an old motte and bailey known as William's Hill, the fortress filled a vital gap along the road between Richmond and Skipton where other important castles had been built. It is possible that all three were initially of timber construction. If so, they were later upgraded in stone.

By 1258, the male line of the family had died out. Inherited by the most senior female, Mary, Middleham entered the hands of the powerful Robert Neville following the pair's wedding two years later. Over the next 400 years, the Neville family proved of enormous importance in the north. Senior among their number was Richard Neville, 16th Earl of Warwick, later dubbed 'the Kingmaker'. The young Richard, duke of Gloucester and later III of England, entered Warwick's household as an 8-year-old boy, following his father's death at the Battle of Wakefield in December 1460. He remained there until 1468, a year before Warwick took his brother, Edward IV, prisoner. This event would play a decisive role in Edward's being forced to flee to the continent in 1470, along with Richard. After Warwick died at the Battle of Barnet a year later, Richard received the castle on becoming Anne's husband. Richard and Anne lived a happy life together at Middleham. Within these cherished walls, their son, Edward, was born in 1473 and perished in 1484. During his short reign, Richard spent little time there. On his death at Bosworth, Henry VII seized the castle.

Unlike the Yorkists, the Tudor monarchs had far less use for Middleham. It remained in royal hands until the reign of James I, after which the neglected fortress spiralled into decline. Ironically, this very lack of care ensured the castle's survival. So limited were its defensive capabilities, the Parliamentarians decided no garrison could realistically be kept there. A garrison was briefly installed in the 1650s, around which time an order to slight the remains wasn't followed. There are also accounts of Royalist prisoners being held there. Further misfortune occurred later that century when poor weather caused the collapse of some of the walls. Parts of the stonework were also plundered and reused for local buildings. After more than two centuries in the ownership of the Wood family, who bought the castle in 1662, Middleham was sold in 1889. During the Wood's tenure, the castle was allegedly used to keep prisoners of the US wars of Independence. In 1984, it entered the care of English Heritage.

A home of nobility and royalty at its best and deemed unfit for soldiers at its worst, Middleham has endured its fair share of ups and downs. Famously the home of an infamous king, Middleham has gained a permanent place in British legend.

According to local legend, it is not only its prominent connection with the alleged nephew murderer that has left its mark. Strange lights are said to flash around the castle at night, most notably over the south wall. The noise of a battle, the footsteps of marching soldiers and the music of centuries past is also reputed to sound from within. Far more frighteningly, the apparition of a medieval knight is believed to haunt the castle. Local stories tell of the knight appearing on horseback and charging menacingly at unfortunate bystanders, only to vanish before their eyes.

The most bizarre of the local legends involves a hidden treasure. Tradition has long told that if one should circle the castle three times, it will be found at the spot where they finish. There remains only one problem. Nobody knows where to begin.

Pickering

Constructed in 1069 to occupy a critical strategic position, Pickering remained in royal hands for many centuries. The original timber fortifications were upgraded to stone in the late twelfth century to complement the natural defences of the west side cliff. A stone shell keep on the motte was added between 1216 and 1236, along with a chapel. An outer ward, curtain wall and three additional towers were built between 1323 and 1326, one of which was to protect the postern.

The name given to the latter was Rosamund's Tower, in honour of an event that reputedly occurred during the reign of Henry II. Famed for her beauty, Rosamund Clifford incurred the wrath of Eleanor of Aquitaine when her husband, Henry II, conspired to make her his mistress. Legend from the fourteenth and seventeenth centuries tells that the king constructed a complicated maze at Woodstock – the predecessor to Blenheim Palace. On finding the pair enjoying an illicit rendezvous, Eleanor gave Rosamund the choice of death by a dagger or to drink poison after giving birth to Henry's bastard. Apart from later conjecture, there is no proof that this event ever happened.

Absent the spirit of fair Rosamund may be from Pickering, a unique atmosphere, nevertheless, imbues the ruins. Situated in the Vale of Pickering, an area abundant in quaint villages and market towns, the locality is sparse compared to many. Having successfully avoided the wars of the fifteenth century onwards, the castle was never upgraded to anything more than a stone motte and bailey. As such, it has been well preserved.

It is perhaps for such reasons, the castle's susceptibility for legends is greater than those in more populated areas. Footsteps on the upper floors have long been heard. Like nearby Helmsley, Pickering is also reputedly the haunt of strange pixie-like creatures.

Undoubtedly most famous among the castle's hauntings is that of a monk. Said to sport a grey robe and a bloodied face, the ghost has been seen numerous times in the vicinity of the keep, carrying some form of ornament. Who the man was remains a mystery. As previously recalled, grey robes were usually the preserve of the Tironesian order. Records also confirm that a chaplain resided there until the Reformation. Before that time, many abbeys and priories existed in the area. Was the monk attacked in his bid to preserve something? Was the invisible object he appears to carry a lost treasure or Catholic icon targeted by reformist iconoclasts? Though we may never know for sure, there is something magical about this part of Yorkshire, almost as if one could close one's eyes and reopen them, only to discover the whole experience of walking the ruins had been nothing but a dream.

Pontefract

Partially razed by the Parliamentarians at the climax of the English Civil War, Pontefract is now a shadow of its former self. Set on a rock to the east of the modern town, the castle was founded by the influential Norman knight Ilbert de Lacy after being granted land in West Yorkshire by William the Conqueror in 1070. The castle appears to have been constructed using wooden fortifications before being developed into a formidable stone stronghold in the following centuries. There is inconclusive evidence that an older structure preceded the original castle. A record exists in the *Domesday Book* for Ilbert's Castle, which was most likely the original name for Pontefract.

For the remainder of the eleventh century, the de Lacy family owned the castle. This changed when Robert de Lacy's support of Henry I was questioned during the king's conflict with brother Robert Curthose. Confiscated from the de Lacys, King John returned the castle to their descendants almost a century later. A decade earlier, Roger de Lacy had paid Richard the Lionheart 3,000 marks for the honour of Pontefract but was never granted possession of the castle. Pontefract remained a de Lacy stronghold until 1311, during which many additions were made, including the magnificent keep.

When the male line died out, the castle passed through marriage to Thomas, Earl of Lancaster. In common with Roger de Clifford – see Clifford's Tower – Lancaster's decision to rebel against the king in 1322 won him no favours. Inside the great hall, the king himself passed judgement on Lancaster and sentenced him to death. Six days after Thomas's defeat at Boroughbridge, he was beheaded outside the walls and condemned to a legacy of martyrdom. His tomb at the nearby priory was viewed a shrine until the Dissolution. Ironically, his ghost is said to haunt the ruins of Dunstanburgh.

In the light of recent events, Edward II gave Pontefract to Thomas's younger brother, Henry, 3rd Earl of Lancaster and, later, his son, Henry of Grosmont, 1st Duke of Lancaster. Under Edward III, it passed to Grosmont's successor as duke of Lancaster, the king's third son, John of Gaunt. Chosen by Gaunt as his principal residence, it was very much a royal home when Gaunt's previously exiled son, Henry Bolingbroke, completed his invasion of England and ascended to the throne as Henry IV in 1399. It was also within the walls of this once lavish residence that Bolingbroke's predecessor, Richard II, was once imprisoned. Conjecture, and Shakespeare, has long told that Richard II perished by Bolingbroke's hand.

With the exception of the Tower of London, no castle in England is more associated with malevolence than Pontefract. Still a royal fortress during the Wars of the Roses, Richard III had two Wydvilles executed there. Sir Richard Grey, the son of Edward IV's queen, Elizabeth, was beheaded there on 25 June 1483 with Elizabeth's brother, Anthony Woodville, 2nd Earl Rivers. Inspired by such actions and the murder of Richard II, William Shakespeare referred to the castle's bloody reputation in his play *Richard III*.

> Pomfret, Pomfret! O thou bloody prison,
> Fatal and ominous to noble peers!
> Within the guilty closure of thy walls
> Richard the second here was hack'd to death,
> And, for more slander to thy dismal seat,
> We give thee up our guiltless blood to drink.

Shakespeare may well also have taken account of the castle's later history. In 1536, Thomas Darcy, 1st Baron Darcy de Darcy, made the controversial decision to hand over the castle to the leaders of the Pilgrimage of Grace. Unimpressed with Darcy's alleged treason, Henry VIII subsequently ordered his execution. Five years later, it was reputedly within the same walls that Henry's fifth queen, Catherine Howard, engaged in her first act of infidelity with Thomas Culpeper. Pontefract is also another in a long line of fortresses that held Mary, Queen of Scots.

A Royalist fortress throughout its history, it remained so during the Civil War when it was forced to withstand three sieges. The first was recorded in December 1644 and continued until the arrival of Royalist forces under the leadership of Marmaduke Langdale, 1st Baron Langdale of Holme, in March 1645. Despite forcing a Roundhead retreat, constant mining and heavy artillery saw the destruction of the Piper Tower. Later in March, the onslaught resumed. The garrison surrendered in July, within days of hearing of Charles I's defeat at Naseby on 14 June. A Roundhead fortress for the next three years, Pontefract was the subject of a surprise coup in June 1648. After the royalists failed to scale the walls under cover of darkness, the parliamentarian commander requested more men and beds from the town. In true Trojan Horse-style, the Royalists disguised themselves as deliverers and hijacked the garrison.

Success, alas, did not last. Almost immediately, 5,000 Roundhead soldiers surrounded the castle, yet even the arrival of Cromwell in November failed to tip the balance. On learning of Charles I's beheading, on 24 March, the garrison, led by Colonel Morrice, surrendered to Major General John Lambert and with it, part two of the English Civil War came to an end. On the requests of the locals, the grand jury at York, and Lambert, parliament ordered the castle's destruction. Though slighting and quarrying occurred, fortunately, they never finished the job. Among the parts that survive are the eleventh-century cellars. Now property of

English Heritage, recent renovations have ensured the castle's future. Never again would it be inhabited.

Deserted since the royalist garrison marched out with their heads held high, local legend tells that within its ruined walls and chequered towers, the ghosts of Pontefract's dreadful past continue to reside. Although the spirit of Richard II has never been alleged to haunt his 'bloody prison', there is no shortage of former inhabitants said to remain confined within the ruins. Over the centuries, the ghost of a black-hooded monk has been spotted walking from the kitchen towards the Queen's Tower. Usually seen around five in the evening, his spirit always seems to be heading in the same direction before vanishing in sight of his intended location. A silent, lonesome spectre, it is strange that many people who report witnessing the holy man are those feeling distressed or upset. Intriguingly, the phantom brother is not the only monk said to haunt the castle. Another former cleric, dressed in grey, has also been witnessed near the old chapel while the ghost of a lady haunts the castle gates. Also dressed in grey, she has been seen after nightfall, her way lit by the ethereal glow of a ghostly lantern.

It is not just the spirits of adults who are thought to linger within the decaying wreck. The ghosts of two children have been seen playing near the dungeons: a rare glimpse of happier times. The inexplicable image of a brown-haired girl with a long, ragged dress has been known to startle visitors by staring vacantly in one of the mirrors of the visitors' centre. It is also believed to be her ghost that has been heard weeping in the ladies' toilets next door. The sounds of a little girl, sometimes screaming, also linger in this area.

For history lovers, the ancient keep remains a fine illustration of splendid Norman architecture. Although tarnished by past sieges, slighting and the forces of nature, the round tower on the eleventh-century mount is one of the more impressive areas. The spectre of a gentleman in black has been witnessed at the summit, reading an old piece of parchment. A distant and thoughtful spirit, his ghost is at odds with another man, armed with a broad axe.

Perhaps unsurprisingly given the circumstances of Pontefract's decline, it is believed that the ghosts of Royalist soldiers also return to the fortress. Joining them are the spirits of former prisoners who haunt the magazine area beneath the surface: the same place where 'guiltless blood' was given 'up to drink'.

Bathed in the blood of the innocent, this once striking Norman edifice is now little more than a relic of former glories. Isolated, lonely and desolate, it is no surprise many locals avoid the castle at night; nor that many aware of its history continue to lament its violent past. As long the castle stands, who knows how many former inhabitants will be destined to reside forever 'within the guilty closure of thy walls'.

Richmond

Occupying a prominent position above the River Swale, the sandstone ruins of Richmond are a timeless sight at sunset. Built by Alan Rufus – a Breton noble who supported William the Conqueror – in the aftermath of the harrying of the north, the original castle, located close to the modern-day town, was called 'Riche Mount': translating 'The Strong Hill'. Unlike many of its contemporaries, the castle was seemingly set in stone from the outset. Some form of fortress was in place at the compiling of the *Domesday Book*, which dubs Richmond 'a castlery'.

Expanded throughout the first half of the following century by Conan IV of Brittany, the 100-foot-high keep appears to have been in progress when Henry II seized it in 1158. Under Henry, the castle was improved with the additions of other towers and an imposing barbican. Work remained ongoing during the reigns of renowned builders Henry III and Edward I.

By the end of the fourteenth century, however, Richmond appears to have fallen out of favour. The castle was unused in the Wars of the Roses, and a survey at the time of the Dissolution of the Monasteries regarded it as a ruin. Renowned for its ascetic appeal in the nineteenth century, it was a regular haunt for many artists, including Turner. As visitor numbers increased, repairs on the keep occurred throughout the Victorian era. In 1855 it became the HQ of the Yorkshire militia and between 1908 and 1910 was also the home of legendary scout founder Robert Baden-Powell.

Thanks to the unexpected revival, Richmond is unquestionably among the best-preserved Norman castles in England. Deprived it may be of a long and bloody history in which loyal garrisons withstood violent sieges, Richmond is home to several fascinating myths and legends. There is an old story that the first bridge was a gift from the Devil. The tale goes that the bridge was given after a local shepherd took pity on the Prince of Darkness on getting lost among the Dales. Legend also says that the Gold Hole Tower designates a treasure trove. The ghost of a nun has been seen stalking the ruins, while other spirits reputed to haunt the castle include one walking between two closed doors.

One of the most fascinating tales is that King Arthur is buried there. Local tradition claims that a potter named Peter Thompson, out one day to escape a feud with his wife, discovered a secret cave and found the Knights of the Round Table sleeping within. How Thompson discovered the cave is unclear, except that he saw a strange gap in the rocks. Espying Excalibur unguarded, the potter attempted to remove the sword. On doing so, the slumbering knights were roused and set upon him. Though he managed to escape, he could never find the entrance again. Till his dying day, he remained haunted by the words of a harrowing voice:

> Potter Thompson, Potter Thompson,
> Hadst thou blown the horn,
> Thou hadst been the greatest man
> That ever yet was born.

Exactly when the strange visitation is said to have occurred is unclear. Though many searches have since taken place, the mysterious cave has never been found. The nearest any appear to have got so far concerns another bizarre tale involving a young drummer. A company of soldiers stationed at Richmond, apparently during the castle's time as a militia HQ in the second half of the nineteenth century, were astounded to discover a slight gap in the nearby rocks. Unable to sneak through themselves, they designated the young drummer who forced his way inside. Tradition tells that the reverberations of ghostly drumming continue to haunt the area, as the doomed boy remains destined to continue his fruitless search.

Similar to the Arthurian tale, finding a source for the story is no mean feat. No record of a location has been found. Nor has any official report survived. Intriguingly, the legend may connect with tales of a secret escape tunnel between the castle and Easby Abbey. Like with the eternal subterranean lodgings of the knights of destiny, no proof of its existence has ever been found.

Ripley

Located close to the spa town of Harrogate, fourteenth-century Ripley is another impressive, aristocratic type of building that falls somewhere between a military stronghold and a noble palace. The home of the Ingleby family throughout its history, Ripley's impressive assortment of coarse squared gritstone and slate may predate Edeline Thwenge, who inherited the medieval manor before her marriage to Sir Thomas Ingleby in 1308.

There is an old story that their eldest son, another Thomas, found favour with the king by protecting him from a wild boar, while out hunting in Knaresborough Forest around 1355. As a mark of thanksgiving, the king knighted him and allowed him the boar as his symbol. He also granted him a charter to hold a weekly market. Sadly, the story is not beyond suspicion. Alive during the reign of Edward III, there is no clear evidence that Edward endured such an encounter, albeit he enjoyed a hunt.

Throughout the Middle Ages, the castle remained the Inglebys' principal seat. Chief among their number was Sir John, who lived 1434–99. On inheriting the castle at the age of five, this pious lad became a monk at Mount Grace Priory and was later enthroned Bishop of Llandaff. Further to building the gatehouse, he left behind a son from his secular days.

Later descendants were also committed Catholics. One, named Francis, became a priest and was executed at York for his faith in 1586. Within the castle exists a priest hole, created by the famed Jesuit St Nicholas Owen, where Ingleby hid before his capture. Catholic tendencies would not prevent Sir William Ingleby from hosting James VI and I in 1603 as he journeyed to London for his coronation. Later that year, he successfully captured a brother of John Ruthven, 3rd Earl of Gowrie, who was then on the run for his part in the 'Gowrie Conspiracy' to kidnap the monarch. Two years later, the castle was also on the fringes of the Gunpowder Plot: the Wintour brothers, Thomas and Robert, being nephews of Ingleby. Robert is recorded as having stayed there as they prepared horses. Ingleby was arrested but later acquitted of treason.

The fervent Catholicism maintained, it is no surprise that the family, now led by the younger Sir William Ingleby, backed the Royalist cause in the Civil War. After being on the losing side at Marston Moor, William made his way back to Ripley. Only by hiding in a hidey-hole did he survive detection when Cromwell stayed a night there. Fortunately for the castle and family, Ripley was never slighted.

During the tenure of the next William, now second baronet, after Charles I had bestowed the original honour on his father, the family fortunes suffered. By 1772, the legitimate baronetcy was at an end; however, the honour was restored nine years later upon Sir John, the illegitimate son of the fourth baronet. On his watch, Ripley underwent significant renovation; however, financial problems inspired him to flee to the continent, and timber from the estate was sold to help pay off the debt.

In later years, the castle's owners became ever more eccentric. The pick of the bunch was another William: a gambler, drinker and MP, who adopted the surname Amcotts-Ingilby and had the local village demolished and rebuilt. Though the castle is often open to the public, it remains owned by the third line of the Ingilby family, the eccentric William having left the estate to his cousin.

A family home for more than seven centuries, the castle is reputedly the haunt of former residents. Dressed in the apparel of the Victorian era, a woman possessed of deep melancholy has been seen walking the corridors. It is believed hers is the ghost of Lady Alicia Ingilby, who lost her two children to meningitis in the 1870s. A harmless and even helpful spirit, Lady Alicia has been seen in the vicinity of what was once her children's bedrooms. She is also believed to have acted as something of a guardian angel over the current brood in more recent times. She is said to be responsible for tucking in bedclothes in the middle of the night as if to prompt the sleeping parent to check up on their offspring.

Joining the worried mother is the unfortunate Father Francis Ingilby, who is believed to reside in the area where he had evaded captivity. From later that century, a far more morbid presence is also said to haunt the castle. Though Ripley was fortunate to escape the Parliamentarian forces, tradition tells that several Cavalier soldiers were executed by firing squad in the aftermath of Marston Moor. The apparitions of Royalist soldiers have been reported at the castle, still bound to the spot where they breathed their last.

Scarborough

Built to stand guard over the North Sea, the magnificent windswept ruins of Scarborough are in every way the epitome of a good castle.

The site's history is traceable back to the Bronze Age. Chief among the revelations from digs conducted in the 1920s was the stunning evidence not only that the hillfort was built on the same headland that now houses the castle but of other finds dating to around 900 BC. Nothing so far discovered at Scarborough has been more impressive than a Bronze Age sword, which was probably a ritual offering given by the original tribe of settlers. Like many such finds, the blade now forms the heart of an exhibition on site. After the hill fort's development in the Iron Age, the Romans used the site as a signal station to warn of potential sea invaders. The settlement was fed by a local spring, known as 'The Well of Our Lady'. The Saxons built a chapel around 1000 AD, which appears to have been destroyed during the invasion of Harold Hardrada shortly before the Norman Conquest.

Due to the defensive capabilities of the cliffs, the well-liked structure appears to have proven of equal appeal to the Vikings. An old Icelandic poem tells of a Viking settlement named *Skarthi* burnt down by Hardrada's forces, which may have been Scarborough. Before Henry II's stone castle was established, the count of Aumale, William le Gros – a grandnephew of William the Conqueror – put down wooden fortifications, most likely a mixture of replacing and adding to those already in place. King Stephen also granted le Gros the earldom of York.

It was from this basic 'adulterine' motte and bailey that the imposing stone castle evolved. According to the chronicler William of Newburgh, it included a gate tower, new chapel, dry moat and an outer curtain wall. Many further improvements and additions followed, all of which helped secure England from invasion while developing Scarborough as a trade port. Of the original castle, only the motte survives in the form of a small mount that juts out from the heart of the inner bailey. By 1169, the three-storey keep appears to have been completed. In the early thirteenth century, King John is recorded as having visited the castle no less than four times and oversaw further work. The trend continued under his son, Henry III, who spent vast sums on its defences, including a new barbican and towers around the gateway. Unlike his father, he never visited it personally.

It has long been reputed that some governors of Scarborough were somewhat unscrupulous with regard to fulfilling their duties. A prime culprit was the thirteenth-century governor, Geoffrey de Neville, who abused his status to confiscate port goods. As governors did not need to be on-site, monies allocated for repairs were also commonly pocketed. Due to such illicit practices, by the late thirteenth century, some of the defences were rotting and the armouries underprovided. Following in Neville's footsteps, in the 1270s, William de Percy blocked the main roads and charged tolls on any merchant travelling to and from the town. Somewhat predictably, officials illustrated far better behaviour when Edward I held court at Scarborough in 1275 and 1280. In 1295, the king also kept hostages from his Welsh campaign there.

By 1308, the castle had come into the possession of Henry de Percy, 1st Baron Percy of Alnwick, whose family would rise to great prominence throughout the following centuries. Following in his father's footsteps, Edward II chose the castle to house some of his key prisoners from the war with Scotland. In 1312, he granted Scarborough, along with Bamburgh, to Isabella de Vesci. That same year, it was chosen by Edward's close friend, Piers Gaveston, as a place of refuge after the Ordnances of 1311 significantly restricted the monarch's powers.

In April 1312, Edward appointed Gaveston governor of Scarborough Castle, thus replacing Sir Robert Felton, who died two years later at Stirling. Yet barely a month passed until de Percy, in league with the earls of Pembroke and Warenne, laid siege to the fortress. Strong as Scarborough's walls were, Gaveston lacked supplies and surrendered on being granted safe passage. Unfortunately for Gaveston, after being tried at Warwick, he was kidnapped and brutally murdered. In retribution for failing to come to their governor's aid, Edward revoked the town's royal privileges.

Due to its coastal location, Scarborough became an important port for wool trade between England and the Low Countries. As a direct consequence, the French attacked the castle throughout the Hundred Years' War. As fears of an invasion grew, a series of repairs were carried out in the late 1390s, and again under Henry VI 1424–29. In 1484, Richard III used the castle to organise a fleet to combat the threat of Henry Tudor.

In the Tudor era, Scarborough's importance continued. Following attacks by the Scots and French in the early 1500s, the castle was also the subject of an unsuccessful assault during the Pilgrimage of Grace. A later attempt at insurrection was led by the rebellious Thomas Wyatt the Younger. In league with Thomas Stafford, Wyatt targeted the castle in the hope of inciting insurrection against Mary Tudor. Good luck initially awaited him in 1557 when he took the castle Trojan-horse-style by dressing his men up as peasants. Ultimately, the endeavour ended in failure and Stafford was executed on Tower Hill.

Like many of England's mighty fortresses, Scarborough's date with destiny occurred in the Civil War. At the outbreak of the war, Sir Hugh Cholmley occupied Scarborough as a Roundhead before defecting, along with his 700-strong garrison, to the Royalists in March 1643. On Cholmley's watch, many improvements were made, including the construction of the South Steel Battery. Unsurprisingly, the loss of the only port then not in Parliamentarian control made retaking Scarborough a vital goal.

On 18 February 1645, the Scottish Roundhead Sir John Meldrum took the town and cut off the Royalists' escape routes. Cholmley's refusal to surrender catalysed one of the bloodiest sieges in British history. At the heart of the Parliamentarian attack was the Cannon Royal: at the time, the largest in the country. On being set up at the nearby twelfth-century church of St Mary, the 55lb plus cannonballs did significant damage to the castle's defences, partially destroying the keep. Nevertheless, the Roundheads' inability to take it caused much frustration, not least when man-on-man fighting close to the barbican ended in Sir John Meldrum's killing. The Royalist resistance continued until July, at which time dehydration, a lack of food, gunpowder, scurvy and fatigue weakened their resolve. On 25 July, the remaining half of the original 500 defenders surrendered, and a company of 160 Roundheads took over.

For the next three years, things went smoothly for the Roundheads. However, things took a turn when a lack of payment prompted new governor Matthew Boynton to defect to Charles I on 27 July 1648. A second Roundhead siege ended on 19 December. Between 1642 and 1648, the castle changed hands no less than seven times. It operated as a prison during the commonwealth and was one of a number to keep Quaker founder George Fox.

As the century progressed, Scarborough again suffered neglect. James II's foolish decision not to garrison the castle saw it fall to William of Orange in the Glorious Revolution. In the Jacobite Rebellion of 1745, the battery was rebuilt, and a barracks of twelve apartments accommodated 120 men. Three more batteries were built overlooking the harbour and town: two facing south, the other north. Contemporary to this period, the Master Gunner's House of 1748 now serves as the exhibition house. Though no action occurred during the Napoleonic era, French prisoners were held there in 1796. After a century of relative peace, two German warships, the *SMS Derfflinger* and *SMS Von der Tann* bombed the town on 16 December 1914. The raid that killed nineteen people also severely damaged the castle, notably the keep. Consequently, the barracks were demolished, and in the Second World War, it operated solely as a listening post.

Possessed of a history that dates back more than 3,000 years, Scarborough's story encapsulates much of the endless transition that is Great Britain. A centrepiece of local life and beyond, it is no surprise that the castle is home to several legends and hauntings. Among them are the ghosts of former Civil War soldiers and a Roman, who are said to haunt the cliff top near the old signal station. Richard III has also been seen on the battlements, gazing out to sea.

Undoubtedly the most famous of the castle's legends concerns Piers Gaveston. Gaveston spent his final free days at Scarborough until he was granted 'safe passage'. A headless ghost who appears to people on their own is believed to be Gaveston. Somewhat unsettlingly, his unhappy spirit is reputedly a violent one. Legend says that he tries to drive his enemies to their death from the battlements. The suggestion is ironic. Historically, Gaveston was assassinated by being dragged out into the road towards Kenilworth and dispatched with a sword. Yet his ghostly motives contain more than a passing resemblance to his portrayed death in the film *Braveheart*. Alas, like so many of history's infamous characters, none has developed his legend quite like the big screen.

Skipsea

A lush green hill is all that remains of Skipsea Castle. Erected the year of the *Domesday Book* on the site of an Iron Age hill fort, Skipsea's early history came on the watch of a Flemish mercenary named Drogo de la Beavrière. Appointed Lord of Holderness, Drogo's importance to William the Conqueror is illustrated by his marriage to the king's niece, as recorded by William Camden.

The original site was likely designed to combat coastal invaders and augment the original tribe's authority over the region. In the Norman era, these purposes continued, along with the added incentive of controlling the maritime trading route. Evidence suggests that an artificial mere separated the motte and bailey: indeed, the term Skipsea is of Scandinavian origin and means lake navigable by ship. The nearby village grew alongside the castle church and, in later years, the fortified town alongside the castle itself.

A dark legend has long claimed that Drogo's marriage to the Conqueror's niece was destined more for tragedy than romance. As William Camden recorded, Drogo became disillusioned with his marriage and concocted a 'love potion' laced with poison. When his wife drank it, he fled to the king's court and successfully borrowed a large amount of money before absconding to the Continent. Only after his departure was the murder discovered. Despite Camden's confidence in the story, the possibility cannot be ruled out that the killing was accidental.

Despite the king's best efforts, Drogo was never caught. Deprived, nevertheless, of his estates, William granted Skipsea to Odo, Count of Aumale. Except for 1096–1102, the castle remained in his family until William de Forz – count of Aumale by marriage – launched his ill-fated insurrection against Henry III in 1220–21. De Forz's motives concerned both an ongoing disagreement over ownership of the estate of nearby Driffield, as well as a protest against the papal mandate that any baron in possession of a royal castle surrender it. Aumale's grievances led to a brief standoff between the pair at Rockingham Castle, which Henry took after a short siege – see Rockingham Castle. A command was also put out to the northern barons to lay siege to William's other castles, including Skipsea. Fortunately for William, his surrender was rewarded with a royal pardon. The lack of ramification for Aumale's treachery was roundly criticised by the famous chronicler, Roger of Wendover, as an act of spinelessness on the part of the king.

At some point during the aftermath of Aumale's rebellion, Henry III put out an order for Skipsea's destruction. To what extent this was carried out is unclear. On William's death, the castle passed to his son and namesake. In 1293, some twenty years after the death of Isabella, the younger William's widow, Skipsea passed to the Crown. In the fourteenth century, both the castle and town were devoid of purpose, and the Aumales' interest was reserved solely for the nearby manor. The mere was drained and reclaimed for farming. The modern-day village has a population of less than 700 and what remains of the original site is now in the care of English Heritage.

The village now more or less a ghost town, it seems strangely fitting that the castle is associated with paranormal activity. Poisoned by her husband before he deceived the king, Lady de la Beavrière is said to haunt the site. Dressed all in white, she has been seen wandering the former earthworks. Legend also records that, before his departure, Drogo hid her body, thus depriving her of a Christian burial. To this day, no remains have been found.

There is another legend that two brothers fought a duel on the ramparts during one of England's civil wars. Exactly when this event took place is unclear. Throughout the country, evidence that the 1640s conflict split families is easily found. That this was true of Skipsea is less likely. Though it cannot be ruled out that the ruins were chosen to end a personal dispute, it is far more likely that the event occurred during the Anarchy or the First Barons' War when Skipsea was of some military importance. According to local lore, four footprints survive in the field where the duel occurred. The story remains an important facet of local tradition, as captured in the following lines:

> E'en yet the marks of their sad fight are found,
> E'en yet their footsteps print th' unhallow'd ground:
> No grass e'er clothes it, and no plants adorn,
> Save the keen thistle, and the savage thorn.

Skipton

The Norman castle at Skipton must rate highly as one of the best-preserved in England. Constructed as a motte and bailey by Robert de Romille around 1090, Romille's lands initially included the estates of Bolton Abbey. These were extended further by Henry I, and the first wooden fortifications were later upgraded in stone. Coupled with the nearby cliffs, the castle proved an impressive defensive structure to combat the Scots.

Like most medieval families, eventually, the male line died out. When this occurred to the Romilles in 1310, Edward II granted the castle to Robert Clifford, henceforth Lord Clifford of Skipton. Plans to improve the castle appear to have been drawn up almost immediately, but due to his death four years later at Bannockburn, it is unlikely much work was done.

For the next three centuries, the castle appears to have enjoyed a relatively peaceful existence, during which improvements were gradual. At the outbreak of the Civil War, Skipton was the only Royalist castle in the north. After putting up a brave three-year resistance, the garrison yielded peacefully to the Parliamentarians in December 1645. There is a legend that sheep fleeces were flung over the walls during the siege to help subdue the impact of the cannon fire. Since that time, the fleece has been a prominent feature of the town's coat of arms.

After the war, the new magnate, Lady Anne Clifford, restored the slighted fortress. The improvements continued until she died in 1676 when the property passed out of the family. In addition to the physical repairs, in 1659, Lady Clifford had a yew tree planted to commemorate the restoration. Thanks in part to her endeavours, the castle remains a private residence and a tourist attraction. It also serves as the starting point of Lady Anne's Way: a pathway that leads to Penrith in Cumbria.

Lady Anne's legacy may be in the form of the walkway and yew tree, but stories abound that her carriage continues to haunt the castle. Tradition cites that the ghostly rattling of wheels on tarmac precedes the arrival of the phantom coach. Owners view this legend with particular unease, as the tale states that her role is to collect the spirit of the castle owner on their death.

Joining Lady Anne in her ethereal visits is reputed to be a little girl who has been spotted and photographed in recent years. A far more famous apparition is that of a lady with red hair. This spirit is yet another to be identified with the ubiquitous Mary, Queen of Scots, who was briefly imprisoned there. The apparition has been seen gazing out of the window in the withdrawing room towards Mary's beloved Scotland.

Chapter 13

Cheshire and Lancashire

Beeston

Few castles in England enjoy a more dramatic position than Beeston. Known locally as the castle of the rock, due to being perched on a sandstone crag some 350 feet above the Cheshire plain, investigations into the local pits have concluded that the site was inhabited as far back as the Stone Age. Supportive of this is the past discovery of flint arrowheads, which appear to precede evidence of a later Bronze Age community and an Iron Age hill fort.

It was on the prehistoric site that construction of the royal castle at Beeston began during the thirteenth century. The instigator of the operation was the Anglo-Norman magnate, Ranulf de Blondevilles, Earl of Chester, described by the Victorian historian Bishop Stubbs as 'Almost the last relic of the great feudal aristocracy of the Conquest.'

The walls of Beeston are incredibly eye-catching and appear to have been influenced by what Ranulf saw in the Holy Land. Ranulf was part of the Fifth Crusade that saw the brief taking of Damascus by the Christian armies. Evidence suggests that he modelled the fortress on Sahyun Castle in north-west Syria. Ranulf's other 1220 strongholds: Bolingbroke in Lincolnshire and Chartley in Staffordshire possess similar characteristics. Of the three, only Chartley boasts a keep, which was cylindrical as opposed to the usual square.

On Ranulf's death in 1232, Beeston and the earldom of Chester passed to Ranulf's nephew, John of Scotland. On John's death without issue in 1237, the Crown subsumed both the earldom and John's castles. Henry III enlarged Beeston considerably as part of his strategy to subdue the Welsh and used it as a prison. In 1254, he granted the castle, along with the earldom and his Cheshire estates, to his eldest son: the future Edward I. Incidentally, the earldom of Chester remains active and is automatically bestowed on the heir to the throne.

For the next three centuries, the Crown regularly maintained the castle until its sale in 1602 to Sir Hugh Beeston of nearby Beeston Hall. By this time, an imposing fortress close to the Welsh border was no longer necessary. At the outbreak of the Civil War, it was one of many defences conscripted by the Parliamentarians. The fortress was seized on 20 February 1643 by the forces of Sir William Brereton, whose relative was beheaded in the reign of Henry VIII for alleged infidelity with Anne Boleyn. In December, by which time repairs had been made, a detachment of the royal army of Ireland landed at Chester. On 13 December, Captain Thomas Sandford and eight soldiers infiltrated the castle under cover of darkness and forced the garrison's withdrawal led by Captain Thomas Steele. Though the Royalists honoured the pledge, Sandford was shot for his sloppiness the following year.

It wasn't long before the Roundheads set about its recovery. A siege that began in November 1644 finally succeeded twelve months later when a lack of food forced the Cavaliers' hands. In 1646, parliament had the castle partially demolished, and the materials were removed throughout the eighteenth century. In 1840, the ruins were sold to the prosperous local magnate John Tollemache, 1st Baron Tollemache, which ensured its future as a tourist attraction.

Uninhabited since the Civil War, tall tales have long held that the castle remains the haunt of past residents. Among the reputed ghosts is one who is undoubtedly a contender for the nation's friendliest apparition. A lovely lady in a white dress is said to appear only to the younger generation. A smiling, happy presence, she has been known to wave to children, especially on school visits and is regarded as something of a guardian angel. Local tradition also speaks of someone being pushed down the well at some point in the castle's past.

In addition to its reputed hauntings, a far more real tale has persisted since 1399 that Richard II buried some form of hoard at Beeston. Richard reputedly chose part of the castle grounds to house his treasure before making his way to Chester in preparation for his crossing over to Ireland to suppress the rebellion there. On the king's return, his cousin, the soon to be Henry IV, dethroned him. Ironically, Henry had been born at Ranulf's other fortress, Bolingbroke.

Since Richard's time, many searches have been made, yet no claim of discovery has come to light. Unlike many stories of castle treasure, the possibility cannot be ruled out that the prize has already been found. Previous writers have stated that Henry recovered Richard's gold and jewellery from their various hiding places. Whether this includes Beeston is unclear. If Richard did bury a hoard at Beeston, it cannot be discounted that something remains undetected.

Lancaster

Situated in the heart of the county town of Lancashire, for more than 800 years, the mighty walls of Lancaster Castle have driven fear into the heart of the local population. A prison since 1196, it has incarcerated hundreds of prisoners, from captured soldiers to the Pendle Witches.

Little is known of the early castle. Tradition holds that it was erected around 1090 on the site of a first-century Roman fort that overlooked the River Lune. Consensus places it as a wooden motte and bailey under the control of the Norman lord, Roger de Poitou, who was most likely the first beneficiary of the 'honour of Lancaster'. Roger fled England in 1102 after rebelling against Henry I. Since 1164, the 'honour' has been in royal control.

Unusually for a castle of Lancaster's status, records concerning its later development are also sparse. After being upgraded to stone during the twelfth and thirteenth centuries, it was caught up in the invasions by the Scots in 1322 and 1389. On both occasions, the marauding Scots accessed the town and inflicted considerable damage on the castle without capturing it. Following the accession of Henry IV, development of the fortress and town assumed greater importance. The castle's impressive gatehouse is one of many features that dates to Henry IV. The reigns of Elizabeth I, James I and Charles I saw the executions of no less than fifteen Catholics there. In 1612, the infamous Pendle Witches followed.

Throughout this period, the castle remained a gaol. In 1554, the religious martyr, George Marsh, was held there before standing trial at Chester Cathedral. When the Civil War came to the north, the castle, which housed only a light garrison, was quickly captured in February 1643. Attempts to retake it proved unsuccessful for the Royalists. Around 1646, orders that 'all the walls about … should be thrown down' was ignored. The decision proved a stroke of luck as the castle played a pivotal role in quashing a Royalist siege led by the duke of Hamilton in August 1648. On 12 August 1660, Charles II visited Lancaster and offered every prisoner a royal pardon.

Militarily redundant due to war damage, the castle's purpose as a prison remained. In the same year as Charles's visit, it was used to incarcerate members of the Quaker community, including the influential George Fox. Also used as a debtors' prison, the site grew a reputation for overcrowding, as noted during a visit by the renowned reformist John Howard in 1776. In the light of that, £30,000 was spent on improvements, while the authorities also relocated the executions to the so-called 'Hanging Corner'. Between 1782 and 1865, no less than 265 criminals were hanged at Lancaster, the spectacle of which drew thousands. By 1916, only POWs remained; however, the gaol returned to use in 1954 until 2011. Though none have been executed there since Thomas Rawcliffe was found guilty of murdering his wife in 1910, Lancaster retains a dark reputation for bringing about the deaths of more people than any other prison in England.

A site whose reputation for unsanitary conditions and hangings was infamous, it is no surprise that Lancaster Castle has earned itself a reputation among the most haunted in England. Alongside the modern updates, the dank cells endured by early prisoners continue to serve as reminders of the harsh conditions. Hushed whispers have been audible in the courtroom, while the thud of heavy footsteps are said to have been heard in otherwise empty rooms. The muffled cries of an invisible entity have also been reported in the Barrister's Library. Intriguingly, CCTV footage from 2013 captured a strange misty shape entering the gatehouse. Reports of staff members being pushed or feeling a peculiar presence also continue to persist.

Of the many spirits said to haunt the castle, one of the most famous is a monk in black robes. Local tradition tells that a monk was once hanged at the prison. The choice of robes may suggest he was a Dominican. Who he was and what he did, however, no record has been found.

The ghost of a young girl has also been seen. Often joining her is a woman of middle-aged features, whose manner is in keeping with that of a parent or guardian. At other times, the woman has been reported as being elderly and haggard. Whether the two women are the same or different remains a mystery. The girl has also been seen running along the main corridors, seemingly oblivious to the general grim ambience.

Undoubtedly the most infamous of Lancaster Castle's former inhabitants are the Pendle Witches. For many years, the level-topped Pendle Hill, often identified as 'The Roof of Lancashire', has been associated with the forces of evil. In the summer of 1612, things came to a head following 'the wonderful discovery of Witches in Lancashire'. Prominent among them was a certain Elizabeth Southerns, also known as Old Demdyke. A resident of Malkin Tower, Demdyke was accused of many strange things, including hosting covens and practising the dark arts. Among the most startling was a plot to blow up Lancaster Castle.

This self-proclaimed coven of twelve entered the realms of infamy after being tried for the murder of ten people by way of witchcraft. Especially troubling was the seemingly coincidental misfortune of a tinker named John Law, who was approached by Demdyke's granddaughter, Alizon Device, for some metal pins, and suffered a stroke when she cursed him on his refusal. Incredibly, though John Law made no claim, not only did Alizon admit her guilt but also implicated members of her own family and that of their local enemy, the Chattoxs. Worse still, when Alizon's mother, Bessie, was arrested and stripped naked, it was discovered she possessed a third nipple. In a two-day trial that took place 18–19 August, all but two of the group suffered inquisition at Lancaster. On the stand with them were the, now less famous, Samlesbury Witches accused of similar but lesser crimes. In the aftermath of the Lancashire Witch Trials, nine of the women and two men, including three generations of the same family, were condemned to the gallows.

Four centuries have passed since the unholy reign of the Pendle Witches, yet local legend tells that at least one of them remains bound to the castle. Senior of the twelve, Demdyke was brought to Lancaster along with her coven. However, unlike the others, she succumbed to age and the harsh conditions. Her ghost is reputed to reside in her cell in the fourteenth-century Well Tower.

Feared at a time when superstition ruled enlightenment, many innocent women were led to their death on being accused of being in league with the devil. While the Demdykes and Chattoxs confessed and accused each other of various oddities, chief among the likely innocents was Alice Nutter of Roughlee: a staunch Catholic charged with attending one of Demdyke's covens. In 1633, 21 years after she went to her death, still protesting her innocence, another group of witches was identified by a young boy named Edmund Robinson. It is a sad reflection of the time that his accusation against local women saw many hanged. Only when it was too late did he admit to making the whole thing up. With this, one can only lament what the judge, Roger Nowell, had previously described as 'the ruine of so many poore creatures at one time'.

Chapter 14

Cumbria

Carlisle

Situated at the heart of this famous cathedral city, Carlisle Castle is steeped in history and legend. At the time of the castle's construction during the reign of William II, the kings of Scotland viewed Cumberland as part of Scotland. For this reason, Carlisle was always destined to be in the thick of the action.

The history of the site goes back to time immemorial. Lying close to Hadrian's Wall, which was begun around 122 AD and named in honour of Rome's emperor, the castle was erected on the first-century Roman fort of *Luguvalium*: a prime contender for the capital of the Province of Valentia. Even before the Normans' arrival, the area had endured its fair share of skirmishes, mostly with local tribes. During Rufus's reign, a decision was made to construct a new castle to stem the threat of invasion from the north. In 1122, William's younger brother and successor – and possible murderer – Henry I, ordered the castle's enlargement and rebuilding in stone. The keep was almost certainly completed before his death in 1135.

Somewhat predictably, tussles to secure Cumberland remained ongoing throughout the centuries, beginning with the Scots' attempts to capitalise on the civil war between Stephen and Matilda. Briefly taken by the Scots, the English recaptured Carlisle in 1157. In 1249, an agreement between Henry III of England and Alexander III of Scotland led to the establishment of the Scottish Marches to provide a buffer zone around the border. This also enabled Carlisle to become the HQ of the Western March. Henry III strengthened the castle, while in 1296, Edward I used it as his HQ for three months.

On 26 March 1296, the lord of Annandale, John 'The Red' Comyn, led an attack on Carlisle; however, the former lord of Annandale, Robert de Brus, oversaw a successful English defence. On being appointed governor by Edward II, Andrew de Harclay, 1st Earl of Carlisle intercepted an army led by Thomas, Earl of Lancaster and defeated them at the Battle of Boroughbridge on 16 March 1322. Despite his initial success, less than a year later, Andrew entered negotiations with Robert the Bruce due to a perceived lack of support from Edward II in defending the north. On learning of this, the furious king executed him in March 1323. In 1461, combined forces of Scots and Lancastrians took the castle following one of the bloodiest sieges of the Wars of the Roses.

In the Tudor era, Carlisle remained of some importance. In 1567, Carlisle became the first of many English fortresses to host Mary, Queen of Scots: her 18 May–13 July stay occurring mainly in the Warden's Tower. In the Civil War, the Royalist garrison held out bravely against an ongoing Scottish siege. So bad had conditions become that their forces had to survive on a diet of 'rats, linseed meal and dogs'. After eight brutal months, Sir Thomas Glemham finally surrendered. A short time later, the Parliamentarians ejected their former allies.

In the following century, Carlisle again became an important location during the Scottish Wars of Independence. After surviving the rebellion of the 'Old Pretender', James Francis Edward Stuart in 1715, Carlisle's walls faced arguably their most significant test yet against the forces of the 'Young Pretender', Charles Edward Stuart – Bonnie Prince Charlie. During the '45 rebellion, Carlisle and its castle were both seized and reinforced by the Jacobites. When the Scots were routed at Culloden, the city and castle were later recaptured by William Augustus, Duke of Cumberland – the son of George II. Those responsible who had been captured were also later executed. The conflict marked the end of Carlisle's role as a military stronghold. Between 1745 and 1959, the castle operated primarily as a state prison as well as an army barracks in the Victorian era. Though still the HQ of the Duke of Lancaster's Regiment, it is now a tourist attraction and hosts a museum.

A key military stronghold in the struggle for control of the border and a prison of captured military and local felons, Carlisle Castle has amassed its fair share of legends. Though prisoners are no longer kept there, one can still find evidence of its brutal past. No better example concerns the worn condition of its 'licking stones', so named due to being absorbed of moisture by thirsty prisoners. Several POWs were executed there, which some believe accounts for the sombre atmosphere.

Many of the castle's apparent hauntings concern the keep. Two medieval soldiers have been sighted on its top floor. A sentry on duty has also been spotted inside an archway of the inner keep, while the spirit of an old caretaker has reportedly been seen seated near the old bell. Intriguingly, a picture of the man seated at Queen Mary's Table has survived from his time in residence. Whether or not there is any connection between these spirits and the mysterious black shape that wanders the inner keep is unclear. A disturbing, misty apparition has been seen by staff members and visitors.

Among the most bizarre stories concerning the castle is that it is haunted by Stephen of Blois, King of England 1136–54. Local legend tells that Stephen appears leaning against a wall in the upper keep, close to the model of the city. Why Stephen's spirit should target this room is a mystery. In 1136, Carlisle was one of many parts of the north that fell to David I of Scotland. When Stephen reached Durham with a large army, a meeting between the two saw an agreement for the return of most, with Carlisle being the main exception. Though the keep appears to have been finished during his reign, it is unclear what connection Stephen had with it.

Beyond the keep, the castle is reputedly the haunt of several other spirits. A yeoman of unknown origin has been seen wandering between the old Regimental HQ and the cellblock. A bizarre anecdote tells that a former caretaker had a conversation with a lost soldier in Ypres Block, only to realise his uniform was of years past. An even stranger story tells of a corporal sent to extinguish a light in an upstairs room one evening, only to find it in darkness. On looking out through the open window to inform his sergeant that the light was off, the corporal was shocked to learn it still shone from outside.

Of all the stories that concern Carlisle Castle, none are more morbid than a chance discovery in the 1830s. When renovations were made of the keep's second floor, the skeleton of a woman was found, bricked up. Dressed in tartan and wearing expensive jewellery – three rings were reported on her fingers – her identity remains unknown. The best guess is that she might have been held prisoner during the rebellion of 1745; however, in reality, many paths could have led the, presumably, Scottish lady to Carlisle. The apparition of a lady in grey is often presumed to be the bricked-up lady's spirit. Indeed, only a short time after her discovery was the grey lady seen for the first time. Stories of her hauntings possess a strange commonality with that of Anne Boleyn at the Tower of London. In 1842, a soldier lunged at her with a bayonet after she failed to answer the call, 'Halt, who comes here?' only to pass right through. After being roused by his colleagues, the shaken soldier again lapsed into unconsciousness before dying of shock.

Muncaster

On first impressions, well-preserved Muncaster is a peaceful sight in a remote part of the English countryside. Built on the remains of a Roman fort and overlooking the tranquil scenery of the River Esk, the castle was assembled on land granted to Alan de Penitone around 1208. Family records suggest it might even date back to 1026. The presence of the fort likely earned 'Muncaster' its name: *castra* being Latin for fort. Over the centuries, the castle has been expanded and developed, while a lack of physical conflict has helped maintain the original structure. The great hall and the Pele Tower are impressive survivors from the castle's early days. Though Anthony Salvin vastly improved it, many of Muncaster's rooms retain the style of the Middle Ages. To this day, the castle remains the ancestral home of the Pennington family and the HQ of the Hawk and Owl Centre, which houses many endangered species of owl.

Successful the castle may have been in avoiding the relentless onslaughts and sieges endured by many of its border region cousins, Muncaster, nevertheless, harbours many secrets. A popular site for tourists, Muncaster is reputedly among the most haunted castles in England.

Of the castle's many ancient chambers, the tapestry room is reportedly the most sinister. Situated in a remote section of one of the wings, paintings from the Middle Ages decorate ancient walls that surround an iron firedog whose appearance is disturbingly reminiscent of a demon from Dante's *Inferno*. If the furnishings alone are not enough to evoke feelings of fear in the minds of its visitors, the disturbing cries of a long-dead baby might. The apparition of a child has been known to terrify unsuspecting visitors, yet this particular spirit is said to be tame compared to the room's other spectres. Mystifying sounds such as footsteps or the turning of the door handle go hand in hand with that of strange mutterings. Sightings of apparitions in black standing over the four-poster bed have also been particularly upsetting to guests. Who they are and why they haunt the castle is unclear. Nor whether the silhouettes are responsible for the crushing sensation some have experienced. Intriguingly, victims of the phenomenon tend to report consistent happenings: reminiscent of a weight being dropped on their chest. Another dark phantom, believed to be a woman, has been seen and heard entering the room before vanishing.

The room is believed to have acted as a nursery, which may account for the child's ghost. A Margaret Pennington apparently died young there.

Further to the bizarre happenings in the nursery room, the spirit of Henry VI is said to appear there. Famously found dead in the Wakefield Tower of the Tower of London, reputedly murdered at the hands of the duke of Gloucester, later Richard III, Henry was king of England 1422–61 and again 1470–71. After regaining the crown following Warwick the Kingmaker's defection to the Lancastrians, Henry's charges lost the Battle of Tewkesbury in 1471 and subsequently lost the crown.

A particularly fascinating story tells that in 1464, Sir John Pennington offered the king shelter after he was found aimlessly wandering the locality after the Battle of Hexham. One version of the story tells that Henry initially sought refuge at Irton Hall but was refused. Consequently, he took shelter in an oak tree in the grounds, which is still called 'The King's Oak'. Sir John and his wife then harboured Henry for nine days. As a sign of gratitude, Henry left behind a Venetian glass drinking bowl. Legend states that Henry offered it with a prayer that the family will enjoy good fortune so long as it remains unbroken. To this day, the 'Luck of Muncaster' remains a part of castle lore. It is perhaps for this reason the apparition of the king is said to return to the chamber where his loyal subjects granted him refuge. A painting of the king kneeling before an altar with the glass in hand hangs in the room in which he is thought to have stayed. About a mile from the castle, the Chapels tower was erected in 1783 to honour the spot where the king is believed to have been found.

The following century was the era of the man many regard as the castle's most prominent character. Employed as the jester of Ferdinand Pennington, Thomas Skelton was renowned for his hostility and playfulness. A chestnut tree outside the castle acts as a tangible reminder of where Skelton passed much of his time. For many hours it is said that he would sit under the tree, providing visitors with directions. Those he liked, he offered the advice they needed. Those he did not, he navigated to their deaths in the quicksand below. Due to his villainous acts, he earned the nickname 'Tom Fool'. The phrase 'Tom Foolery' originated from this man. It is also possible Shakespeare based the fool in *King Lear* on Skelton.

Always one to please his master, Skelton got his chance when Pennington learned that his daughter – Helwise – had been enjoying secret liaisons with a local carpenter. After Pennington instructed the jester to take care of this inconvenience, Skelton invited the carpenter to the castle for drinks one fateful night. After the young man became intoxicated, Skelton hacked off his head with the carpenter's tools. The ghost of the carpenter has been witnessed at the castle, seemingly disoriented without his head. The terrifying sounds of banging on the stairs, as well as that of dragging, are assumed to be a replay of the dreadful event.

Of the story's exact happening, the facts are difficult to establish. Other versions depict the victim as the carpenter's son and Skelton's employer Helwise's betrothed. Conflicting sources also refer to Sir Alan or Ferdinand. A portrait of the larger-than-life character hangs at the end of one of the castle's many corridors. His presence is also said to haunt the battlements. The jester's will resides next to his painting and intriguingly appears to have predicted his death by drowning. Local lore tells that irony played its own trick on the fool, who drowned around 1600 in the cold waters of the Esk.

Further to the many spirits believed to haunt the castle, sightings of a woman have been witnessed near the gate. Dressed in white, her apparel that of the 1800s, the apparition lingers at the site where history records a local woman named Mary Bragg met a horrific end. Though she did not have any direct links with the castle, she fell deeply in love with one of the castle footmen. Unfortunately, another also desired the man in question and collaborated with some local thugs to have Mary murdered.

One night, this group of men ventured to the village to see Mary. Informing her that her love was fatally ill, Mary obliged in journeying in a coach with them under the impression she was to be taken to her lover's side. Instead, they took her to a secluded location and shot her. According to legend, she was murdered near a tree, named in her honour and now decayed. After the murder, the thugs threw her body into the river.

As in the case of Skelton, justice had a strange way of catching up. The doctor who examined Mary's recovered body two weeks after the murder – and allegedly paid to find no suspicious cause of death on his autopsy – was found drowned within 200 yards of where authorities had earlier recovered Mary's body. Within a short space of time, all involved in Bragg's murder met with bizarre ends.

Pendragon

There is a legend that the present-day ruins of the castle at Mallerstang Dale were built on the site of a fortress constructed by the mythical Uther

Pendragon. Regarded by the twelfth-century Welsh chronicler, Geoffrey of Monmouth, as the father of King Arthur, Uther allegedly settled in Cumbria after killing a dragon. A more realistic tale tells that the powerful chieftain took up his sword against the invading Angles and died after drinking contaminated well water. How the water came to be undrinkable is a matter of uncertainty. One version of the story suggests that Saxon intruders poisoned him and 100 men. Another says that the water was already undrinkable. Uther's building of the original castle is said to have involved a failed attempt at creating a moat by diverting water from the River Eden. As a local couplet recalled:

> Let Uther Pendragon do what he can,
> Eden will run where Eden ran.

Possible though it is that a fifth-century chieftain once resided there, little evidence of anything pre-Norman has been found at Pendragon. A Roman coin is a solitary find from the era: a tantalising possibility, yet meaningless without earthworks or foundations.

Better evidence concerns the origin of the present remains. The stone keep dates from the time of Ranulph de Meschines, 3rd Earl of Chester. Some forty years after Chester's death in 1129, the castle was the property of Lord of Westmorland, Hugh de Morville, one of the quartet who rid Henry II of the 'turbulent priest' Becket in 1170. The nearby point of Hugh's seat at Mallerstang Edge is named in his honour. It is also likely that Hugh was responsible for some of the original stonework. A later owner, Lady Idonea de Veteripont, founded St Mary's Church in the local hamlet of Outhgill around 1311.

At least twice in its history, the castle was the subject of pirate attacks. The first occurred in 1342 by Scottish raiders as part of the ongoing border wars between Edward III and the monarchs of Scotland. A second raid in 1541 ruined much of the medieval fortress. Fortunately for Pendragon, Lady Anne Clifford restored it in 1660, with additions that included a brewhouse, bakehouse, coach house and stables, see also Skipton Castle. A favoured residence of Clifford until her death in 1676, her successor and descendant Nicholas, 3rd Earl of Thanet stripped it for the metal value. By the 1770s, the site was mostly decrepit.

A picturesque ruin in an area that is often shrouded in mist, the air of mystery at Pendragon has survived far longer than its walls. In the

Second World War, the castle's owner, Edward Frankland, wrote a book about the Arthurian legends. Disappointingly, the lack of evidence for the pre-Norman fortress, coupled with what is known of the Arthurian romances, makes any connection with the actual castle unlikely. Stories of Merlin inhabiting the castle and visiting the nearby Castlerigg Stone Circle – one of the most significant prehistoric stone circles in Britain – are tantalising but fanciful.

Reputed to join Uther and Merlin, ladies in white are said to float around the castle on moonlit nights. A ghostly horseman has also reportedly been seen galloping noiselessly around the ruins. Local lore often paints him as either an Arthurian knight or the controversial sacrilegious murderer, de Morville, taking sanctuary after his evil deed at Canterbury Cathedral.

Strangest of all of Pendragon's rumours is that a great treasure is buried among the ruins, guarded by a gigantic black hen. According to legend, the chicken keeps a constant eye on the ruins and endeavours to frustrate any treasure hunter by refilling any hole they have dug. What came first, the chicken or the golden egg remains unclear!

Sizergh

No less than twenty-seven generations of the Strickland family have occupied this sumptuous mansion. Gifted to the National Trust in 1950, part of the house remains the home of the Hornyold-Strickland family.

While many visitors enjoy Sizergh as a grand home with impeccable gardens, parts of the building date back much further. Edward III permitted Sir Walter Strickland to enclose the land around the castle as his exclusive parkland. The great stone tower most likely dates from that time, with other additions following between the Wars of the Roses and the Georgian period.

Furnishing the stunning oak-panelled rooms, for which the castle remains famous, paintings of former inhabitants hang side by side with those of the Stuart family. Due to their shared Catholicism, the family retained a strong affinity with the exiled Stuart court. Indeed, following the Glorious Revolution, Sir Thomas Strickland was exiled with the dethroned James II. A century earlier, Catherine Parr, the sixth wife of Henry VIII, almost certainly occupied one of the bedrooms when visiting her Strickland relatives. It is commonly thought that around 1533, Parr lived at Sizergh for a time. Her second husband, Lord Latymer, was also a relation of the dowager Lady Strickland.

Prior to the castle passing to the Stricklands through marriage in 1239, Henry II granted the estate to Gervase Deincourt, who built the pele tower: the small stone tower that formed the castle's origin. An insecure and insanely jealous man, Deincourt reputedly locked his wife in a room when he left to join the king in battle against the Scots. Local legend laments that either due to the servants' forgetfulness, deliberate intent or an act of suicide, his wife starved to death. Since that time, her wretched ghost has reportedly been seen stalking the corridors: a somewhat gaunt figure, whose movements are often accompanied by the lingering echo of her sullen cries. It is a sad thought indeed that even in death, a spirit never meant to be caged remains bound to her place of captivity.

Chapter 15

County Durham

Barnard Castle

Begun by the Picardian baron Guy de Balliol between 1095 and 1125 on land granted to him by William Rufus, the castle in the modern market town of Barnard Castle came into its own during the first half of the twelfth century. Guy's nephew Bernard de Balliol and Bernard's son, Bernard II, extended the original fortress far beyond the initial defences.

After experiencing no mishaps in the Anarchy, the castle faced its first test in 1216 when Alexander II of Scotland laid siege to the castle as part of a complex argument concerning its ownership. Prior to the siege, John is recorded as having enjoyed the lodgings there. Despite Alexander's best efforts, the walls stood firm. Throughout the reigns of Henry III and Edward I, the Balliol family were engaged in a similarly fierce dispute with the bishops of Durham. The matter was briefly resolved on the dethronement of the king of Scotland, John Balliol, in 1296; however, only four years later, Edward granted it to the earl of Warwick, which passed in marriage to the Nevilles. The future Richard III, then duke of Gloucester, himself a Neville after marrying Anne, daughter of Warwick the Kingmaker, took possession of Barnard Castle in 1477. Richard's love for it remains celebrated locally, as well as an inspiration to Shakespeare.

When the Rose Wars ended, the castle returned to Neville control. Over the coming century, vast improvements were made to the estate. Devout Catholics, the family were prominent players in the Rising of the North, aimed at usurping Elizabeth I in favour of Mary, Queen of Scots. On the rebellion's failure, Sir George Bowes took refuge at the castle and was forced to surrender after an eleven-day siege due to running low on provisions. Found guilty of treason, the family were confiscated of their properties, including Barnard Castle. The Crown sold it to Sir Henry Vane in 1626, after which it fell into further disrepair. Having also acquired the Neville fortress of Raby, Vane prioritised the latter and used Barnard's materials to improve it. Despite the owner's important role in the English Civil War, the downgrading of Castle Barnard ensured it played no part.

Though abandoned since the 1600s, local lore tells that the castle is far from empty. Still said to reside there is Lady Ann Day, who was murdered at the castle. A resident from a young age during the sixteenth century, Day lived much of her life at Barnard Castle. Her ghost, dressed in white, has reportedly been seen falling into the river below, re-enacting the scenes of her gruesome death.

Such has been the castle's impact on the area, the phrase 'Barney Castle' is a recognised part of the County Durham dialect, literally translating as 'pathetic excuse'. It is thought that the original phrase concerns Sir George Bowes's retreat in 1569, though it is difficult to prove this all together. In more recent times, the castle and town have re-entered the public spotlight as the location that the former advisor to the Prime Minister, Dominic Cummings, travelled to during the height of the Covid-19 crisis. Some aspects of the media even criticised Cummings's reasoning as a 'Barney Castle', confirming, for a time at least, the castle's fame and the term remain very much alive.

Bowes

Little now remains of the Roman fort of *Lavatrae*. In the first century, the Romans constructed the fortress with wooden ramparts on the road that forms the modern A66, as a waypoint on the northern leg of Watling Street that connects Carlisle to York. Around 130–140 AD, approximately sixty years after the initial building work, the timber fortifications were either upgraded to stone or protected by outer stonework. Also added was an external settlement, or *vicus*, along with a bathhouse. Evidence suggests that the site remained occupied until the fourth century.

What transpired at *Lavatrae* until the Norman era is a mystery. The route was regarded as an important one since it is one of the few upland passes that connects England and Scotland. *Lavatrae* itself means 'summit', which accounts for the fort's purpose to guard the eastern entrance of the Stainmore Pass that cuts a path through the Pennines. The view would have been almost identical in 1136 when the count of Brittany, Alan de Bretagne – Alan the Black – built the original castle. From this time onwards, Bowes made up part of the honour of Richmond, which was the preserve of the counts of Brittany throughout the medieval period – see also Richmond Castle.

In keeping with many castles of the era, Bowes was initially of timber construction. The location chosen was the north-west corner of the old fort, which allowed them to take advantage of the original work. It is likely little more was done during Alan's tenure or that of his son, Conan. On the latter's death in 1171, the castle passed to the Crown. Henry II's concern that the walls would fare poorly against invaders from the north convinced him to spend around £600 over the next two decades. Chief among the additions was the hall-keep: a three-storied structure of extended length, which was a rare design in England. Only Middleham and Pendragon are remotely similar. From Henry's upgrade, the village of Bowes followed. Like the design of the keep, planned dwellings were rare in England.

Developments at Bowes were likely still to take full shape in 1173 when an attack by William the Lion provided the castle with its first significant test. Severely damaged but still standing, new work began in expectation of renewed attacks, which came the following year. Fortunately for Henry and his new castle, a relief force led by Geoffrey, Bishop-elect of Lincoln – a bastard of the king – saw things return to normal. Successful in quelling the revolt of his son, Henry the Young King, Henry also captured William the Lion at the second Battle of Alnwick and imprisoned him until the pair agreed to a peace treaty.

After the treaty, life in the north of England became far more peaceful. King John visited the castle in 1206 and 1212. It was also used for a time as the prison of his niece, Eleanor of Brittany: viewed by some as the rightful monarch as the daughter of John's elder brother, the late Geoffrey, Duke of Brittany. In 1241, Peter of Savoy acquired Bowes on being granted the long-coveted earldom of Richmond. The castle remained in the hands of Peter's successors until 1322. By this time, the castle had fallen into severe decline. When Edward II granted Bowes to John de Scargill, the local tenants, loyal to the Richmond earls, practically destroyed what was left of the castle and drank all the remaining wine.

Over the coming decade, ongoing skirmishes with the Scots caused further damage to both the castle and the surrounding fields. By 1340, the manor was deemed worthless, and in 1361 it was claimed by the Crown. In 1444, what remained became yet another Neville stronghold before reverting to the Crown again in 1471. There it remained until the reign of James I. After seeing little or no action in the Civil War, what remained of the fortifications were further dismantled. In 1928, the owner, strapped for cash, gifted the castle to the state after which it became the property of English Heritage.

Battered by its enemies – human and meteorological – and neglected by past owners, little except the long keep survives from the building's heyday. Despite the lack of raw materials, a story from the site's pre-Norman days continues to arouse intrigue. A legend from Roman times tells that the inhabitants of the old fort raided the local village and stole a hoard of gold. Though the villagers launched a counter raid, the gold was never found.

A fascinating epilogue to the legend comes with the story that the ghosts of Roman soldiers have been seen close to the castle, seemingly burying something. According to a later tale, two locals in the 1700s saw the ghosts and died violently shortly afterwards. Because of this, it is often assumed that vicious death is associated with the sightings. To this day, apparitions of Roman soldiers are reported at the site, along with malevolent black shadows that float like wraiths above the ruins. Given the area's reputation for bloodshed and greed, it hardly surprises that some believe the site to be cursed.

Durham

William the Conqueror constructed a motte and bailey at Durham around six years after the Norman Conquest. Located a stone's throw from Durham Cathedral, the king allocated the castle to the bishop of Durham after a short tenure under the guardianship of Waltheof, Earl of Northumbria, the last of the Anglo-Saxon earls. He was also the only nobleman to be executed for treason during William's reign. On the earl's death in 1076, royal authority was granted to Bishop William Walcher on his purchase of the earldom from the Crown. The title of prince-bishop remained unique to Durham until 1837.

The residence of noblemen and prelates as opposed to a great military citadel, the strange blend of sword and frock did little to help Durham escape the rough and tumble of British history. Due to its location close to the Scottish border, the castle was key to England's northern defences. That the castle was also built 'to keep the bishop and his household safe from the attacks of assailants' was equally logical. William's first earl, Robert de Comines, was murdered in 1069, along with his entourage. In May 1080, a brutal four-day siege by Northumbrian rebels also failed to protect Bishop Walcher. Whether the castle had been erected in stone by then is unclear. Contemporary records state that the keep was initially wooden.

Most of Durham's significant challenges came in its early days. In 1177, Henry II confiscated the castle from the prince-bishop, Hugh de Puiset, following a quarrel. Hugh was responsible for the cathedral's famous Norman archway and the Galilee – the iconic porch at the west end. Over the coming centuries, further enhancements included the great hall and a wooden minstrels' gallery.

For modern visitors, the Norman chapel located on the way out remains a jewel in the crown. Although the painted walls have faded, the Anglian architecture remains rich in early Christian symbolism ranging from early gravestones to images of the Green Man. The castle remained in good condition when the bishops of Durham moved to nearby Auckland Castle in 1832. With this, the home of the bishops of Durham for more than seven centuries was donated to form part of University College.

Today, many students are intrigued by the ghost stories reported there. The apparition of a lady in grey has been seen gliding up and down the black staircase. According to local legend, she is Isabella van Mildert: believed to have been the wife of one of the Protestant bishops, who either committed suicide by jumping from the tower or suffered an unfortunate fall. Confirming the story has not been easy, not least as there are different tales about the lady belonging to either the seventeenth or the nineteenth centuries. A bishop William van Mildert held the see 1826–36, thus making him the last bishop to reside at the castle. That a scandal would have been confirmed at the time would have been unthinkable at such a prestigious and religious institution. That a cover-up existed cannot be proven either way. Van Mildert married a Jane Douglas in 1795, but whether he had another wife is unclear.

A similar story concerns the tragic lot of one of the university's earliest students. Frederick Copeman was reputedly a precocious scholar who occupied room 21: the highest in the castle. On the morning exam results were due out, Copeman rose early before hurrying to Palace Green. Finding that his name was not on the pass list, the distraught lad sadly took matters into his own hands. After pacing around his room, he marched to the top of the cathedral and tragically threw himself from the tower. To make matters worse, Copeman's fears had been unfounded. Hidden behind a second sheet of paper was confirmation that he had been awarded the highest distinction possible and had come top of the entire year.

Since Copeman's suicide, campus legend tells that Frederick's pacing can still be heard inside room 21, which often carries an air of solemnity. Regardless of the exact circumstances, we are left with timeless lessons. It never does well to dwell on things that cannot be changed. Nor jump to unwarranted conclusions.

Lumley

Reputedly one of the most haunted castles in England, fourteenth-century Lumley has welcomed many people through its doors. Situated in the pleasant market town of Chester-le-Street, the castle was created around 1389 when Sir Ralph Lumley upgraded his manor house into something more elaborate on his return from the wars with Scotland. However, Sir Ralph's lot would take a turn for the worse on being found guilty of conspiracy to kill Henry IV, thus leading to his execution. In 1421, his grandson, Thomas, regained the property from the earl of Somerset, John Beaufort.

Throughout the centuries, the castle remained primarily in the same family. A fortified home as opposed to a military stronghold, Lumley enjoyed a relatively peaceful existence. James I visited it on his accession to the throne of England as the guest of Lord Lumley. In the present-day hotel, the King James Suite was once the chapel and named in his honour rather than any room in which the king stayed. In the 1800s, the castle served for a time as residence of the bishop of Durham on Bishop Van Mildert's gifting of Durham Castle to the new university. When the bishops moved to Auckland Castle, Lumley operated for a time as a hall of residence for first years at Durham. This ended in the 1960s when the university sold Lumley. In the coming years, the new owners converted it into a hotel.

Although the Lumleys, the bishops and the students have long been gone, the seventy-three-room hotel welcomes thousands of visitors every year. Among the stories any visitor is likely to be regaled with is that of Sir Ralph's wife: 'the Lily of Lumley'. Allegedly a disciple of the controversial religious reformer, John Wycliffe, legend tells that when Sir Ralph was away, a cell of monks from Durham Cathedral visited Lily to expunge her reformist ways. Adamant in her rejection of Catholicism in favour of the new wave of Lollardy – a precursor to Protestantism – it is said that the monks hacked her to death in one of the bedrooms and threw her body down the castle well. To cover up the heinous crime, the monks reputedly scoured the nearby village for a woman of similar age yet close to death. On finding one, they brought her to the local convent and informed the nuns that the woman was Lily. When the woman died, the nuns bore witness that Lily had passed of natural causes. On his return, Lily's disappearance aroused Sir Ralph's suspicions, and after establishing the truth, he swiftly ordered the execution of the guilty parties.

An intriguing tale, evidence that the story is historical is limited. Records from the time tell that Ralph, 1st Baron Lumley was married to one Eleanor Neville. In a contemporary romance, *The Lily of Lumley*, Lily is identified as an earlier wife. The romance is also heavily based on a concurrent legend and remains unidentified in family records. In other versions of the story, the murderers are a pair of Catholic priests rather than brothers of the cloth.

Despite the lack of proof, the legend of Lily continues to arouse intrigue. Local tradition tells that Lily's ghost remains bound to the castle and reportedly rises from the well and floats throughout the modern corridors. Similar reports concern the monks but outside the castle.

This tale aside, the castle still has a reputation for strange happenings. Due to its location close to Durham County Cricket Club's Riverside Ground, the hotel is a firm favourite with visiting cricket teams and has welcomed many stars of the game. Intriguingly, the Indian, West Indian and Australian national sides have reported unexpected encounters there. Headlines were also made during the 2005 Ashes series that at least one of the Australia players was too spooked to be alone. In an interview with journalists, the Australian media officer even claimed that she had seen a procession and 'someone looking in through the window'. Though initially adamant, she later reasoned, 'I think perhaps the shadows and the moonlight were playing tricks on my mind.'

Regardless of what was seen, reports of paranormal activity continue to trouble the castle. It also shows that even the most committed sports star can be affected by fear of the unexplained.

Raby

Set among 200 acres of deer park near the large village of Staindrop, Raby Castle was initially the home of John Neville, 3rd Baron Raby de Neville, between 1367 and 1388. Local records also confirm that the Neville family owned the manor from the previous century. Though possessed of no official title, in 1295, the first baron, Ralph Neville, was summoned to attend Edward I's legendary Model Parliament as Baron of Raby. Early in the next century, his heir, John, joined the household of Thomas, 2nd Earl of Lancaster, who lost his life in 1322 for rebelling against Edward II.

Records confirm that some form of impressive house, if not a fortified manor, existed on the site before the castle's construction. In 1378, the bishop of Durham granted the third baron permission to fortify, thus converting Raby from 'a defendable house into a palace-fortress'. It was within this new stronghold in 1415 that Cecily Neville was born: the countess of Richard, 3rd Duke of York and the mother of Edward IV, George, Duke of Clarence and Richard III.

A unique, imposing structure formed of nine towers, a four-storey gatehouse and three strong portcullises around a strong keep, Raby has proved a formidable opponent. In honour of Ralph's loyalty to Richard II, the king created the earldom of Westmorland. In hindsight, that seemed unwise when Ralph defected to Bolingbroke following his invasion of July 1399. Indeed, Neville was influential in Richard's decision to abdicate, after which Henry IV made Neville Earl Marshal of England, as well as a Knight of the Garter. Five years after the death of Henry Neville, 5th Earl of Westmorland in 1564, his son, Charles, was a leading player in the failed Rising of the North. In the aftermath, no less than 800 Catholic participants were executed, while Neville and fellow leaders, Thomas Percy, were exiled. Two years later, his lands were confiscated by an act of attainder.

For forty-three years, the castle was the property of the Crown before being purchased by the devout royalist Sir Henry Vane the Elder. Already the owner of Barnard Castle, Vane embarked on a modernisation project, during which he deprived Barnard of many of its materials. After avoiding any form of attack in the Civil War, alterations were carried out in the early Victorian era to the plans of architect William Burn. On 17 March 1849, William – at the time prince of Orange – was a guest of Raby's then-owner, the duchess of Cleveland, when he became king of the Netherlands. The title Duke of Cleveland became extinct in 1891 when the fourth duke's death saw the castle become the property of his relative.

An elegant, attractive building whose pleasing characteristics and backdrop once caught Turner's eye, Raby is both a home that has inspired many paintings and home to many inspiring paintings. Sir Joshua Reynolds, Sir Anthony van Dyck and Luca Giordano are just a handful of the famous artists whose works are housed within its walls. Joining them are impressive portraits of past family members, the likeness of whom offers a tangible link with bygone days. According to some, Raby's famous art collection isn't its only connection with former inhabitants.

Prominent among the castle's alleged hauntings is Charles Neville, 6th Earl of Westmorland, whose ghost has reportedly been seen on the grand stairs and in the baron's hall. Having been forced into exile in the Netherlands on being found guilty of treason, Charles was deprived of his estates and never returned to Raby.

Joining Neville in frequenting Raby is Lady Barnard. According to tradition, she has been seen marching the corridors at night, preoccupied with her knitting. Known in life as 'the old hell cat', Barnard bore a grudge against her son, Gilbert, who married against her wishes. Eyewitness reports describe her as an older woman with piercing eyes that glow like a jaguar's in the dark.

Other spirits said to haunt the castle include an unknown entity that vanishes before the gate and an older man who appears in the library, writing at the desk. The latter, a somewhat portly gentleman, appears with his body upright but with his head lying on the nearby table, his lips moving as though engaged in conversation. Conjecture identifies this spirit as that of Sir Henry Vane the Younger, who was executed at the Tower of London on 14 June 1662. An opponent of the regicide of Charles I, Vane was later involved in the Commonwealth and, thus, charged with treason against the new king. After time incarcerated at the Tower, Vane was further imprisoned on the Isles of Scilly, where he passed the time writing: a pastime he had often enjoyed at Raby. The famous diarist, Samuel Pepys, recorded of his execution:

> He made a long speech, many times interrupted by the Sheriff and others there; and they would have taken his paper out of his hand, but he would not let it go. But they caused all the books of those that writ after him to be given the Sheriff; and the trumpets were brought under the scaffold that he might not be heard. Then he prayed, and so fitted himself, and received the blow ... he changed not his colour or speech to the last, but died justifying himself and the cause he had stood for; and spoke very confidently of his being presently at the right hand of Christ; and in all things appeared the most resolved man that ever died in that manner, and showed more of heat than cowardise, but yet with all humility and gravity.

Walworth

The present castle at Walworth dates from around 1600 on the site of a fortress from about 1150. Whether the previous building was a castle is now unclear. The original family, the Hansards, lived there until the Black Death, after which Walworth briefly became another Neville stronghold. Ownership returned to the Hansards in 1391 and remained so until 1539 when Elizabeth Hansard married one Sir Francis Ayscough, whose number were later related to Sir Isaac Newton.

For around forty years, the castle remained in Ayscough hands until the family line died out. It was bought by Thomas Jennison, auditor general of Ireland. Evidence suggests that Jennison's purchase included a manor house or castle, which he demolished apart from the south-west tower that was incorporated into the new building. It is believed that the renowned Thomas Holt – architect of many of the University of Oxford's fine buildings – designed the modern castle, completion of which occurred after Jennison's death on the watch of his widow, Elizabeth. During her tenure, Walworth welcomed King James I on his way to his coronation at Westminster. Family lore tells that James knighted her son-in-law, George Freville, in thanksgiving for his enjoyment at the entertainment.

Following Elizabeth Jennison's death, her son William's imprisonment on recusancy charges saw the castle enter a period of decline. In 1679, Francis Jennison sold the estate before emigrating to the continent. A year earlier, Thomas Jennison was sent to Newgate Prison for his alleged involvement in the fictitious Popish Plot that reputedly intended the assassination of Charles II. Although the family divided up the estate in 1681, the castle remained in the Jennison family. The authorities ordered a search in 1689 in response to allegations that the Catholic owners were engaged in potential plots against William III and Mary II. Though no evidence was found, due to the costliness of upkeep, the castle passed through a succession of owners. In the Second World War, it was used as a prisoner-of-war camp, after which it became a boarding school and finally a hotel in 1981.

An impressive building set in appealing grounds, Walworth Castle has all the hallmarks of an esteemed residence. Historical suits of armour line many of the corridors and stairways, from which a regal feel pervades. In typical years, the hotel welcomes thousands of guests, many of whom enjoy the opportunity to eat, drink and sleep in rooms frequented by royalty and nobility.

Yet, in contrast to the many delights, Walworth also has a darker side. Many guests might well be unaware that a dank dungeon lies beneath the ballroom. Local legend holds that one of the maids was impregnated by the lord during the castle's early years and subsequently bricked up alive. Eyewitness reports speak of her mournful ghost being seen close to the Honeymoon Suite. The wall by the stairway is also reputedly a regular haunt. Whether it is the spirit of the maid who has been spotted in an armchair is unclear. The same is true of the often-heard footsteps on the stairs that lead up to one of the turrets.

Chapter 16

Tyne & Wear

Featherstone

Places of war, prisons, murder and tragedy, it is hardly surprising that the bitter memories of the past are believed to haunt many of Britain's ancient castles. Yet, despite being designed to keep enemies out, these historic chambers have witnessed countless scenes of laughter and joy. Many folklorists believe that any action or event that evokes strong emotions, good or bad, will leave a permanent imprint on the fabric. Even in the modern-day, castles remain popular locations for parties and banquets of all shapes and sizes. Few occasions are happier than weddings. However, in the case of one English castle, the memory of one such event seems destined to forever act as a reminder of a day intended for joy that ended in tragedy.

Situated more or less in the centre of Great Britain, Featherstone is a castle of contrasts. To modern visitors, a large castellated country house of iconic turrets and ivy-clad walls fits well with the image of a modern wedding venue. A grade I listed building that also acts as a conference and activity centre, the origins of this former family home overlooking the South Tyne can be traced to an eleventh-century manor house. The Featherstonehaughs constructed the castle as a thirteenth-century hall house on the site of the original manor, itself built in an area once inhabited by the Romans. The square three-storey pele tower followed in 1330, after which the castle remained the property of the same family until the seventeenth century.

Due to its location in an area of strategic importance, the castle served an important role during the ongoing disputes between Scotland and England. In later years, it endured an equally colourful history up until the family lost their estates during the Civil War. Acquired by Sir William Howard, whose son would become the earl of Carlisle, the castle was greatly enlarged and remodelled. Indeed, it was a far superior home that

Matthew Featherstonehaugh purchased in 1711, described in a survey taken four years later as 'an ancient and well-built structure'. For the next seventy-four years, the family once again enjoyed possession of their ancestral home before Sir Matthew Fetherstonhaugh relinquished it to James Wallace. Further alterations between 1812 and 1830 preceded more developments in the following century. It was partly within the parkland that a POW camp named Camp 18 in which 7,000 German officers were held operated in World War II. Though the base closed in May 1948, evidence of its existence remains visible. Two years later, by which time the camp contents had been sold, the estate entered new ownership. After serving for a time as a prep school, the castle became a centre for students.

A family home, a POW camp and a school, Featherstone is a castle rich in history and mystery. In 1825, it was subject of further intrigue when farmers working the nearby lands dug up an oaken coffin. Though the bones immediately turned to dust, four more were subsequently found in the same area. Tests have confirmed an early medieval origin, which fits well with similar discoveries in the north of England. It is unclear whether this predates the Featherstonhaugh family.

Local lore tells of no less than three hauntings associated with the castle. The ghost of a lady in a green and brown dress has been seen gliding the corridors. The spirit of Sir Reginald FitzUrse has also been seen. Tradition maintains that Sir Reginald was kept prisoner in one of the towers and, either as a means of torture or neglect, cruelly starved to death. Although the founding family no longer inhabit the castle, many affiliated with Featherstone claim their connection has lived on in other ways. Most specifically, one terrifying event that reached levels of such intensity its memory has remained imprinted ever since.

Believed to have occurred during the seventeenth century, one of the baron's daughters, Abigail Featherstonehaugh, was said to have fallen in love with a boy from a local family, the Ridleys of Hardriding. Sadly, she could not marry the lad on account of a feud between the families and a pre-engaging match to the son of a neighbouring baron – also a distant relative – negotiated by her father. Though Abigail contented herself to marry her chosen suitor, her decision went down badly with Ridley, who vowed to take his revenge.

With this, the scene was all set for a tragedy of Shakespearian proportions. When the big day came, proceedings started without complication, and Abigail was married. In keeping with the traditions of the time, most of the party set out on a post-wedding hunt. Remaining behind were the baron and his wife, who oversaw preparations for the lavish banquet that would follow.

The evening drew on, and the arrangements were completed. Yet, to the baron's great surprise, no sign of the party was forthcoming. As night fell, and with no word of their return, worry set in. What should have been a routine hunt was taking far too long. Time continued to pass, and, on the stroke of midnight, the sound of horses on the drawbridge confirmed the party's return. Initially relieved, the baron's peace of mind soon turned to horror. Confused on watching them enter without making a sound, their cheeks devoid of colour, all present witnessed the returners walk straight through tangible objects as if they weren't there. As the terrified servants backed off, a strong wind blew all away.

Rocked to the core by the bizarre event, all witnesses must have known that they had experienced a supernatural occurrence. A search of the locality the following day confirmed the party had been slain. Their bodies were found in nearby Pinkyns Cleugh: ambushed, so it seemed, by the Ridleys. Tradition holds that Ridley and Abigail's husband clashed violently, and Abigail was accidentally killed. Both fought valiantly but succumbed to their wounds. As for the baron, unable to come to terms with the horrific loss of his daughter and loved ones, he went mad with grief and died broken-hearted.

Though the cursed wedding happened long ago, it is said that every year on 17 January, the doomed party make their way back to the castle and disappear once again into the darkness until the next anniversary comes to pass.

Hylton

Home throughout its history of the Hylton Family, this neo-gothic stone fortress located in the North Hylton suburb of Sunderland is another that traces its history back to the Norman Conquest. The Hyltons themselves can document their origins earlier still. The family were already settled in England during the reign of the Saxon king Æthelstan (894–939). Another early record shows one Adam de Hylton offering either a pyx or a crucifix emblazoned with the family coat of arms to Hartlepool Abbey.

When the Normans invaded, the sons of Lancelot de Hilton pledged allegiance to William and were granted a large area of land on the banks of the Wear in gratitude. There Henry de Hilton put down the first castle, most likely a typical timber motte and bailey around 1072. In the late fourteenth century, his descendant Sir William Hylton upgraded it in stone as a four-storey fortified manor house. In 1448, records of the castle first came to light as 'a gatehouse constructed of stone'. It is likely that other buildings also existed on the site.

For all but a brief period, the impressive tower house remained the property of the same family. That rare exception concerned the somewhat eccentric Henry Hylton. On his death in 1641, the baron left the castle to the City of London Corporation on the premise that they strictly use it for charity purposes on a lease of ninety-nine years. In reality, the interlude lasted only twenty, as the castle was returned at the restoration to Henry's nephew. Under later generations, a significant upgrade in the 1700s took it to new heights. Work was likely ongoing when the final baron passed away in 1746. Since that time, periods of refurbishment and neglect followed, including additions in the gothic style and brief use as a school. In the twentieth century, a local coal company owned it before passing it to the state in 1950. Management and ownership now lies with English Heritage and a local trust.

A family home for much of its history, even today, reminders of the Hyltons survive. A small coat of arms above the west entrance is just one of many heraldic devices located there. Close by, the arms of local gentry and lords of the late 1300s to early the following century decorate the walls: most notably those of the Eures, Percys, Washingtons, Lumleys and Greys. Later legend reports that a certain George Washington adapted the family coat of arms to the design of the Star-Spangled Banner.

Within the old walls, it is said that other reminders of the castle's past can also be found. Most prominent among the reputed hauntings is that of a small child. Described as a 'shivering, naked boy', the apparition is said to haunt the fifteenth-century gatehouse tower that was originally the heart of the mansion. He has been identified as a stable boy named Robert Skelton, who worked there in the early 1600s. Sadly for Robert, working at the castle proved a tiring occupation. So much so that on one fateful day, he was caught sleeping on the job and violently stabbed by his master, Sir Robert, later 13th baron. Another version states he was in love with the baron's daughter. The poor boy's body was later tossed into the nearby lake or well to cover up the crime. In 1609, the baron was pardoned; however, rumour has abounded that the authorities were bribed.

The baron's crime may have gone unpunished, but retribution, it seems, would come in another form. Much poltergeist activity has been reported at the castle in the days and years since the horrific murder. Intriguingly, some staff at Hylton grew increasingly fond of the lad dubbed 'the cauld boy'. A well-meaning employee in life, Robert is said to have maintained his work ethic beyond the grave. Over the years, many staff discovered that their chores had been done for them. Even more bafflingly, when little needed doing, Robert would show off a more violent streak and often throw things around. To calm the busy spirit, the staff deliberately left him chores to do.

As time passed, the ghost of young Robert drew mixed reactions. Beloved for his helpfulness, perceived glimpses of the wet boy's nakedness caused severe fright to apparent eyewitnesses. As a gift to the young lad, it is said that a green cloak was left out for him by the fireplace, which he duly accepted on appearing on one occasion on the stroke of midnight. Local legend tells that the boy was somewhat enamoured with the gift, not that it changed his nakedness. Conflicting reports suggest that the acceptance of the cloak ended his haunting.

An interesting addendum to the story is that James VI of Scotland – later I of England – in his 1597 work, *Daemonologie*, defined a being known as a 'brownie' as a devil that would take the appearance of a naked or hairy man and haunt 'divers houses, without doing any evil, but doing it as it were necessarie turnes up and down the house'. Understandably, many regarded the 'brownie' as the most welcome of spirits. In 1584, Reginald Scot wrote in his *Discoverie of Witchcraft* that 'if the maid or good wife of the house, having compassion of his nakedness, laid any clothes for him' this would end the haunting.

Thirlwall

Believed to have benefitted from the reuse of stones taken from Hadrian's Wall, twelfth-century Thirlwall was of vital significance to the border wars. Lying on the banks of the Tipalt that later merges with the Tyne, the castle was erected as a defence against border raiders around 1330 by John Thirlwall, whose family had owned the site since its creation. Among the family's claims to fame are the antics of the former owner, Sir Percival Thirlwall, who carried Richard III's standard at Bosworth. Legend says that he valiantly held the standard aloft after losing his legs.

Occupied throughout the Middle Ages, the castle was abandoned as a residence when the final Thirlwall, Eleanor, married Matthew Swinburne of Capheaton Hall in 1738. A decade later, the property was sold to the earl of Carlisle and fell into decline. Since 1999 the Northumberland National Park Authority has worked hard to ensure its survival and offers access to the public free of charge.

The home of royal standard-bearers and chivalrous barons who fought hard against Frenchman and Scot, there is a bizarre legend that a magnificent treasure is buried there. The story concerns the baron of the day, John de Thirlwall, who returned home around 1360 with a train of spoils, most likely from the Hundred Years' War. Prominent was a solid gold table, which de Thirlwall entrusted to one of his retainers: a dwarf, who possessed strange and wondrous powers.

These powers would be put to the test one fateful day a short time later when a Scottish raid resulted in the butchering of every last Englishman. On discovering that the table was gone, one of the attackers spied the dwarf throwing it down a deep well. When the Scots sought to attack him, the dwarf also jumped inside. Local legend reports that in doing so, the dwarf sealed the well and that only the son of a widow can ever break it.

Tynemouth

Standing close to where the River Tyne meets the North Sea, the combined ruins of the castle and priory at Tynemouth together pay testament to a long and eventful past. Founded on a rocky headland around 617 AD, the priory developed as a site of religious importance that included serving as the burial place for the ancient kings of Northumbria. Evidence from the time indicates no less than three important kings were buried there, namely the Northumbrian warlords: Oswin of Deira and Osred II, as well as Malcolm III of Scotland, who died at the Battle of Alnwick in

1093. Malcolm's body was sent north in the reign of his son Alexander I for reburial. It was in their honour that the town chose the three crowns as the coat of arms.

Despite being gutted in the Dissolution, much remains of the buildings. Nor was the Reformation the site's first encounter with violence. After the Vikings plundered the priory around 800, the monks set about fortifying it. After successfully repelling a second attack in 832, the defences proved less effective in 865. After destroying the monastery and church, the Nordic raiders slaughtered the nuns of St Hilda taking refuge there. Five years later, the priory was again plundered and finally destroyed in 875.

In the reign of Edward the Confessor, the Saxon Earl Tostig Godwinson – brother of Harold Godwinson – chose Tynemouth as his new base. Little is known about the early castle, except that it was close to the lost priory and an old fort. According to legend, the ghost of St Oswin appeared to a novice named Edmund in 1065 and showed him his forgotten place of burial. A year later, Tostig was slain at the Battle of Stamford Bridge. In 1074, the final Anglo-Saxon earl of Northumbria, Waltheof II, granted the church to the monks of Jarrow, along with St Oswin's remains. In 1090, the Norman earl, Robert de Mowbray, had the priory re-founded. Legend says that some of William II's seafarers plundered Tynemouth a year later, which inspired one victim to appeal to St Oswin for assistance. A day later, Rufus's ships ran aground in fair weather, which convinced the king a miracle had transpired.

Slain at Alnwick by Robert de Mowbray in 1093, the monks interred Malcolm III's body at the re-established priory before its removal, most likely to Dunfermline Abbey. Two years later, Tynemouth's defences kept Rufus out for more than two months after Mowbray rebelled. Though the king took the castle, Mowbray initially fled to Bamburgh before later returning. When the castle fell a second time, Mowbray was dragged out in chains and suffered life imprisonment.

Exactly what state the castle was in at the time is uncertain. Most likely, the structure was of timber construction, consisting of earthen ramparts and a wooden stockade. In 1296, Edward I granted the prior permission to surround his monastery with stone walls, which appear to have been in place when Edward II took refuge there with Piers Gaveston – see Scarborough Castle. In 1594, the Elizabethan poet Christopher Marlowe dramatised these events in his play *Edward II*. The priory was also the chosen burial place for the king's bastard, Adam FitzRoy, who fought during the Scottish campaigns of 1322 before dying of unknown causes. Edward is recorded as having purchased a silk cloth with gold thread to cover his body.

The Plantagenet monarchs added more defensive features later in the fourteenth century: primarily an imposing gatehouse and a barbican in 1390. By this time, thick walls surrounded the castle and priory until those on the north and east side fell into the sea. Like for most monasteries, the Dissolution proved a watershed moment. Following Henry VIII's seizing of their land, he granted the priory and attached lands to Sir Thomas Hilton. As the monastery's dismantling left only the church and prior's house, both served the local parish until 1668. The ruins still exist, beneath which lies a small oratory devoted to the Virgin Mary. Two important features have also survived: the painted ceiling, with coats of arms, which acts as a fitting memory of the local families, while a rose window in the east wall is also a valuable reminder of the ancient time.

For a time, the castle remained the property of the king. Due to its coastal location, new fortifications were built onwards of 1545 and the walls upgraded with gun ports to help stave off the threat of foreign invaders. It was likely around that time a coal-fired brazier began to burn above one of the turrets of the priory church, acting as a form of a lighthouse. Though the exact start date is unrecorded, a source from 1582 refers to the 'kepinge of a continuall light', which remained until a new lighthouse was established on the headland.

Although comparatively little remains of the castle, its strategic significance made it a useful defensive site during both World Wars. During the late nineteenth century, new buildings were added to house military barracks, part of which was removed following a fire in 1936. In the 1970s, more modern buildings housed a coastguard station; however, this was closed in 2001. Much of what remains of the entire site is open to the public.

Dilapidated or destroyed over time and juxtaposed with the more recent additions, Tynemouth is very much a site of continuous transition. For this reason, it seems somehow fitting the castle's legends are a mix of the new, the old and the ancient.

The original lighthouse appears to date from the tenure of the eighth earl of Northumberland. In 1564, it was also the birthplace of the future ninth earl, Henry Percy, who the authorities arrested for being on the fringes of the Gunpowder Plot in 1605. He was imprisoned in the Martin Tower: located on the opposite side of the Tower of London from Sir Walter Raleigh in the Bloody Tower. Together the pair began collaborating in scientific experiments, which led to Percy's nickname, 'The Wizard Earl'.

Eleven years before the plot, the English politician Sir George Selby and lieutenant of the castle, Thomas Power, captured a pair of fugitives who had stolen precious jewels from the court of Anne of Denmark. Jacob Kroger and Guillaume Martyn – a German goldsmith and a French stableman – were kept at Tynemouth for five weeks before being transferred to Edinburgh. On being found guilty of robbing the queen of Scotland, they were summarily tried and executed.

A claimant for the castle's most colourful legend concerns a bizarre discovery made in 1849. According to the accounts of local fishermen, the carcass of a terrifying monster was discovered floating in the sea and brought back to land. Whether it was genuine, perhaps a case of mistaken identity or another mystery of the waters, the whereabouts of this inexplicable find remain unknown.

An area famously harassed by Norse raiders, the ruins are claimed to be haunted by an ancient Viking, who appears with a solemn look in his eye. The reason for the Norseman's despair is believed to lie in a story from the ninth century. During one of the violent raids on the area, it is said that a warrior named Olaf was wounded and taken to the local priory. Nursed to health by the kindly monks, he graciously accepted their hospitality and subsequently stayed in the community. A short time later, Olaf's comrades returned, among them his brother, determined to either locate his missing sibling or avenge his death. According to tradition, the brother was gravely wounded during the raid and passed away soon after. Broken-hearted by his brother's death, Olaf soon joined him in the afterlife, apparently dying in the chapel while praying for his brother's soul.

More than 1,000 years have passed since the days of the Vikings. Yet Olaf is still said to return to the site where he met his end. He has been seen, wandering the ruins, dressed in the armour of his people. On days when the breeze blows softly, it is claimed that he appears gazing out to sea in the direction of Scandinavia. In so doing, his story perhaps represents the stories of England's castles most aptly. Something of military might yearning for home.

Chapter 17

Northumberland

Alnwick

Overlooking the River Aln and surrounded by forty-two acres of green pastures, magnificent Alnwick is rightly celebrated as one of England's most beautiful buildings. Described by some as a 'fairy-tale castle', a reputation developed from masterpieces by Turner and Canaletto, Alnwick's lonely location and lack of action in the post-Tudor conflicts has helped ensure its preservation. For such reasons, it has featured in many television sitcoms and films: most famously, the Harry Potter films.

Built around 1096 AD on land granted by William Rufus to the Norman knight Yves de Vescy, medieval legend offers the castle – along with Bamburgh and Dunstanburgh – a possible connection with one of the most legendary characters of all time. Arthurian lore, notably the *Vulgate Cycle*, placed the fifth-century fortress of Dolorous Gard in Northumberland. So named after an evil enchantment placed on it, Sir Lancelot captured the castle and broke its curse. Legend also tells that Lancelot uncovered an empty tomb with his name carved into it: confirmation that the fortress was destined to be his home.

The legend of Lancelot is, of course, a famous one. The *Vulgate Cycle* tells that, after a visit by Arthur and Guinevere, the castle was renamed Joyous Gard in honour of the curse being broken. In later years, Lancelot rescued Guinevere as she was to be executed in retribution for their affair. On returning to the castle with the king's disgraced wife, the enchantment returned, and the castle was once more Dolorous.

What became of Lancelot and Dolorous – or Joyous – Gard remains a mystery. With Lancelot buried in the crypt after his death in exile, the castle disappeared altogether. Local legend maintains that the Normans built on the site of the ancient Northumberland castle. Sadly, proof is non-existent.

Evidence of Alnwick's early post-Norman history is easier to piece together. Yves de Vesci, Baron of Alnwick, put down the first stones to guard the Aln. The castle later became part of the Fitz John family by marriage before David I of Scotland captured it in 1136. Other sieges followed in 1172 and 1174 when William the Lion attempted to take advantage of Henry II's distraction with the rebellion of his son Henry the Young King. Unfortunately for the Scottish king, he was captured during or after the Battle of Alnwick.

In 1212, Alnwick's future was threatened when Lord of Alnwick, Eustace de Vesci, was accused of entering a conspiracy with the controversial rebel baron, Robert Fitzwalter, to murder King John or else abandon him on his Welsh exploits. Fortunately for Alnwick, while John's orders to dismantle Fitzwalter's Baynard's Castle in London were carried out, the similar order at Alnwick was not. In the reign of Henry III, as Eustace's heir, John de Vesci, was underage, the king conferred wardship of Alnwick to Antony Bek, later a bishop of Durham. Vesci later took the side of Simon de Montfort during the Second Barons' War, and Bek sold the estates to the Percy family.

Few families would prove more prominent in the context of English history than the Percys. Though Henry Percy never lived to see his reconstructions complete, under his son, the once modest home became an imposing military fortress and esteemed residence, albeit often less preferred than nearby Warkworth. As the castle's might increased, so did that of the family. The first earl of Northumberland, another Henry Percy, was influential in the dethroning of Richard II in 1399. Along with his son, he later rebelled against Henry IV. The son in question was none other than Sir Henry Percy, aka Harry Hotspur, whose exploits in the wars against the Scots and the Hundred Years' War earned him lasting fame. After defeating Hotspur at the Battle of Shrewsbury in July 1403, Henry IV attacked the Percys and forced Alnwick to surrender.

By 1461, Alnwick was one of three castles still held by the Lancastrians. That changed following their defeat at the Battle of Towton. That winter, Sir William Tailboys recaptured the castle, only to surrender to Lord Hastings, Sir John Howard and Sir Ralph Grey in July. In the autumn of 1462, Grey failed to withstand a brutal siege, while forces led by Edward IV and Warwick the Kingmaker forced Margaret of Anjou to sail to Scotland. A substantial counterforce led by Margaret with help from the king of Scotland secured Bamburgh and Dunstanburgh, but Alnwick initially survived. In May 1463, the castle returned to Lancastrian hands when Grey betrayed and imprisoned the Yorkist commander, Sir John Astley. Warwick finally took the castle on 24 June. When the fourth earl pledged fealty to Edward IV during his second period on the throne, Alnwick was once more a Percy stronghold.

During the century that followed, Alnwick enjoyed an increasingly peaceful existence. That changed, however, when the deeply Catholic Thomas Percy, 7th Earl of Northumberland, was executed. Another renowned for his devotion to the Old Faith, Henry Percy, 9th Earl of Northumberland, was incarcerated in the Tower for association with his 'bad relative' Thomas Percy, one of the thirteen members of the Gunpowder Plot. Increasingly uninhabited, Cromwell used Alnwick as a prison in the aftermath of the Battle of Dunbar in 1650. The Percys returned in the 1700s, during which restoration work included landscaping by Capability Brown. Further work continued in the nineteenth century under Anthony Salvin. It was essentially due to Salvin that the work on display to the public survives to this day.

A magnificent family home, coupled with the capability to withstand attack, Alnwick Castle is an exceptional place. Even in the absence of Arthurian lore and Hogwarts, there is something about Alnwick that cries out to castle enthusiasts. Although the castle lacks hauntings, it is no surprise that it is shrouded in other mysteries. Indeed, the great knight of Joyous Gard is not the only former occupant said to rest at the fortress. Legends from the twelfth century tell that Alnwick was once the home of a vampire.

According to ancient tradition, this spirit of the living dead was connected to a one-time lord of the estate. His remains interred in the castle crypt, it is said that he would return, not as a ghost, but as a victim of a terrible curse. Although the exact circumstances of his death remain unknown, convinced that his wife was guilty of infidelity, he fell from the roof to his death on the grassy verge below while awaiting her return.

Vampires have a unique place in popular culture. Folklore has long told that the living dead would return to the place they frequented in life, causing mischief to loved ones or deaths to the locals. In the case of Alnwick, the lord supposedly rose from its grave at night and sucked the blood of locals. As death and famine took a hold, it was believed that the evil magic of the former lord was responsible. Determined to put an end to the demon-like creature's reign of misery, the locals marched to the late lord's grave one night and opened the casket. On finding his remains, his skeleton was incinerated. The vampire has reputedly not been seen for 900 years.

Bamburgh

Regarded by the famed Arthurian writer Sir Thomas Malory as a more likely candidate for Joyous Gard than Alnwick, Bamburgh is known to predate the Norman era.

Situated on a dolerite outcrop, the site was originally home to a Celtic Brittonic fort named Din Guarie, which is believed to have been the capital of Bernicia during the fifth and sixth centuries. After toing and froing between the ancient Britons and Anglo-Saxons, the fort was taken under Saxon control in 590. In the seventh century, King Oswald of Northumbria became the first Christian ruler to live there, a move that prompted St Aidan, the bishop of Lindisfarne, to take him by the hand and utter, 'Never let this hand consume of whither.' A combination of local legend and the writings of Bede tell that Oswald later succumbed to wounds in battle, after which the hand in question was retained as a relic. Later legend relates that the hand was moved by monks of Peterborough in the eleventh century when Norse raiders plundered the castle. The worst, coming in 993, destroyed the old fort and removed the final trace of the ancient royal kingdom of Northumbria.

Rebuilt in part by the powerful Norman, Robert de Mowbray, the castle was besieged in 1095 when Robert rebelled against William II. Unsuccessful in breaching the walls, Rufus captured Robert and later the castle after threatening Robert's wife that her husband would be blinded if she withstood. In Royalist hands, Henry II erected the keep, after which Richard the Lionheart entrusted governorship to Sir John Forster in light of his service at the siege of Acre in 1191. In the First Barons' War, responsibility lay with Philip of Oldcoates.

Like many English castles, strong walls made good prisons. Such was the experience of David II of Scotland on suffering defeat at the Battle of Neville's Cross in 1346. Inhabited by loyal Lancastrians in the Wars of the

Roses, Bamburgh fell in 1464 to Richard Neville, 16th Earl of Warwick, after a nine-month siege, thus making it the first castle in English history to be defeated by heavy artillery. From that time, members of the Forster family commonly governed Bamburgh up until 1700, when Sir William Forster was declared insolvent after his death. Consequently, the castle was sold to Lord Crew, Bishop of Durham, who was married to Forster's sister. Refurbishments under local curator Dr John Sharp followed until the Victorian industrialist William Armstrong purchased the castle in 1894. By that time, Sharp had established Britain's first lifeboat station there. In World War II, pillboxes were established in the dunes to help deter coastal invasion, and a naval warship was named in the castle's honour.

Both inside and out, Bamburgh remains the epitome of a solid medieval castle. When taking a stroll through the dunes, the combination of medieval walls and sea air provide an alluring mix. Of all the counties in England, Northumberland is one of the few that rivals Cornwall in its ability to charm the eyes and arouse the senses.

A ballad from the twelfth century tells of 'The Laidly Worm of Bamburgh' – alternatively 'Spindleston Heugh' – a monster not dissimilar to the Lambton Worm. In the tale, the beast was none other than the king of Northumbria's daughter, upon whom her stepmother had placed a curse. Unaware that his new wife was a witch, the king willingly gave in to her charms, after which the worm laid waste to the local country. Sometime later, the king's son, Childe of Wynde, learned of his sister's new identity, which ended the spell. The story tells that the wicked stepmother was changed into a toad and kept in Bamburgh's dungeons. Legend says that the door is opened every seventh Christmas Eve. The spell can, it is claimed, be broken if one unsheathes Childe's sword three times, blows three times on his horn and kisses the toad. Then, frog and princess-style, the curse shall be lifted. No better example exists of the castle's continued ability to mix history and legend than in 1971 when a seventh-century gold plaque containing the emblem of a mythical beast was discovered during restorations. In more recent years, the creature has been adopted as the castle's motif.

Should a visitor be fortunate, they might even catch a glimpse of the castle's most famous ghost. Reputed to have been a tenth-century Northumbrian princess whose father refused her the right to marry her love, the lady in pink is something of a celebrity at Bamburgh. Local tradition describes how the princess's father, the lord of Bamburgh, assigned the unfavoured suitor overseas to ensure they remained apart. On the lad's departure, the lord told the princess her love had married elsewhere. Such was her heartache, she jumped from the battlements, yet not before her father had commissioned a pink dress.

While the lad's fate remains unclear, reports over the centuries have spoken of the lady in pink's embittered shade stalking the battlements. Tradition tells that her spirit returns every seven years to wander the corridors. She is also reported to appear on the shore, gazing out to sea, her mind tormented by thoughts of her lost love. Of the tale's historical validity, little is known. The seven-year return compares with the story of the worm and may be of connection. Joining the princess is the lady in green. Reports tell that she has been seen near the top of the castle before disappearing mid-air as she falls. She is believed to be the ghost of a woman named Jane, who was reportedly mocked on begging for bread and tragically fell with her babe in arms on being turned away. A knight in armour is also reputed to stalk the corridors, his movements accompanied by the rattling of chains.

Far more benignly, a strange atmosphere has been detected in the library where a misty apparition has been seen. Being tapped by unseen hands is also reported. That this man is Dr Sharp is unlikely to be confirmed. It is a comforting thought, however, in a castle plagued by stories of tormented loves and rampaging knights that the man who oversaw such significant renovations is still there in spirit, perhaps still watching over a project so close to his heart.

Chillingham

Another of England's finest castles, Chillingham's origins are something of a rarity. Originally a monastery, it was converted into a home in the twelfth century and stormed in 1246 by the Grey family, whose descendants still own it.

Due to its location at a critical strategic point between England and Scotland, Chillingham proved a crucial player in the ongoing border wars. Henry III chose the castle as his lodgings in 1245. In 1298, Edward

I also stayed there on his way north to battle William Wallace. A window put in for the king's visit survives from that time.

Thomas Grey petitioned Edward III for a licence to crenellate, which was granted in 1344. Five years later, Grey was a founder member of the Knights of the Garter. Consequently, Chillingham underwent a series of developments, which continued during the Tudor era. Following Elizabeth I's death, it was chosen as the lodging of James I, his Queen, Anne of Denmark, and their children on 6 June 1603. Fourteen years later, James also stayed there to break his journey as he headed north. Towards the end of the Civil War, James's son, Charles I, also spent three nights within the walls.

As the unification of the two nations ensured repeats of the historic wars became less common, Chillingham's military purpose became increasingly redundant. With this, the medieval stronghold was gradually converted into an opulent home. The refinements to the grounds and gardens in the eighteenth and nineteenth centuries remain a fitting testament to the work of Sir Jeffry Wyatville, who carried out similar success at Windsor Castle and Chatsworth House. The moat was filled, and the battlements were converted into residential wings. A library was also added, along with a banquet hall. All were in place when the prince and princess of Wales, the future Edward VII and Alexandra of Denmark, visited in 1872. In the previous century, Chillingham was again the subject of ongoing restoration. Used as an army barracks in the Second World War, the castle fell into disrepair until its sale to Sir Humphry Wakefield, 2nd Baronet, husband of Katherine, a Grey descendant. The property was used in the 1997 film *Elizabeth* and is usually open to the public and partly available for holidaymakers.

A grand family home that loving care has helped restore, Chillingham has a reputation for living up to its name. Indeed, deep within the walls, a darker side is said to dwell. On pulling up in the leafy car park, little can prepare the unsuspecting visitor for the strange charge of electricity that seems to linger in the air. Visiting the castle for the first time in 2010, this author was shocked by the bizarre outcome of several photographs. A walled section, intercepted by an iconic archway, separates the main façade from further woodland. In at least two photos, irregular shapes appear to be present among the leaves, while the odd shape of what many viewers have described as a female form can be seen. What caused the oddities is, frankly, anyone's guess.

Even without the strange sightings, the exterior and parkland are not without curiosities. Since the thirteenth century, a rare breed of white cattle with red ears have grazed in the 300-acre park. Today, they are the only survivors in Britain of a type that roamed all over Europe before the Roman invasion. Legend tells that the cattle have the same colourings as 'fairy cattle', and death awaits anyone who touches them. Local tradition also relates that a phantom funeral procession has been seen in the Topiary Garden before vanishing without a trace.

On entering the castle, its reputation becomes all the more real on seeing the faceless statues on the walls. Such things are further intensified by the presence of a medieval torture chamber that once housed Scottish prisoners of war, some of whom are believed to have resorted to cannibalism. The dungeon remains essentially unchanged from its role in the medieval border feuds. If reports can be believed, their ghosts are just a handful of the castle's former residents who continue to plague their old home.

Regarded as an omen of ill tidings, the 'blue boy' was once the most prominent of the castle's spirits. Said to linger within the Pink Room, the radiant child has been seen on many occasions and is one of several similar hauntings reported in the North. Local lore tells that the peculiar boy would appear at midnight, accompanied by the shrill sounds of a child crying.

Witnessed on numerous occasions over the centuries, the sounds of the boy's restless spirit always seemed to originate near a secret passage cut through the wall that leads into the next tower. After lingering for several moments, the silence that followed would be replaced by the inexplicable appearance of a hazy mist of blue light cutting the darkness near the four-poster bed. Many people who have slept in the Pink Room have reported witnessing the strange aura, described as the ghostly image of a child from Charles II's reign.

Although the boy is famous in these parts, his identity and reasons for haunting the castle remain unknown. However, it may relate to a startling discovery made in the 1920s. During restoration, the skeleton of a young boy was found, accompanied by fragments of an old blue dress and the remains of a man. It has also been reported that some form of paper or document was present. The bones, found where a fireplace is now placed, were entombed near a trapdoor that overhangs the castle vaults. Sadly, the condition of the fingers suggests the boy was alive when he was incarcerated. The skeletons were given a fitting burial shortly after. Despite the peace of the grave, visitors who have stayed in the room reputedly continue to report the strange spectre of a blue apparition forming in the darkness.

Dubbed 'The ghost in the portrait', the apparition of a lady has also been seen at the castle. She is believed to be Lady Mary Berkeley, who lived a happy life at Chillingham in the 1600s before her life was turned upside down in a blaze of bitter turmoil. Married to Ford, Lord Grey of Wark, Mary's joy turned to despair when her husband had an affair with her sister, Lady Henrietta. Stories abounded that the pair had eloped; however, that was not the case. Centuries after Lady Mary lived out her days in the castle in the sole companionship of their baby girl, her lonely spirit is said to return. Footsteps, accompanied by the rustling of a dress, are said to precede an inexplicable drop in temperature. Following this, she has reputedly been seen stepping out from her portrait and terrifying any who bear witness.

The castle pantry is regarded as a strange area. Famously used to prepare sumptuous banquets, on one particular evening, a frail-looking figure in white appeared before a duty footman and asked him for a glass of water. Assuming the lady was a guest, he turned away to oblige her request only to discover that the woman had vanished. Local tradition records that a woman succumbed to poison at the castle, be it deliberately or accidentally.

In addition to the castle's more famous apparitions, an unseen spirit has been felt in one of the bedrooms. Beneath the chamber, two male voices have been heard in the library. Who they are and what they discuss is unclear. The conversation appears destined to cease in mid-speech and fade to silence.

Dunstanburgh

Overlooking a jagged cliff, the ruins of Dunstanburgh certainly look like a castle steeped in legend. Officially the largest in Northumberland, the rugged Norman stronghold continues to dominate the skyline along the North Sea coast as it has done since the fourteenth century.

Built between 1313 and 1322 by Thomas, Earl of Lancaster on the site of an Iron Age hill fort, Dunstanburgh served as a refuge for Lancaster's rebels who suffered defeat at the Battle of Boroughbridge in March 1322. Despite being Edward II's cousin – his father, Edmund 'Crouchback' having been Henry III's second son – Thomas began a rebellion after a falling out. Sadly for the earl, defeat at Boroughbridge culminated in his capture. He was later arrested and tried at Pontefract Castle – see also Pontefract Castle. Found guilty of treason, he was executed on a hill close to St John's Priory.

Inherited by Thomas's successors as earl, and duke, of Lancaster, the castle was later enlarged by John of Gaunt. Impressive though Gaunt's efforts were, the thick walls were no match for the heavy artillery unleashed upon it. Ownership changed hands regularly during the Wars of the Roses.

Besides minor repairs carried out in 1470, no substantial upkeep took place. By the sixteenth century, the castle had fallen into disrepair and reputedly served as a base for piracy. A year after James I's accession, Dunstanburgh was sold. A year later, it became property of the Grey family, whose descendants owned it for several centuries. Of its general state at this time, records are sparse. That things improved from 'a very ruinous house and of small strength' in 1538 and 'in wonderful great decaye' twelve years later is unlikely. Though the nearby lands were used to grow crops, it was likely never inhabited.

A beautiful yet sinister-looking ruin, the castle has long been a popular site for tourists. Partly due to its picturesque location overlooking the choppy waters, the ruins have been a favoured haunt for artists and poets. In the nineteenth century, artists from Turner and Thomas Girtin were known to have found inspiration within the ruins. Yet, while the feeling among visitors in the day is almost entirely positive, the medieval walls are said to take on a much different form at night.

Among the ghosts said to haunt Dunstanburgh is that of Earl Thomas. Accounts of his execution tell that his head needed three strokes before it was finally severed from his body. Seven centuries have passed since the gruesome event, yet local legend recalls that his tortured spirit returns to his former home. The disoriented ghost has reportedly been seen stumbling through the darkness, carrying his decapitated head under his arm.

Further to Earl Thomas, Dunstanburgh is home to many legends. According to local lore, a child once escaped the castle and threw her dungeon key into a nearby field to the north-west. Though the landing place is unknown, since that time, the land is said to be infertile.

Another of the castle's legends dates from the tenure of Margaret of Anjou, queen consort of Henry VI. At some point in the 1450s, Margaret entrusted control of the castle to a man named Gallon, whose duties included the safekeeping of valuables. When the Yorkists captured Dunstanburgh, he managed to escape before returning to salvage six Venetian glasses. Exactly what became of Gallon is a mystery. Records from the fourteenth century tell that there were receivers and bailiffs at the castle named Galoun. That a man of a similar name was descended of them is highly plausible, albeit challenging to prove altogether.

A far less easy story to prove is Dunstanburgh's most colourful legend. While riding along the Northumberland coast, a bold knight called Sir Guy the Seeker was close to the ruins when a sudden downpour caught him exposed. Seeking shelter, the knight made his way to the long-abandoned castle and sought refuge inside the gatehouse. Although successful in escaping the thunderous storm, a short time passed before Sir Guy sensed that an enchantment had been placed. Aware he was being watched, the knight became deeply disturbed by the inexplicable appearance of a hideous creature dressed in white – in other versions of the tale, the beast was a wizard, perhaps Merlin. On being approached, Guy was instructed to follow the ghostly form and bear witness to the fantastic reward of a 'beauty bright'.

Pushing his fears to one side, the knight followed the strange being up a long, winding staircase and entered a room where 100 knights lay sleeping by their horses. In the middle of the chamber, a sparkling crystal casket housed a beautiful sleeping maiden, the sight of which enthralled him. Wishing a closer look, Guy realised that his path was blocked by two serpents: one holding a sword, the other a horn. The apparition in white instructed the knight that the maiden could only be awakened by one or the other, but he must choose wisely, as only the correct choice would rouse her. After deliberating for a time, Guy blew on the horn and was soon surrounded by the awakening knights, their swords drawn. Several hours passed before the knight regained consciousness. Once again alone in the gatehouse, the seeker was mystified by what he had encountered. Was the experience real or nothing more than a dream?

Distraught that his chance to awaken the maiden had gone, legend tells that Sir Guy vainly searched the remains, devastated to find it devoid of any clue to what had unfolded. For the remainder of his life, the brave knight was said to have searched for the gorgeous maiden. His ghost still resides within the ruined fortress where the strange events brought him to the point of madness.

Like many legends of the type, pinning down an exact point of origin is difficult. Intriguingly, in keeping with the tale of the Lambton Worm, the story of Sir Guy draws clear parallels with legends of nearby Hexham and the Eildon Hills. The first recorded evidence of the adventure appears to date from Matthew Lewis's 1808 poem, *Sir Guy the Seeker*, after which there are at least two similar versions from different authors in the 1820s. That Lewis's tale was based on an earlier tradition seems likely. The story has an Arthurian ring to it, albeit seemingly separate from the medieval romances. Speculation has also been made that Dunstanburgh's design was influenced by Arthurian mythology. Thomas, Earl of Lancaster, was one of many barons who held an interest in Arthurian lore and even used the nom-de-plume, King Arthur, to correspond with the Scots. An ancient fort surrounded by water offers clear parallels with Camelot. Even more intriguing, of all of Northumberland's mighty castles, Dunstanburgh bears the closest similarities to Lancelot's Joyous Gard.

Home to many legends, a far more tangible one may concern a longstanding rumour that a series of underground tunnels connect Dunstanburgh to the nearby Georgian mansion, Craster Tower. Similar stories concern Embleton and Proctor Steads, in addition to a different tunnel between the well and the castle's west side. That the stories concern anything more than drainage pipes remain elusive.

Described in the modern-day as 'one of the most imposing structures in any English castle', there is no denying that there is something extraordinary about Dunstanburgh. Though lacking the traditions of Tintagel, it is this author's humble opinion that this is one of the few castles that comes close. Coupled with the majesty of the distant sea views, the feeling of the salty air spraying softly against the skin as one wanders the ruins is an alluring combination. Close one's eyes for a second, it isn't difficult to let the natural enchantment of the area dominate the senses.

Undoubtedly, never did Sir Guy the Seeker lay witness to beauty bright before narrowly escaping with his life. Yet, in Dunstanburgh, we have a castle that allows the visitor to wonder. In doing so, we have a cautionary tale. Rarely does it pay to build our castles in the air when it serves so much better to do so on the ground!

Lindisfarne

For more than 1,000 years, the Holy Island of Lindisfarne has been steeped in legend. Located off the Northumberland coast in an area plagued by the wind, rain and Vikings, the tidal island is connected to the mainland by a causeway at low tide and a short boat ride at other times. On a clear day, the mighty walls of Bamburgh are visible from the island. Since the sixth century, both have played significant parts in the area's history.

It was from the original fortress at Bamburgh that Lindisfarne's date with destiny truly began. Around 635 AD, King Oswald of Northumbria summoned the renowned Irish monk and preacher St Aidan from Iona in Scotland to Bamburgh, thus marking the introduction of Christianity to the area. Though Oswald was slain in battle around seven years later by the pagan warlord Penda of Mercia, from his tiny base on the nearby island, Aidan set about his mission. According to legend, as Aidan watched Penda prepare to torch Bamburgh, a sudden change in the wind answered his prayers and spared the wooden walls.

The priory on Lindisfarne was likely constructed immediately after Aidan's arrival, albeit as little more than a cell. On Aidan's death in 651, legend tells that his replacement had a vision. Fourteen years later, that replacement would, at last, make his way to Lindisfarne, thus beginning a journey that inspired the Venerable Bede. Brought up close to Melrose Abbey, St Cuthbert spent about twelve years on the island, from which he developed a reputation that has become inseparable from the island. After nine years as a hermit among the Farne Islands, he returned to Lindisfarne around 685 and inherited the bishopric. On his death two years later, his remains were buried in the priory church and remained so until 875 when the loyal monks salvaged his relics during a Viking raid. In time, they found a more permanent place of rest inside Durham Cathedral.

Between Cuthbert's death and the removal of his body, the so-called 'Holy Island' became an unlikely heart of a golden era of Christian culture. Thanks in part to saints Aidan and Cuthbert – and later that century Eadfrith and Earberht – the area became a centre of art and learning. It was there that a set of stunning gospels, bearing the island's name, were written. Today, the Lindisfarne Gospels are among the most precious illuminated manuscripts in existence.

Located off England's north-east coast, Lindisfarne was always susceptible to attack. In 793, the Anglo-Saxon chronicler wrote that 'portents appeared over Northumbria' as the 'harrying of the heathen miserably destroyed God's church in Lindisfarne'. That those portents extended to dragons and whirlwinds or that the damage was bad enough to destroy the saints' bodies seems unlikely. On Cuthbert's burial at Durham Cathedral, Eadfrith and Earberht were reinterred alongside him. More plausible is the suggestion that the monastery was destroyed, as records from the time do indicate the original was little more than a wooden hut. The monastery was re-established in stone after the Norman Conquest and survived unscathed until the Dissolution. Local legend also tells that when the priory was re-created, the labourers replenished their energy with bread made from thin air and wine from a bottomless cup.

In the monks' absence, Lindisfarne began a new chapter. Using some of the raw materials made redundant by the monastery's closing, Henry VIII ordered a new fortress to help protect against foreign raiders. Lying on a whinstone hill, which serves as the island's highest point, the small fort was blessed with near-perfect observation. Such views, however, did not prevent the castle from falling briefly to Jacobean rebels in the eighteenth century. After being captured shortly after, the Jacobites were imprisoned. According to local tradition, they dug their way out and waited nine days before heading to Bamburgh and then back to Scotland. As the need for a military presence faded, the castle operated as a coastguard point and tourist attraction. In 1901 it was acquired by the owner of *Country Life* Magazine and served as his retreat. Notably revamped, it passed to the National Trust in 1944 and remains open to visitors.

A place of pilgrimage since its formation, little now remains of the Saxon church and monastery in which Cuthbert and his brethren lived their simple existence. The sandstone ruins and iconic arches that formed part of the medieval priory are now a desolate yet romantic reminder of the society that once flourished. In some cases, human remains may still lie beneath the rain-battered grave slabs. Anyone fortunate enough to visit will almost certainly agree that Holy Island is indeed an extraordinary place. When the tide is out, views across the mudflats towards the seemingly endless sea is a truly magical sight. At such times, the wider area possesses an air of timelessness. Local legend claims that apparitions of white-robed monks still walk the causeway, their translucent shades appearing like shadows before disappearing into the vastness. A similar story concerns a spectral monk reading from parchment within the old ruins. Another stands on the seashore, as though on the lookout for unfriendly visitors. From later times, the ghost of a roundhead soldier reputedly stalks the castle's interior. More bizarrely, a white dog is rumoured to jump down from the ruins and run towards the shoreline.

Of the many spirits said to remain tied to Lindisfarne, none surpass the legendary monk and bishop whose presence there has ensured the island's fame. Dressed in simple robes, St Cuthbert's friendly ghost has reputedly been seen wandering the island for centuries. Among the earliest reported sighting was before a young Alfred of Wessex, to whom the saint foretold greatness. His ghost has been reported within the remains of the Norman priory and by the nearby rocks, affectionately known as St Cuthbert's Beads. Local legend tells that the fossils are the product of Cuthbert himself, who sits on a rock and bangs out the shape using an anvil. A strange hammering sound has been reported there: the noise, so it is claimed, of Cuthbert doing his work. The story served as the inspiration for Sir Walter Scott in his epic poem, 'Marmion', which includes the lines:

> If, on a rock, by Lindisfarne,
> St Cuthbert sits, and toils to frame
> The sea-born beads that bear his name

Though the monks have been gone for centuries, Lindisfarne's reputation for pilgrimage remains strong. Some of the quirkiest local customs concern brides jumping over the so-called 'Petting Stone', which is believed to have once formed the socket of St Cuthbert's cross. Like passing from the mortal plains to the heavenly, the custom symbolises the beginning of the new journey. So long as the tradition remains, Lindisfarne's age-old reputation as a crossing point will undoubtedly be preserved.

Prudhoe

Standing on a ridge on the south bank of the Tyne, Prudhoe is the third castle of prominence along the famous river, after Tynemouth and Newcastle. Henry I granted the barony of Prudhoe to Robert d'Umfraville, whose family had built the original motte and bailey following the Norman Conquest. It was likely under Robert that the wooden palisade was upgraded with the usual twelfth-century stonework. Those extra defences proved effective in repelling two invasions by William the Lion 1173–74 in his quest to inherit the Earldom of Northumberland.

A d'Umfraville fortress until late 1381, the castle passed to the Percy family when Gilbert III's widow, Maud Lucy, married Henry Percy, 1st Earl of Northumberland. After bearing no children to either husband, on her death, the castle formally passed to the Percys, whose number influenced many fortresses in the north. A new great hall appears to have been added before Hotspur took up arms against Henry IV at the Battle of Shrewsbury in 1403. Consequently, the king deprived the family of their estates until 1440, during which time Prudhoe spent thirty years in the hands of the king's third son, John of Lancaster. In 1461, Henry Percy's grandson and namesake, by then the third earl, fought and died for the Lancastrians at Towton. On seizing the Percy estates, Edward IV granted Prudhoe to his younger brother, George, Duke of Clarence, and later Lord Montague, before it was returned to the Percys in 1470.

For the next fifty years, the family presence there was inconsistent. Things changed in 1536 when Henry VIII confiscated the family estates as punishment for their role in the Pilgrimage of Grace. A survey from the time described the castle as requiring repair. Such was its condition in 1557 when Thomas Percy, 7th Earl of Northumberland, revamped it when Mary Tudor returned the family their lost estates. Thomas was executed in 1572 after initially escaping in the aftermath of the Rising of the North three years earlier. Though beatification awaited Thomas, Prudhoe's decline set in. Despite being rented out to tenants, the castle's days as a residence were probably over by the 1660s. In 1808, its ruinous condition prompted Lieutenant General Hugh Percy, 2nd Duke of Northumberland, to carry out a major overhaul and replace the redundant dwellings within the walls with a Georgian manor house built adjoining the keep. Like most ruins, it is now managed by English Heritage.

Many oddities reputedly haunt this former family home and military fortress. A white horse has reportedly been seen pacing the outer ward, while ghostly chanting has been heard from within the chapel. Sounds have also been heard on stairs where a young boy who grew up to become a priest once played with a ball. Alleged poltergeist activity has included water being thrown against a door and a substantial oak table being tipped over.

Further to such mysteries, Prudhoe is said to remain the home of two other spirits. The ghost of a knight with a thick beard has been reported there. The same is true of a lady in grey. A nearby road, 'Grey Lady Walk', appears to have been named in her honour. In more recent years, the spirit of a young girl was reputedly caught on camera.

Perhaps the most fascinating of Prudhoe's legends is that an underground passage links it with Bywell Castle three miles away. The tale is almost certainly untrue as the tunnel would need to have been constructed beneath the nearby river. Built by the Nevilles in the 1430s, Henry VI took refuge within Bywell after the Battle of Hexham in 1464.

Warkworth

Seated at the summit of a steep hill less than a mile from England's north-east coast, the imposing remains of Warkworth act as a further reminder of the border wars that once plagued the region.

Exactly when the first fortress was erected at Warkworth is a mystery. Local tradition places construction to the mid-twelfth century, at the behest of Prince Henry of Scotland, Earl of Northumbria. Equally possible is that the renowned castle builder Henry II began construction as part of his bid to control the northern counties. Warkworth appears documented for the first time in a charter dated 1157–64, at which time the king granted the timber fortress to Roger Fitz Richard. The primitive structure performed poorly and was left to burn or rot during the Scottish invasion of 1173. A contemporary record makes no specific mention of the area beside the local population taking refuge in the local church. The village of the same name, whose residents still enjoy a peaceful existence alongside the River Coquet, developed alongside the castle.

On Roger's death, the beneficiary was his son, Robert, under whom many improvements were made. A number were in place for King John's visit in 1213 before more still were added to welcome his grandson, Edward I, in 1292. When the family line died out in 1345, Warkworth passed to the Crown, but not before Edward II invested heavily in the northern defences. In 1319, he reinforced the garrison: a move that seemed all the more prudent when the Scots failed twice to breach the walls in 1327. Unfortunately for the king, that same year, his barons dethroned him.

On the death of the widow of John de Clavering – a descendant of Roger Fitz Richard – in 1345, Edward III granted the castle to Henry Percy, 2nd Baron Percy of Alnwick. Later that century, Henry Percy, 1st Earl of Northumberland, added a keep. Later developments followed during the time of the fourth earl. Among the notable changes was the remodelling of the bailey and the building of a collegiate church, which was abandoned on his death. Inconsistent supporters of the Crown throughout their history – especially the monarchs of protestant leanings – the loyalty of Algernon Percy, 10th Earl of Northumberland, rested solely with parliament at the outbreak of the English Civil War. Despite Percy's roundhead leanings, a royalist garrison inhabited the walls until Cromwell's Scottish allies forced them to surrender in 1644. Although the castle avoided destruction, it was badly damaged.

Within twenty years of the Civil War, the eleventh and final Percy earl died. Two years later, his widow allowed Warkworth's raw materials to be quarried for the benefit of Chirton Hall, including some 272 cartloads from the keep. Though the pure Percy line had died out, a mid-eighteenth-century marriage between one Hugh Smithson and Lady Elizabeth Seymour – an indirect Percy heiress – saw the family name revived. With this unusual step of taking his wife's ancestral name, a second Percy dynasty was founded: one that would inherit the dukedom of Northumberland. During the lives of the pair's descendants, the decrepit walls enjoyed an Anthony Salvin-led overhaul, the highlight of which was the keep's restoration. In 1922, the eighth duke gifted the castle to the Office of Works. Sixty-two years later, it entered the preserve of English Heritage, in whose hands it remains to this day.

Uninhabited since the days of the original Percys, like many of England's beleaguered fortresses, Warkworth has gained a reputation as a romantic ruin. On a visit to the area around 1799, the crumbling walls attracted the interest of Turner, who painted the pre-Salvin castle. At that time, the curtain wall east of the gatehouse had been demolished, and the keep awaited restoration. Should the revered artist have toured the interior, he might well have been interested in the unique carvings on the walls, including those of Christ and his apostles. Captivated, he might also have been to view the Grey Mare's Tail Tower once used to house prisoners.

Yet of all the possible charms that awaited him, few compare with the castle's reputation for alleged hauntings. Among the most prominent is Margaret Neville, wife of Henry de Percy, 1st Earl of Northumberland, who appears as a lady in grey. Joining her is her famous son, Sir Henry Percy, better known as Harry Hotspur. Captured by the Scots at the Battle of Otterburn in 1388, Hotspur was successfully ransomed, after which he helped Henry IV claim the crown from Richard II. Influential in imposing a crushing defeat on the Scots at Homildon Hill in 1402, Hotspur's loyalty to the king turned to disillusionment. Among his grievances was his frustrations on being deprived of the ransoms due from his Scottish prisoners. After rebelling against the king, he was slain at the Battle of Shrewsbury in 1403.

Exactly how Hotspur died is the subject of conflicting accounts. The chronicle *Historia Anglicana*, written by Thomas Walsingham, stated, 'while he led his men in the fight rashly penetrating the enemy host, he was unexpectedly cut down, by whose hand is not known'. A differing account states that he was struck in the face by an arrow on opening his visor. Shakespeare's presentation that the prince of Wales, the future Henry V, killed him is fictitious.

On being shown the young rebel's body at the battle's end, the king is said to have wept. Around the time the body of his former friend was taken by Thomas Neville, 5th Baron Furnivall, to Whitchurch in Shropshire for burial, rumour abounded that Hotspur remained alive. To dispel the stories, the king had the corpse exhumed and displayed in Shrewsbury. His head was put on display in York, and his quartered body spread throughout the four corners before being returned to his widow. Eventually buried at York Minster, he was posthumously declared a traitor and the Percy lands forfeited until 1440.

Downed in battle more than six centuries ago, local lore states that Hotspur's ghost haunts the castle. He has been known to stare quietly from one of the windows, his eyes on the horizon. Eyewitnesses have reported that his mind is troubled, perhaps ruing the circumstances of his rebellion: how one destined for glory would instead be forced to suffer ignominy.

Joining Hotspur, a young man has been seen running along the walls. Though his identity is unknown, he appears to be carrying a message of some importance.

About half a mile from the castle is an ancient hermitage hewn in the rock on the wooded riverbank. Within lies a quaint chapel and basic quarters. Due to the area's seclusion, it can only be reached by boat.

The inhabitant of this isolated spot was Bertram de Bothal, who hailed from nearby Bothal Castle, which owed allegiance to Hotspur. A brave young man, Bothal fell for the charms of Lady Isabel Widdrington. Though fond of the young man, the lady requested further proof of his love. On presenting him with an engraved helmet, she asked that Bertram wear it in battle as a sign of his devotion.

Determined to prove himself, Bertram joined up with Hotspur's force that crossed into Scotland in 1402. The young man fought well but was severely injured, forcing his return to England. On hearing of his mishap, a distraught Isabel hastened to his aid; however, a week passed, and there remained no sign of her. Despite not being fully recovered, the wounded romantic set out to explore the borderlands.

Sure enough, not long passed until news reached Bertram that Isabel had become the prisoner of a local border raider. On reaching the castle in question, he kept watch from a nearby cave as he planned his next move. Two nights later, he awoke to watch a woman climb down a rope and embrace a man in tartan awaiting her. Bertram waited till the time was right and pounced on the unsuspecting man. After striking him hard, Isabel instinctively blocked a second swipe, which mortally wounded her. Only then did Bertram realise he had accidentally killed his love, who had been rescued by her brother – disguised as a Scot.

Heartbroken beyond words, Hotspur granted Bertram refuge at Warkworth. In a bid to make amends for his rashness, he gave up his possessions and built the hermitage. Local legend relates that his mortified spirit continues to haunt the area, ever tormented by his dreadful mistake. The story appears to originate from a ballad from 1771. In reality, the chapel predates Bertram's arrival. An insight into the young man's mindset can be found in an inscription he apparently engraved into the rock.

'My tears have been my meat, by day and by night.'

Chapter 18

Best of the Rest

Writing a book on the castles of England has been an enormous privilege. Not to mention a unique challenge. Due to limited space, including every story was sadly not possible. Nor every castle. The two appendices at the end of this book include a list of important castles from the Middle Ages, both royal and baronial. This section contains my best attempt at including some of the more exciting stories not present in the main section.

Constructed between 1379 and 1400, Powderham Castle in Devon is one of the oldest family homes in England. Another property of the Courtenays, it was built by Sir Philip Courtenay, a minor son of Hugh, the second earl of Devon, who played an influential role in the Hundred Years' War. While the main branch enjoyed the ancestral home at nearby Tiverton Castle, Powderham developed as the seat for the so-called 'cadet' line. Somewhat unsurprisingly, relations were often tense.

Debatable though it is that Powderham was anything more than a manor house – the appellation castle added for reasons of prestige – the presence of a curtain wall and the likely former presence of a barbican or bulwark as recorded by Leland is enough in this author's view to warrant its inclusion. Some 300 Royalists garrisoned the castle during the Civil War. The Parliamentarian stalwart, General Thomas Fairfax, tried unsuccessfully to capture it, following which Colonel Robert Hammond met with better success. On the restoration of the monarchy, the castle was returned to the family and is now their ancestral seat. Among the eighteenth-century additions was a long carpet, at the time reportedly the longest ever made. This stunning building is often open to the public and also the site of splendid concerts.

The medieval rooms within this ancient fortress have mostly survived intact. Among them are those of the Guard Tower, in which renovations revealed a shocking secret. After discovering that one of the walls was hollow, workers subsequently uncovered a secret room where a mother and her baby had been holed up. Precisely who the unfortunate pair were is unknown. A short time after, their remains were laid to rest in Powderham Church. The holy ceremony, local tales tell, was not enough to calm their restless spirits and their ghosts now haunt the area.

A second haunting is the ubiquitous lady in grey. Believed to be Lady Frances – wife of Viscount William Courtenay from 1741 until her death – she has been seen strolling between the castle and the church or frequenting the library. Tradition states that her appearance is a sign the head of the family is not long for this world.

A final footnote of some interest is that since the Middle Ages, the castle has reputedly been home to a unicorn's horn capable of detecting poison. So helpful was the rare artefact that should the horn be lowered into the poisonous liquid, the colour would change. The tale, of course, is too good to be true. The nine-foot horn is the tusk of a narwhal.

Close to the gorgeous Lulworth Cove near the village of Wool in Dorset, restored Lulworth Castle is a magnificent sight. Originally an early seventeenth-century hunting lodge, the owners transformed it into a fine country estate in the eighteenth century. The façade is different from practically every other castle in Britain, not least for the time. Often dubbed a revival-fortified castle, Lulworth was purposely built to recreate the aura of the Middle Ages and is now one of only five of its type from the Elizabethan or Jacobean era.

Despite enjoying a relatively peaceful existence, the history of the opulent building is surprisingly colourful. Gutted by fire in 1929, the castle has served chiefly as home to the Weld family. Family tradition tells that throughout their time there, the apparition of a grey lady has stalked them. Even more bizarrely, when the fire laid waste to the property, one of the estate workers was alarmed by the frantic cries of a woman from one of the burning rooms. On attempting to save her, he was shocked to learn that the floor had caved in sometime earlier.

Another of the castle's legends is a strange tale concerning one of the upstairs rooms. For reasons unknown, the room tended to glow brightly from the outside at night. Stranger still, investigations into the cause invariably came up with nothing. When the fed-up family decided to have it knocked down and rebuilt, the same phenomenon occurred. Completing the trilogy of intrigue, Sir Simon Marsden also recorded that a statue of a Roman soldier on a plinth in the nearby park would come to life around lunchtime and enter the castle for his food. An intriguing prospect indeed that standing around all day made of stone works up an appetite.

Like many of its Sussex counterparts, delightful Amberley played no role in England's history either before the Norman Conquest or during the ebb and flow of the Anarchy. Bishop William Reade of Chichester built the great curtain wall and gatehouse around 1377 on the site of an earlier hall after Richard II granted a licence to crenellate. Over the centuries, such impressive beginnings were built upon further. When the Dissolution changed the country's landscape, the property was requisitioned by the Crown. A century later, it suffered minor involvement in the Civil War. It has been claimed, among other places, that Charles II took a night's shelter after the Battle of Worcester before heading to Shoreham and a nine-year exile. Easier to verify are his two visits there as king. Purchased by the duke of Norfolk in 1893, the castle was last sold in 1989 and now operates as a hotel.

Beloved by past owners and modern guests alike for its beautiful setting and strong walls, at least one tale of tragedy is associated with the castle. Tradition states that a serving wench named Emily, believed to have been employed there during its early days, endured the cold shoulder of the resident bishop on falling pregnant with his child. Exactly which bishop was responsible is unclear. Stories also vary concerning her death during childbirth or committing suicide by jumping from the battlements. Reports tell of her walking the hallways or battlements, accompanied by maniacal laughter. Joining Emily is another maid, this time in Victorian dress, who appears in a far calmer state. Strange male voices have also been heard in the dead of night. The same is true of heavy footsteps, believed to be those of Cavalier soldiers.

Little now remains of Betchworth Castle. Lying on a sandstone spur overlooking the River Mole in Surrey, the castle was recorded in the *Domesday Book* as the seat of the manor of West Betchworth after beginning life as an earthworks fortress. Granted to Richard FitzAlan, Earl of Arundel, in 1373, it was rebuilt by his son in stone around 1378 before further development as a fortified house followed in 1448. In 1834, by which time a large mansion had been added, banking dynasty co-heir Henry Thomas Hope bought the remains and predominantly used it as a quarry. From this time onwards, the once impressive property became famed as something of a folly.

Despite experiencing a mostly uneventful history, Betchworth does have two legends. One concerns the haunting of a black dog that is said to stalk the ruins on moonlit nights. One of the Hopes is also said to roam the grounds, part of which is now a golf course. According to local legend, the errant lord accidentally killed his son, who he believed to be an intruder. There is no proof whatsoever that such an event occurred here.

The ruined walls of fifteenth-century Baconsthorpe, located in the Norfolk village of the same name, are believed to stand on the remains of a far older manor house. The present castle, whose iconic gatehouse and jagged stone walls are surrounded by rugged greenery and a murky moat, is believed to have been built by Sir John Heydon and his father, William. A lawyer of humble origins, John made many enemies, not least as he continuously switched sides in the Rose Wars. When the wars were over, his descendants fared far better, particularly his son, Sir Henry. After marrying a wealthy Londoner, Henry enjoyed life as a sheep farmer, the proceeds of which helped upgrade the property into an elegant country home with vast grounds that included a deer park.

By the end of the sixteenth century, a decline in the wool trade coupled with reckless spending forced them to mortgage the estate. This did not stop the creation of new formal gardens, complete with a shallow lake or wetland area. By the Civil War, the owner was the stout Royalist Sir John Heydon III, who parliament declared delinquent in 1646. The Royalists' fortunes of war equated closely with those of the family. When the war was over, the walls were partially destroyed for their stones. John died in debt in 1653, and the quarrying process continued under his son, Charles. The gatehouse was converted into a private residence and remained inhabited until the 1920s. It is now cared for by English Heritage.

Reached by the quiet back lanes of rural Norfolk, the castle possesses a wonderful tranquil nature: quite the place to pass the time without a care in the world. Such a pastime seems the way of its ghost, a harmless sentry who lobs pebbles into the moat. Over the years, many have reported seeing ripples appear in the moat, accompanied by the customary 'plopping' sound. On investigation, the sight of the sentry on the walls tossing stones is revealed as the culprit. Of all the hauntings mentioned in this book, the phantom idler lays claim to the crown of most harmless. An underground passage reputedly runs from below one of the turrets.

Excavations in modern times have revealed a drain that sends sewage into the moat. Unless that is the source of the tale, the tunnel is still to be found.

Once dubbed the 'lordship house', sixteenth-century Bruce Castle in Tottenham is one of England's oldest surviving brick-built dwellings. It is widely believed that the present house stands on the site of an older castle, forfeited by the House of Bruce on Robert the Bruce's accession to the throne of Scotland in 1306. The first owner is believed to have been Sir William Compton, groom of the stool to Henry VIII. An interesting mention from 1516 tells that Henry himself met sister Margaret 'at maister Compton's house beside Tottenham'. In the early 1800s, Bruce was the home of the renowned postal reformer Sir Rowland Hill and now holds the historical archives of the London borough of Haringey and a museum.

Though little of extremity appears to have dogged the castle, Lady Constantia is believed to have committed suicide there on 3 November 1680 due to her possessive husband, Lord Coleraine, locking her up. A further sad note is that she may have carried her young baby as she jumped from the balcony.

Precisely what transpired there is somewhat murky. Constantia's late husband confirmed she was buried in the local All Hallows Church, yet no burial record has survived. After her death, Coleraine married Sarah Alston, widow of the duke of Somerset, who died in 1675. As the pair wed soon after and were engaged years earlier, it has been conjectured that Constantia's death was linked to an affair between the two. The earliest recorded reference to Constantia's ghost was not until 1858. Reports also tell of echoing screams accompanying her apparition, which was said to appear on the balcony on the anniversary of her death. In the early twentieth century, a clergyman held a prayer service in her room, after which the screams reportedly ceased. There are also accounts of people being seen dressed in eighteenth-century costume and acting in the manner of a never-ending ball. Unlike Constantia, their identities remain a mystery.

Constructed by the justiciar of England, Geoffrey Fitz Peter, 1st Earl of Essex, in the twelfth century, Kimbolton Castle in Cambridgeshire became the property of Sir Richard Wingfield in 1522 before being sold to the first earl of Manchester, Sir Henry Montagu, in 1616. The seventeenth-century mansion served as the main family home for more than three centuries until the tenth duke sold it around 1950 to Kimbolton School.

The most famous of Kimbolton's ghosts is Catherine of Aragon, who took up residence following her divorce from Henry VIII. Just three weeks after her arrival, she played host to the bishop of Durham, who put to her the king's demand that she swear an oath acknowledging Henry as head of the church and Anne Boleyn as queen. To this, Catherine responded: 'Hold thy peace, bishop. These are the wiles of the devil. I am queen and queen I will die. By right, the king can have no other wife. Let this be your answer!' When the bishop warned her that refusal might result in her execution, she retorted: 'And who will be the hangman? If you have permission to execute this penalty on me, I am ready. I ask only that I be allowed to die in sight of the people.'

Life in the Fenlands did little to suit Catherine, and she died there on 7 January 1536. Later that evening, the castle's chandler carried out an autopsy and discovered to his horror her heart contained 'a black growth, all hideous to behold'. When he cut the heart open, it 'was black inside'. While academic consensus explains the development as a malignant tumour, others have speculated that she was poisoned. Much of the accusation concerned Anne Boleyn, something Henry himself found disturbing. At the time, Henry organised a ball to celebrate the diminished threat of war with Spain. There is also a disturbing story that Sir John Popham threw his newly born baby out of the window. Local legend claims that the stone on which it landed glows red on the anniversary. Another female ghost has been seen walking the field north-east of the castle.

A burnt-out shell is all that now stands of Astley Castle. Held by the Astley family since the twelfth century, the sixteenth-century fortified manor in North Warwickshire stands on the site of a far older manor. Records from 1266 confirm that Henry III granted the family a licence to crenellate; it is less clear whether anything more than a fortified manor house ever existed.

Due to its connection with the Grey family, Astley has an affinity with three former queens of England. The first was Elizabeth Wydville, whose first husband, Sir John Grey, owned the castle. Among Elizabeth's daughters with her second husband, Edward IV, was Elizabeth of York, queen consort of Henry VII. Completing the bizarre trinity, Frances Brandon, the granddaughter of Henry VII and Elizabeth of York, married her cousin, Henry Grey, Duke of Suffolk: a union that saw the birth of three sisters, including Lady Jane Grey.

Disgraced by a combination of the failed plans of John Dudley, 1st Duke of Northumberland, chief schemer in 1553 to put Lady Jane on the throne, and the ill-advised rebellion of Sir Thomas Wyatt, the castle was slighted and sold by the Crown. During the English Civil War, it served as a Parliamentarian base before being sold in 1674 to the Newdigate family, who maintained it until 1902.

Gutted by fire, neglected, its moat overgrown, a covering of trees now shields the crumbling red walls from easy view. Although the spirit of Lady Jane Grey appears to be absent from her former home, the ghost of her father, Henry Grey, 1st Duke of Suffolk, is believed to linger. Local legend tells that Suffolk spent three days hiding in a tree in the adjacent churchyard during Wyatt's rebellion before being betrayed by his groundskeeper. Later executed on Tower Hill, his headless ghost is alleged to wander the property where he encountered joy and fury.

Famously the ancestral seat of the earls of Durham, it is unlikely that a medieval castle ever existed where the nineteenth-century Lambton Castle now stands. Nevertheless, a strange story has survived. During the crusades, the heir to the lordship of Lambton was John Lambton – other sources say Henshaw. Regarded as something of a jack the lad, John was more of a fisherman than a churchgoer. Nor would the warnings of a local soothsayer convince him otherwise.

That was until one Sunday when John caught a hideous wormlike creature while out fishing. A second meeting with the doomsayer led to a severe warning that John had caught the devil himself, prompting John to dispose of the creature in the castle well. While John grew up to fight in the crusades, in the hidden depths, the demonic creature grew. Murmurs in the village claimed that the water had become poisoned, and livestock suffered. Mystified, the lord asked two servants to keep watch and recounted how the worm appeared in the dead of night. Some versions of the story also tell of it coiling itself around a local hill – either Worm Hill in Fatfield or Penshaw Hill on which the Penshaw Monument was erected in honour of John Lambton, 1st Earl of Durham around 1844.

Seven years after leaving for the crusades, John returned to an estate plagued by missing children and torn-up trees. Accepting his responsibility for the creature's reign of terror, John sought out the soothsayer and was advised to stud his armour with razor-sharp spears and knives. On being instructed to fight it in the river, he was told of the need to sacrifice the first living thing he then saw. The penalty for failure would be a curse on his family that nine generations would not die peacefully.

On discussing the instructions with his father and men, a plan was made to slaughter one of the castle dogs. With this, John set off and found the creature coiled up by the river. After an energy-sapping struggle, the bladed armour vanquished the serpent, and the river washed it away. Forgetting the plan, John's father emerged to great delight and the following nine generations were doomed to suffer.

So what exactly happened in Lambton all those years ago? Mention of the crusades, coupled with the known history of the early estate, may date the tale to the twelfth century. Yet traditionally, it is dated to the fourteenth century, which fits with the Lithuanian crusades of 1283–1410 or the Ottoman Crusades that occurred sporadically 1366–1481. Other possibilities include the crusade of Smyrniote 1343–51, the Alexandrian Crusade of 1365, or the Barbary Crusade of 1390. Intriguingly, later members of the Lambton family did meet with misfortune. One Robert Lambton drowned at Newrig. Sir William Lambton, a colonel of foot, lost his life at Marston Moor. A William Lambton also died in one of the Wakefield battles. On 26 June 1761, Henry Lambton suffered an injury when his carriage attempted to cross Lambton Bridge. Further to being celebrated in pantomime and song, Bram Stoker's 1911 novel, *The Lair of the White Worm*, has much in common with the story, while the Sockburn Worm, the Laidly Worm and the Worm of Linton all warn of similar threats.

Bellister in Northumberland is another prime example of an evolving castle. Now a nineteenth-century mansion in the care of the National Trust, the present building lies on a mount on which a motte and bailey probably stood. In the century after its acquisition by Robert de Ros around 1191, a moated manor house existed on the site. In the century after the family's departure in 1295, a fourteenth-century tower was constructed to the western end, thus confirming the manor house's upgrade to castle status.

A survey from 1541 confirms that Bellister was the property of the Blenkinsop family – whose chief seat was Blenkinsop Castle – and in a 'measurable good' state. After the family sold their broader portfolio in 1697, it was upgraded to a three-storey castellated house, after which the architect John Dobson oversaw a period of rebuilding, beginning in 1826. Among the additions was a castellated east front. Refurbishment also followed fire damage from around 1900.

Primarily a familial residence, Bellister has attracted few war stories. A tree in the west part of the grounds was apparently used for executing Cavaliers during the Civil War. Most prominent among Bellister's legends is that of the grey man. Tradition tells that a minstrel visited the castle during the residency of Lord John Blenkinsopp, who purchased it around 1480. After the minstrel sang for his supper, Lord Blenkinsopp suspected the stranger of ulterior motives. On instructing his men to keep watch, the minstrel's sneaking out instead of retiring to his bed confirmed his fears. His men tracked him to the banks of the Tyne, where their dogs tore him limb from limb.

The old lord may have been correct in his suspicions, but his troubles were not at an end. For the remainder of his life, legend tells that Blenkinsopp was forced to endure the musician's vengeful wraith. Tales continue to circulate that the old man's screams have been heard at the castle. The same is true of the noise of a hound attack. In such ways, Bellister may offer a strange twist on the story – that the phantom cries are from one terrified on coming face to face with a ghost.

Newcastle's Black Gate is a notable feature in the modern city centre. Added by Henry III 1247–50, this fortified gatehouse is one of two components of Newcastle Castle. The other, the keep, dates back about seventy years further to the reign of Henry II. Evidence suggests Henry II's choice of master mason was the same man he had earmarked for Dover Castle, recorded merely as 'Maurice the Engineer'. It was this 'New Castle' that lent the city its name.

A Roman settlement, *Pons Aelius* – Bridge of Aelius – was built across the Tyne in the mid-second century, along with a fort. In 1080, Robert Curthose, eldest son of William the Conqueror and brother of both William Rufus and Henry I, erected a timber motte and bailey on his return from the campaign against Malcolm III of Scotland. The fortifications proved helpful when Robert de Mowbray, Earl of

Northumbria, rose against Rufus in 1095, at which point the Crown gained the castle. It was also there where the two Henrys replaced the earlier work, including the Roman fort and seventh-century Saxon cemetery. Both stone fortifications were already in place when the town wall was built in the 1260s.

Ironically, it was those same outer walls that led to the castle's neglect. By the 1590s, it was in a ruinous condition. Over the next century, urban sprawl and the development of shops and houses on the site saw its condition worsen further. Only in 1643 did the Royalist mayor, Sir John Marley, carry out essential repairs of the keep and attempt to refortify the walls. Invaders came in the form of the Scots a year later, who besieged the city for three months before finally securing its surrender on 19 October. Like the castles in Norwich, Oxford, Lincoln and Lancaster, it then served primarily as a gaol for prisoners of war, local felons and debtors. Meanwhile, the number of houses within the site continued to increase until their demolition in 1809. The castle was then sold to a private company, and the Black Gate leased out to the Society of Antiquaries of Newcastle-Upon-Tyne.

Often viewed as a place of incarceration instead of protection, the Black Gate has long held a reputation as being haunted. Echoing footsteps, ghostly chanting, strange lights and eerie mists are just some of the unexplained happenings for which the site has become famed. The queen's chamber, in the keep, is viewed with particular apprehension, not least due to the chanting. The ghost of a woman has also been seen there and in the chapel.

The most famous spirit said to inhabit the former castle is 'Poppy the flower girl'. Tradition tells that the poor girl was imprisoned due to her debts and badly beaten by the unruly incarcerates. Her ghost is most commonly seen on the stairway, before which a soothing fragrance permeates. A harmless spirit, her tragic ghost is viewed as a likeable one for spreading warmth and love in an area in which the feeling was often lacking.

Close to the village of Humshaugh on the west bank of the North Tyne, Haughton is another great fortress that began life as a simple manor. Like nearby Featherstone, the original mansion was rebuilt as a thirteenth-century tower house and expanded and fortified in the following century. Initially owned by the Widdrington family, and later the Swinburnes, by the sixteenth century, the castle's condition had already deteriorated. A regular victim of so-called 'Border Reivers' – gangs of criminals who plagued the border regions until the unification of Britain – in 1541, a report into its condition confirmed that the building's floor and the roof had decayed. Purchase in 1640 by the Smith family failed to save it from being described as ruinous in a further survey conducted in 1715.

Haughton's fortunes changed for the better under the guidance of renowned architect John Dobson and restorer Anthony Salvin. Local legend tells that the castle served as the inspiration for the famed local song 'Waters of Tyne'; however, this is difficult to prove. Similar is true of the castle's ghost story. On being captured in the reign of Henry VIII, clan leader Archie Armstrong was accidentally left to starve in the dungeons, as Cardinal Wolsey had summoned the owner, Sir Thomas Swinburne, to York. On realising his critical error, he returned to find the Scot dead. Local legend tells that the hungry captive had gnawed on his arm and that an exorcism was required to quieten his ghost.

A stone's throw from the Lake District, Penrith Castle dates from around 1397. Most likely built on the site of a Roman encampment, Penrith was another of those stout defensive fortresses constructed to repel the Scots, who razed the town in 1345. Held by the Neville family, the castle fell to the Crown after Richard Neville, 16th Earl of Warwick died without a male heir: two of his daughters famously married the younger brothers of Edward IV. In the Civil War, Penrith was initially royalist before its capture by the roundheads, after which it served as the HQ of General Lambert. Like many of England's castles, the war caused considerable damage, and parliamentary orders led to its dismantling.

Nearly a century on, a strange story came to light of a farm labourer espying ghostly soldiers marching close to the castle on Midsummer's Eve 1735. Over the years, several more saw the army on the same date, which seemingly increased in size. The ghostly forces' identity has never been solved.

Lying on the banks of Cumbria's River Eden, the red-sandstone tower house near the village of Great Corby is thought to date to the thirteenth century. Formerly the prime residence of the Howard family who acquired the castle in 1611, Corby avoided the bloodshed endured by many other English castles in the north. It was remodelled in the nineteenth century and incorporated the fourteenth-century Pele-Tower, also known as 'the old castle'. Lots of impressive statues litter the grounds, in which a cascade takes water down to the river.

Just a casual look at Corby is enough to conjure up images of Dickensian-style plots or Edgar Alan Poe horrors. Indeed, accounts passed down tell of an apparition perhaps more famous than any other in the country. Overlooking the main court and reachable via a narrow passageway, the so-called 'haunted room' isn't used very often. Prior to its sale in 1994, ancient tapestries and portraits of deceased members of the Howard family accompanied strange figures carved into the antique wood. Despite the gloomy atmosphere, many guests are known to have slept there. At least one complained of having been awaken by the spectre of a child.

Described as a beautiful boy with long locks of pure blond hair and dressed in a white nightshirt, the 'radiant boy' has been reported at many castles. Although rarely seen, sightings of the apparition are rightly met with a degree of anxiety. In the case of Corby, the boy's appearance is said to serve as a prelude to the acquisition by the witnesses of a vast fortune before ending their lives in violent circumstances.

Described by one Mrs Crowe in her 1848 book, *The Night Side of Nature*, the apparition was witnessed by one Reverend Henry Redburgh, Rector of Greystoke, and his wife who stayed at the castle in the autumn of 1803:

> Soon after we went to bed, we fell asleep; it might be between one and two in the morning when I awoke. I observed that the fire was totally extinguished; but, although that was the case, and we had no light, I saw a glimmer in the centre of the room, which suddenly increased to a bright flame. I looked out, apprehending that something had caught fire, when, to my amazement, I beheld a beautiful boy, clothed in white, with bright locks resembling gold, standing by my bedside, in which position he remained some minutes, fixing his eyes upon me with a mild and benevolent expression. He then glided gently towards the side of the chimney, where it is obvious there is no possible egress, and entirely disappeared. I found myself again in total darkness, and all remained quiet until the usual hour of rising. I declare this to be a true account of what I saw at Corby Castle, upon my word as a clergyman.

Although the ghost is associated with subsequent fortune and horror, the rector was never cursed by the so-called prophecy. Intriguingly, another member of the Howard family at a different estate would recount a different story. Captain Robert Stewart, a Howard and later Lord Castlereagh, was a humble captain when he saw the boy while attending a hunting party in Northern Ireland in the 1790s. In later life, the future lord served as a war minister in William Pitt the Younger's cabinet before slitting his own throat aged 53 after suffering bouts of insanity.

The origins of the radiant boy remain one of the great mysteries of British lore. According to one explanation, the child comes from a German tradition of 'Kindermorderinn': children murdered by their mothers. The apparitions are commonly associated with Northumberland and Cumberland, where German settlers lived in the distant past. Since the rector's visit, there have been no confirmed sightings of the ghost of Corby Castle. With the prophecy unfulfilled, perhaps peace has finally come to the murdered child.

The fourteenth-century moated manor house near the village of Dacre in Cumbria is rare in England. Owned by the Dacre family until the seventeenth century, the 66-foot-tall Sandstone tower house was a helpful site for defence against raiders from the north. On the death of Randal Dacre in 1634, the Crown briefly claimed the castle until Thomas Lennard, Lord Dacre, restored it around 1675. After he died in 1715, the castle was sold to the Hassell family, under whose ownership its fortunes declined. In modern times, it has undergone a period of restoration, including a state visit in 1967 from the daughter of the King of Nepal.

During the fifteenth century, the young heir, Sir Guy Dacre, reputedly fell in love with Eloise, the daughter of a French nobleman – a friend of his father. Before going off to war with Scotland, Sir Guy persuaded his friend, an Italian tutor, to help woo her. Though seemingly successful, in his absence, Eloise had an affair with the tutor. When Guy came back, she agreed to marry him. Only when he set off to fight a second time did he learn of their illicit relationship. Consequently, Guy imprisoned Eloise in the dungeon, in which the Italian tutor was already chained up. When she tried to kiss him, the tutor's head rolled to the floor, and the cramped conditions drove her to the point of madness.

Eloise and her lover are not the only ghosts said to haunt Dacre. The second floor of the keep consists of a single chamber, in which a priest hole was discovered behind a fireplace. The room is known locally as the 'Room of the Three Kings' to commemorate an old legend conjectured by the prominent twelfth-century chronicler, William of Malmesbury, that Dacre was the site of a meeting between three ancient kings: Constantine III of Scotland, Owain ap Dyfnwal, King of Strathclyde and Æthelstan, King of the English, concerning a peace treaty. Used due to its location of geographical convenience, the conference proved unsuccessful. Local lore tells that their ghosts return on the anniversary of the meeting, attempting in vain to secure peace from beyond the grave.

During the late seventeenth century, the first Viscount Lonsdale, John Lowther, ordered the rebuilding of Lowther Hall on a grand scale. This was surpassed between 1806 and 1814 by a castellated mansion on the designs of the English architect Robert Smirke, for 1st earl, William Lowther.

As the following years would show, a combination of grand ambition and reckless spending would bring about the rise and fall of an elegant and ostentatious mansion, yet also the creation and loss of some of the most extensive gardens that England has ever seen. At its height, the estate was a regular haunt for artists, including Turner. Under the fifth and final earl, whose unthrifty ways led the estate to ruin, the castle became something of a socialite's paradise. Welcomed within the walls were the kings of Italy and Portugal, an actress and alleged mistress of Edward VII, and, perhaps most famously, Kaiser Wilhelm I, whose visit in 1895 to shoot grouse saw the imperial flag fly in his honour. In World War I, the earl helped found the Blue Cross animal welfare organisation and had a Pals Battalion, most of whom were killed on the Somme.

Lowther is also home to a legend unlike any other. The strange tale concerns Sir James Lowther – wicked Jimmy – who inherited the hall in 1784. Although married, the story goes that he fell in love with a local farmer's daughter, who tragically died young. Determined to hold on to his lost love, Sir Jimmy kept the body, even bringing it to dinner. At other times, he kept her in a glass coffin. This despicable charade continued for some time until he moved her to another of his properties: Maulds Meaburn Hall. Following her eventual burial, the heartbroken laird took long walks alone and neglected his duties to the point wild horses ran free across the estate. Legend says that in 1802, his coffin swung violently during the burial. His ghost driving a phantom coach also reputedly appears in the long driveway.

Thanks to the Lowther Estate Trust, since 2011, much progress has been made. The ruins remain standing, and the grounds are a lush green. Yet, it is a sad thought that the once magnificent gardens are now lost. Only the occasional illustration and description survives of what was once a paradise of Edenic proportions. With this, Lowther leaves us with something of a puzzle. James Lowther was only too correct when he pointed out that the castle 'was a place that exemplified gross imperial decadence during a period of abject poverty'. Such things being said, praise can also be reserved for the creativity that surrounded them. As the British statesman, George, 1st Earl Macartney, commented in 1793 when visiting the summer retreat of the Chinese emperor in Chengde:

> If any place in England can be said in any respect to have similar features to the western park, which I have seen this day, it is Lowther Hall in Westmoreland, which (when I knew it many years ago) from the extent of prospect, the grand surrounding objects, the noble situation, the diversity of surface, the extensive woods, and command of water, I thought might be rendered by a man of sense, spirit, and taste, the finest scene in the British dominions.

Postscript

'What a realm will England be when his grace hath set walls according to the ditches that run round about us. England will then be much like a castle than a realm.'

So wrote Richard Morrison, Henry VIII's ambassador to the German court, in 1539. Morrison was also the protégé of chief minister Thomas Cromwell, who oversaw the creation of more than twenty new fortresses on the coast to help combat the threat of foreign navies. One can easily see that there was wisdom in Morrison's words. Though the age of gunpowder had required an evolution in military engineering, as the following century would show, this new breed of castle would help ensure England never again fell victim to foreign invaders.

For the inland castles, it was a different story. By the 1650s, the Roundheads had slighted more than 100 castles and fortified towns in England. As Oliver Cromwell had come to learn, the process was no easy task. The workforce and expertise needed made it almost as complicated as building them. Parliament was constantly at odds over which castles should be slighted and which continue to be used. A single vote shot down a parliamentary debate to break down Windsor Castle.

How perilous the castle's position in England had become.

Thank you for reading. Researching and writing about these magnificent fortresses has been an immense pleasure. In truth, I could easily have written a book three times longer. The *Castellarium Anglicanum*, published in 1983 and perhaps the most authoritative index of castles in England ever compiled, made the bold claim that more than 1,500 castle sites can be found in England alone. In some cases, these once mighty fortresses no longer exist. For example, Henry III's great hall of Winchester Castle is all that remains of one of the most important fortresses of the age. Famous in the modern-day for Edward I's mock round table, created for a tournament around 1280, the hall is a rare survivor of a former royal residence obliterated by Cromwell. Impressive castles such as Bristol, Gloucester and Northampton were also destroyed to make way for railways or other modern buildings.

While some have left no trace, many still exist in their entirety. Including every castle in this book was sadly not possible. For this reason, some genuinely spectacular fortresses have been left out. For those of you who were hoping to read about the castles located in what were historically the Welsh Marches – Goodrich and Ludlow, for example – rest assured, these will be included in *Castles of Wales*.

Throughout our journey exploring the castles of England, many aspects repeat themselves. The same is true of certain stories. That said, no two are ever exactly alike. We all have our favourite castle. Be it the picturesque ruins or the preserved stately home, it matters not. Regardless of how their journey ended, assuming it has ended, the impact of all of these fine fortresses on England's history will always be worthy of memory. Many gave rise to the cities of medieval England. Indeed, for every castle built in England, a church would precede or follow: if not an abbey, priory or cathedral. With this, we have also faced one of history's great mysteries. Why some thrived while others fell into ruin, if not vanished altogether.

Thanks to the collective efforts of many devoted people and organisations, the preservation of many castles can almost be taken for granted. I, for one, hope this never ends. By preserving the castles of England, we are keeping alive not only an essential part of England's history but part of the souls of those who lived within them. In this author's view, there is a unique beauty in England's castles – particularly the ruins. As Reverend William Gilpin, the man who coined the term 'picturesque', rightly said:

> After all that art can bestow, you must put your ruin at last into the hands of nature to finish. If the mosses and lychens grow unkindly on your walls – if the streaming weather-stains have produced no variety of tints – if the ivy refuses to mantle over your buttress; or to creep among the ornaments of your Gothic window – if the ash cannot be brought to hang from the cleft; or long, spiry grass to wave over the shattered battlement – your ruin will still be incomplete – you may as well write over the gate, Built in the year 1772. Deception there can be none. The characters of age are wanting. It is time alone, which meliorates the ruin; which gives it perfect beauty and brings it, if I may so speak, to a state of nature.

Appendix A

Royal Castles in the Middle Ages

Bamburgh, Northumberland
Bedford, Bedfordshire
Berkhamsted, Hertfordshire
Bolsover, Derbyshire
Bridgnorth, Shropshire
Bristol, South-West
Bytham, Lincolnshire
Cambridge, Cambridgeshire
Canterbury, Kent
Carlisle, Cumbria
Chichester, Sussex
Colchester, Essex
Corfe Castle, Dorset
Devizes, Wiltshire
Dover, Kent
Exeter, Devon
Fotheringhay, Northamptonshire
Gloucester, Gloucestershire
Guildford, Surrey
Haughley, Suffolk
Hedingham, Essex
Hereford, Herefordshire
Hertfort, Hertfordshire
Kenilworth, Warwickshire
Knaresborough, Yorkshire
Lancaster, Lancashire
Launceston, Cornwall
Lincoln, Lincolnshire

Marlborough, Wiltshire
Newcastle, Tyne and Wear
Norham, Northumberland
Northampton, Northamptonshire
Norwich, Norfolk
Nottingham, Nottinghamshire
Odiham, Hampshire
Orford, Suffolk
Oxford, Oxfordshire
Peveril, Derbyshire
Pickering, Yorkshire
Portchester, Hampshire
Rochester, Kent
Rockingham, Northamptonshire
Salisbury (Old Sarum), Wiltshire
Sauvey, Leicestershire
Scarborough, Yorkshire
Sherborne, Dorset
Shrewsbury, Shropshire
Southampton, Hampshire
Tower of London, Middlesex
Wallingford, Oxfordshire
Winchester, Hampshire
Windsor, Berkshire
Wolvesey, Hampshire
Worcester, Worcestershire
York (Clifford's Tower), Yorkshire

Appendix B

Important Private Castles in the Middle Ages

Alnwick, Northumberland
Barnstable, Somerset
Beeston, Cheshire
Berkeley, Gloucestershire
Bolingbroke, Lincolnshire
Chartley, Staffordshire
Chester, Cheshire
Cockermouth, Cumbria
Conisborough, Yorkshire
Durham, County Durham
Egremont, Cumbria
Farnham, Surrey
Folkingham, Lincolnshire
Framlingham, Essex
Harbottle, Northumberland
Helmsley, Yorkshire
Kimbolton, Cambridgeshire
Knepp, Sussex
Lewes, Sussex
Mitford, Northumberland
Mountsorrel, Leicestershire

Newark, Nottinghamshire
Newbury, Berkshire
Newcastle-under-Lyne, Staffordshire
Plympton, Devon
Prudhoe, Tyne and Wear
Rayleigh, Essex
Richmond, Yorkshire
Sandal, Yorkshire
Sleaford, Lincolnshire
Sheriff Hutton, Yorkshire
Skipsea, Yorkshire
Skipton, Yorkshire
Stogursey, Somerset
Sudeley, Gloucestershire
Tickhill, Yorkshire
Tonbridge, Kent
Totnes, Devon
Trowbridge, Wiltshire
Tutbury, Staffordshire
Wormegay, Norfolk

Bibliography

AA, *Exploring Britain's Castles*, Basingstoke: AA Publishing, 2011
——, *Treasures of Britain and Treasures of Ireland*, London: Drive Publications Ltd, 1968
Abrahams, Paul and Marc Alexander, *In Search of Britain's Haunted Castles*, Stroud: The History Press, 2011
Alexander, Marc, *Phantom Britain*, London: Muller, 1975
Arnold, Neil and Kevin Payne, *Haunted Rochester*, Stroud: The History Press, 2011
Ashe, Geoffrey, *Mythology of the British Isles*, York: Methuen Publishing, 1990
Barlow, Frank, *William Rufus*, New Haven and London: Yale University Press, 2000
Bartlett, Robert, *England Under the Angevin Kings 1075–1225*, Oxford: Oxford University Press, 2000
——, *The Making of Europe: Conquest, Colonization and Cultural Change, 950–1350*, Harmondsworth: Allen Lane, 1993
Beer, Anna, *Patriot or Traitor: The Life and Death of Sir Walter Raleigh*, London: OneWorld Publications, 2018
Borman, Tracy, *Henry VIII and the Men who Made Him: The Secret History Behind the Tudor Throne*, London: Hodder & Stoughton, 2018
——, *Thomas Cromwell: The Untold Story of Henry VIII's Most Faithful Servant*, London: Hodder & Stoughton, 2014
Bradbury, Jim, *Stephen and Matilda: The Civil War of 1139–53*, Stroud, Gloucestershire: The History Press, 2005
Brooks, J.A., *Ghosts and Legends of the Peak District*, Peterborough: Jarrold Publishing, 1991
Brown, R. Allen, *English Castles*, London: B.T. Batsford, 1976
Camm, Bede, *Forgotten Shrines: An Account of Some Old Catholic Halls and Families in England and of Relics and Memorials of the English Martyrs*, London: MacDonald & Evans, 1910
Carpenter, D.A., *Henry III*, New Haven: Yale University Press, 2020
——, *The Minority of Henry III*, Berkeley and Los Angeles: University of California Press, 1990
——, *The Struggle for Mastery: Britain 1066–1284*, Oxford: Oxford University Press, 2003
Cathcart, King, D.J., *Castellarium Anglicanum: An Index and Bibliography of the Castles in England, Wales and the Islands: Vols 1-2*, London & New York: Kraus International Publications, 1983

Chandler, David, *Sedgemoor 1685: From Monmouth's Invasion to the Bloody Assizes* (Spellmount Classics), Staplehurst: Spellmount, 1999
Chandler, John, *John Leland's Itinerary: Travels in Tudor England*, Stroud: Alan Sutton, 1993
Clancy, Michael, *England and its Rulers*, Oxford: Oxford University Press, 1998
Clarke, David, *Ghosts and Legends of the Peak District*, London: Jarrold Publishing, 1991
Cogswell, Thomas, *James I (Penguin Monarchs): The Phoenix King*, London: Phoenix, 2017
Curran, Bob, *Lost Lands, Forgotten Realms: Sunken Continents, Vanished Cities, and the Kingdoms that History Misplaced*, Franklin Lakes, New Jersey: New Page Books, 2007
Danziger, Danny, Gillingham, John, *1215: The Year of Magna Carta*, London: Hodder and Stoughton, 2004
Davis, John Paul, *A Hidden History of the Tower of London: England's Most Notorious Prisoners*, Barnsley: Pen&Sword History, 2020
———, *King John, Henry III and England's Lost Civil War*, Barnsley: Pen&Sword History, 2021
———, *The Gothic King: A Biography of Henry III*, London and Chicago: Peter Owen Publishers, 2013
———, *Robin Hood: The Unknown Templar*, Peter Owen, 2009
———, *Pity for the Guy: A Biography of Guy Fawkes*, London and Chicago: Peter Owen Publishers, 2010
Dunne, John J., *Folklore, Myths and Legends of Britain*, London: Readers Digest Association Ltd, 1977
Edwards, John, *Mary I: England's Catholic Queen* (The English Monarchs Series), New Haven and London: Yale University Press, 2011
Fissel, Mark Charles, *The Bishops' Wars: Charles I's Campaigns Against Scotland 1638–1640*, Cambridge: Cambridge University Press, 1994
Foss, Arthur, *Country House Treasures*, London: Book Club Associates, 1980
Fraser, Antonia, *Cromwell, Our Chief Of Men*, London: Phoenix, 2002
———, *The Gunpowder Plot: Terror and Faith in 1605*, London: Phoenix, 2002
———, *King Charles II*, London: Phoenix, 2002
———, *Mary, Queen of Scots*, London: W&N, 2018
———, *The Six Wives of Henry VIII*, London: Phoenix, 2002
Fry, Plantagenet Somerset, *Castles: England, Scotland, Wales, Ireland: The Definitive Guide to the Most Impressive Buildings and Intriguing Sites*, Newton Abbot: David & Charles, 2001
Gascoigne, Christina, and Gascoigne, Bamber, *Castles of Britain*, London: Book Club Associates, 1976
Giles, J.A., *The Life and Times of Alfred the Great*, London: George Bell, 1848
———, *Matthew Paris's English History from the Year 1235 to 1273*, Vols 1-3, London: Henry. G. Bohn, 1852–4
———, *Roger of Wendover's Flowers of History, Comprising the History of England from the Descent of the Saxons to AD 1235*, Vols 1–2, London: Henry. G. Bohn, 1849

Gillingham, John, *Richard I* (The English Monarchs Series), New Haven and London: Yale University Press, 1999

———, *The Wars of the Roses: Peace and Conflict in Fifteenth Century England*, London: Phoenix, 2001

Hallam, Dr Elizabeth (General Editor), *Chronicles of the Age of Chivalry: The Plantagenet dynasty from 1216 to 1377: Henry III and the Three Edwards, the Era of the Black Prince and the Black Death*, London: Salamander Books Ltd., 2002

———, *The Plantagenet Chronicles: Medieval Europe's Most Tempestuous Family, Henry II and His Wife, Eleanor of Aquitaine, Richard the Lionheart, and His Brother King John, Seen Through the Eyes of Their Contemporaries*, London: Salamander Books Ltd., 2002

Hamilton, Dave, *Wild Ruins: The Explorer's Guide to Britain's Lost Castles, Follies, Relics and Remains*, Bath: Wild Things Publishing, 2015

Hesketh, Robert, *Writers' Walks on the Cornish Coast*, Otley: Bossiney Books, 2019

Hicks, Michael, *Richard III*, Stroud: Tempus, 2003

Higham, Robert and Philip Barker, *Timber Castles*, Exeter: University of Exeter Press, 2004

Hogge, Alice, *God's Secret Agents: Queen Elizabeth's Forbidden Priests and the Hatching of the Gunpowder Plot*, London: Harper Perennial, 2009

Holt, J.C., *Magna Carta*, Cambridge: Cambridge University Press, 1965

———, *The Northerners: A Study in the Reign of King John*, Oxford: Oxford University Press, 1961

Horspool, David, *The English Rebel: One Thousand Years of Trouble-making from the Normans to the Nineties*, London: Viking, 2009

Hume, David, *History of England from the Invasion of Julius Caesar to the Abdication of James the Second*, Vol. III, Boston, MA: Phillips, Sampson & Co, 1858

Hunt, Tristram, *The English Civil War At First Hand*, London: Phoenix, 2003

Hutchinson, Robert, *House of Treason: The Rise and Fall of a Tudor Dynasty*, London: Phoenix, 2009

Jeake, Samuel, *Charters of the Cinque Ports: Two Ancient Towns and Their Members*, Bernard Lintot, 1728

Jenkins, Simon, *A Short History of England*, London: Profile Books, 2012

Johnson, Matthew, *Behind the Castle Gate: From Medieval to Renaissance*, London: Routledge, 2002

Johnson, Paul, *The National Trust Book of British Castles*, London: Book Club Associates, 1978

Jones, Dan, *The Hollow Crown: The Wars of the Roses and the Rise of the Tudors*, London: Faber & Faber, 2015

———, *Magna Carta: The Making and Legacy of the Great Charter*, London: Head of Zeus Ltd., 2014

———, *The Plantagenets: The Kings Who Made England*, London: HarperCollins Publishers, 2012

———, *Summer of Blood: The Peasants' Revolt of 1381*, London: HarperCollins Publishers, 2010
Jones, Richard, *Haunted Castles of Britain and Ireland*, London: New Holland, 2003
———, *Myths and Legends of Britain and Ireland*, London: New Holland, 2006
Keay, Anna, *The Last Royal Rebel: The Life and Death of James, Duke of Monmouth*, London: Bloomsbury, 2016
Keen, Maurice (ed.), *Medieval Warfare: A History*, Oxford: Oxford University Press, 1999
Kenyon, John, *The Popish Plot*, London: Phoenix Press, 2000
Kinross, John, *Discovering Castles in England and Wales*, Princes Risborough: Shire Publications Ltd, 1995
Lander, J. R., *The Wars of the Roses*, Stroud, Gloucestershire: Sutton, 2000
London, Pete, *Castles of Cornwall and the Isles of Scilly*, Redruth, Cornwall: Tor Mark, 2014
Luard, Henry Richards, *Annales Monastici, Vols I–V*, Longmans, Green, Reader & Dyer, 1866–73
Macculloch, Diamaid, *Thomas Cranmer: A Life*, New Haven and London: Yale University Press, 2016
Maddicott, J.R., *Simon de Montfort*, Cambridge, MA: Cambridge University Press, 1994
Marsden, Sir Simon, *The Haunted Realm: Ghosts, Witches and Other Strange Tales*, Exeter: Webb and Bower, 1986
———, *Phantoms of the Isles: Further Tales from The Haunted Realm*, London: Guild Publishing, 1990
———, *This Spectred Isle: A Journey Through Haunted England*, London: English Heritage, 2005
Mason, Emma, *William II: Rufus, the Red King*, Stroud, Gloucestershire: Tempus, 2005
Mason, John, *Haunted Heritage*, London: Collins and Brown, 1999
Maurer, Helen E., *Margaret of Anjou: Queenship and Power in Late Medieval England*, London: Boydell Press, 2005
McLynn, Frank, *1066: The Year of Three Battles*, London: Pimlico, 2005
———, *Lionheart & Lackland, King Richard, King John and the Wars of Conquest*, London: Vintage Books, 2007
Miller, John, *James II* (The English Monarchs Series), New Haven and London: Yale University Press, 2000
Montgomery, J.G., *Haunted Castles of England: A Tour of 99 Ghostly Fortresses*, Woodbury, Minnesota: Llewellyn Worldwide, 2018
Moorhouse, Geoffrey, *The Pilgrimage of Grace: The Rebellion that Shook King Henry VIII's Throne*, London: Phoenix, 2003
Morris, Marc, *Castle: A History of the Buildings that Shaped Medieval Britain*, London: Windmill Books, 2012
———, *A Great and Terrible King: Edward I and the Forging of Britain*, London: Windmill Books, 2009

——, *King John: Treachery, Tyranny and the Road to Magna Carta*, London: Windmill Books, 2016
——, *Kings and Castles*, London: Endeavour Press, 2018
——, *The Norman Conquest*, London: Windmill Books, 2013
Mortimer, Ian, *The Fears of Henry IV: The Life of England's Self-Made King*, London: Vintage, 2008
——, *The Greatest Traitor: The Life of Sir Roger Mortimer*, London: Vintage, 2010
——, *The Perfect King: The Life of Edward III, Father of the English Nation*, London: Vintage Books, 2008
——, *The Time Traveller's Guide to Medieval England*, Vintage, 2009
Mortimer, Richard, *Angevin England 1154–1258*, Oxford: Blackwell, 1994
Nicolle, David, *Medieval Siege Weapons: Western Europe AD 585–1385*, Oxford: Osprey Publishing, 2002
Pearse, B., *Ghost Hunters Casebook: The Investigations of Andrew Green*, Stroud: The History Press, 2007
Penn, Thomas, *Winter King: The Dawn of Tudor England*, London: Penguin Books, 2012
Pettifer, Adam, *English Castles: A Guide by Counties*, Woodbridge: Boydell Press, 1995
Plowden, Alison, *Lady Jane Grey: Nine Days Queen (Classic Histories Series)*, Stroud: The History Press, 2016
Pollard, A.J., *Richard III and the Princes in the Tower*, Stroud: Alan Sutton, 1991
——, *The Wars of the Roses (British History in Perspective)*, Basingstoke: Palgrave MacMillan, 2013
Powicke, Maurice, *King Henry III and the Lord Edward*, Vols 1-2, Oxford: Clarendon Press, 1947
——, *The Oxford History of England: The Thirteenth Century 1216–1377*, Oxford: Clarendon Press, 1962
Prestwich, Michael, *Edward I* (Yale English Monarchs), New Haven and London: Yale University Press, 1997
Prestwich, Michael, Britnell, Richard, and Frame, Robin, *Thirteenth Century England X*, Woodbridge: Boydell Press, 2005
Purkiss, Diane, *The English Civil War: A People's History*, London: Harper Perennial, 2007
Readers Digest, *The Most Amazing Places of Folklore & Legend in Britain*, London: Vivat Direct Ltd, 2011
Reese, Peter, *The Life of General George Monck: For King and Cromwell*, Barnsley: Pen & Sword Military, 2008
Rex, Peter, *1066: A New History of the Norman Conquest*, Stroud: Amberley Publishing, 2011
Ritson, Darren W., *Paranormal County Durham*, Stroud: Amberley Publishing, 2012
Ross, Charles, *Edward IV* (The English Monarchs Series), New Haven and London: Yale University Press, 1997

Saul, Nigel, *Richard II* (The English Monarchs Series), New Haven and London: Yale University Press, 1999
Seward, Desmond, *A Brief History of the Wars of the Roses*, London: Robinson, 2007
——, *The Last White Rose: The Secret Wars of the Tudors*, London: Constable, 2010
——, *Richard III: England's Black Legend*, London: Thistle Publishing, 2013
Skidmore, Chris, *Bosworth: The Birth of the Tudors*, London: Weidenfeld & Nicolson, 2013
——, *Edward VI: The Lost King of England*, London: Phoenix, 2008
Soden, Iain, *Ranulf de Blondeville: The First English Hero*, Stroud: Amberley, 2009
Somerset, Anne, *Elizabeth I* (Women in History), London: Phoenix, 1997
——, *Unnatural Murder: Poison at the Court of James I*, London: Phoenix, 1998
Spencer, Charles, *Killers of the King: The Men Who Dared to Execute Charles I*, London: Bloomsbury, 2014
Stoughton, John, *Windsor: A History and Description of the Castle and the Town*, Ward & Co, 1862
Swanton, Michael (ed.), *The Anglo-Saxon Chronicles*, London: Dent, 1996
Thompson, M.W., *The Decline of the Castle*, Cambridge: Cambridge University Press, 1987
——, *The Rise of the Castle*, Cambridge: Cambridge University, 1991
Tout, Thomas Frederick, *The History of England: From the Accession of Henry III to the Death of Edward III (1216–1377)*, London: Longmans, Green & Co., 1906
Trevelyan, Raleigh, *Sir Walter Raleigh*, London: Allen Lane, 2002
Underwood, Peter, *A Gazetteer of British, Scottish and Irish Ghosts: Two Volumes*, New York: Bell, 1985
——, *Ghosts of Hampshire and the Isle of Wight*, Farnborough: St Michael's Abbey Press, 1983,
——, *Ghosts of Kent: Authentic Ghost Stories From the Garden of England*, Sittingbourne: Meresborough Books, 1984
——, *Ghosts of North-West England*, London: Forfana, 1878
——, *Queen Victoria's Other World*, London: George C. Harrap & Co Ltd, 1986
——, *This Haunted Isle*, London: Javelin, 1986
Warner, Kathryn, *Blood Roses: The Houses of Lancaster and York before the Wars of the Roses*, Stroud: The History Press, 2018
Warren, W.L., *King John*, London and New Haven: Yale University Press, 1997
Weir, Alison, *Henry VIII: King and Court*, London: Pimlico, 2002
——, *Lancaster and York: The Wars of the Roses*, London: Vintage, 2009
——, *The Princes in the Tower*, London: Pimlico, 1992
Westwood, Jennifer, *Albion, A Guide to Legendary Britain*, London: Book Club Associates, 1986
Wolffe, Bertram, *Henry VI* (The English Monarchs Series), New Haven and London: Yale University Press, 2001

Websites

www.castlefacts.info
www.castlestudiesgroup.org.uk
www.ecastles.co.uk
www.english-heritage.org.uk
www.gatehouse-gazetteer.info
www.landmarktrust.org.uk
www.nationaltrust.org.uk
www.savebritainsheritage.org
www.ukapt.org.uk

Index

Abberbury the Elder, Sir Richard, 90
Abingdon Chronicle, 95
Agincourt, 34, 54, 72, 114, 129, 152
Aidan, St., 212, 221–22
Albert, Prince, 62, 95
Alexander, Bishop of Lincoln, 135
Alexander I of Scotland, 206
Alexander II of Scotland, 128, 189
Alexander III of Scotland, 180
Alexander III, Pope, 155
Alfred the Great, 16, 115–16, 121, 223
Alnwick, battles of, 191, 205–06
Alnwick Castle, 168, 209–12, 226, 247
Amberley Castle, 231
Anarchy, the, xvi, 33, 43, 54, 76, 89, 96, 103, 110, 112, 113, 116, 127, 142, 172, 189, 231
Anglo-Saxon Chronicle, the, xv, 9, 26, 37, 56, 73, 222
Aragon, Catherine of, 79, 81, 100, 129, 234
Armstrong Archie, 239
Armstrong, William, 213
Arthur, King, 1–3, 10–13, 30–31, 78, 164, 186–87, 209, 211–12, 220
Arundel Castle, 60–63,
Arundel, earls of, 60–65, 108, 231
Arundell family, 50–51
Ashburnham, Roger, 87
Ashe, Geoffrey, 31
Aske, Robert, 150
Astley Castle, 234
Astley, Sir John, 211
Astor, William Waldorf, 80
Aubigny family, d', 60–61, 83, 108
Aubrey, John, 29
Auckland Castle, 193, 195

Augustinians, 37, 154
Augustus, William, Duke of Cumberland, 181
Aumale, Odo, Count of, 171
Aumale, William de Forz, Earl of, 128, 131
Aumale, William le Gros, Earl of, 167
Austria, Leopold of, 137–38
Ayscough family, 198

Babington Plot, 124
Baconsthorpe Castle, 232
Baden-Powell, Robert, 163
Bader Alfred, 71
Badlesmere, Bartholomew of, 81
Baile Hill, 149
Baillie, Lady, 81–82
Baker, Geoffrey le, 41–42
Balliol family, 189
Bamburgh Castle, 168, 206, 209, 211–14, 221–22
Bankes family, 27
Bannockburn, Battle of, 173
Baring-Gould, Sabine, 5, 7
Barnard Castle, 189–90, 197
Barnet (Barnet field), Battle of, 117, 157
Barnwell, 84, 127–28
Battle Abbey, 69, 75
Bayeux Tapestry, the xvi, 68, 73
Beatrice, Princess, 57
Beamont family, de, *see* earls of Warwick
Beavrière, de, family, 170–72
Bec, Bernard le, 9
Becket, Thomas, 69, 155, 186
Bede, 106, 212, 221
Beeston Castle, 174–76
Bek, Antony, 210

256 Castles of England

Bellister Castle, 236–37
Belvoir Castle, 132–34, 154
Berkeley Castle, 40–43, 61, 109, 138
Berkeley family, 40–43
Berkeley, Lady Mary, 217
Berry Pomeroy Castle, 9, 13–16
Betchworth Castle, 231–32
Bickley, Augustus Charles, 102
Bigod family, 103–04, 110–12
Bingham, Colonel, 27
Birch, Lieutenant-Colonel John, 61
Black Shuck, 7, 82, 103, 107–08
Blake, Admiral, 4
Blake, Colonel, 33
Blanchminster, Sir Ranulph de, 3
Blandy, Mary, 96
Blenkinsop Castle and family, 237
Blois, Henry of, Bishop of Winchester, 37, 89
Blois, Stephen of, King of England, xvi, 37, 40, 44, 48, 73, 89, 103, 142, 144, 167, 180, 182
Bloody Assizes, the, 17, 38–39
Blount, Richard, 87
Bloxham, Moll, 119
Bodiam Castle, 63–66, 70
Bohemia, Anne of, 61, 81, 90
Boleyn, Anne, 44, 55, 79, 92, 175, 182, 234
Boleyn (Bullen) family, 79
Bolingbroke Castle, 174–75
Bolingbroke, *see* Henry IV
Bolsover Castle, 140–42
Bolton Abbey, 172
Bolton Castle, 147–48
Boroughbridge, Battle of, 150, 160, 181, 218
Bosworth, Battle of, 34, 44, 150, 154, 157, 205
Boteler, Ralph, 43–44
Bothal, Bertram de, 228
Boudica, 97
Bowes Castle, 190–91
Bowes, George, 189–90
Boynton, Matthew, 169
Boys, Sir John, 90–91

Bragg, Mary, 185
Bramber Castle, 66–68
Braose family, de, 26, 66–67, 92
Breauté, Falkes de, 144
Brereton family, 120, 175
Bretagne, Alan de, Count of Brittany, 190–91
Breton, Richard le, 155, 163
Bristol, 28, 40, 245–46
Brittany, Conan IV of, 163
Brittany, John of, Earl of Richmond, 129
Brown, Lancelot 'Capability, 118, 211
Bruce Castle, 233
Bruce family, 85, 181, 233
Brus, Robert de, 180
Brut Chronicle, the, 136
Buckingham, George de Villiers, dukes of, 154
Bulstrode, Richard, 118
Burgh Castle, 106–08
Burgh, Elizabeth de, Queen of Scotland, 85
Burgh, Hubert de, 1st Earl of Kent, 76–77, 83, 100, 128–29
Bushel, Sir Edward, 46

Caen, Roger de (le Poer), Bishop of Salisbury, 28, 48
Cambridge, 110
Camden, William, 106, 120, 170–71
Camelot, 30–31, 114, 220
Camlann, battle of, 2–3
Canaletto, 116, 209
Canterbury, xv–xvi, 82–83, 155, 187
Cantilupe family, 145
Capo, Sir Ralph de, 85
Carey family, 153
Carey, William, 79
Carisbrooke Castle, 56–58, 93
Carlisle, 99, 147, 148, 180–82, 190, 200, 205
Carr, Robert, 1st Earl of Somerset, 21, 28
Cassiterides, 2–3
Castle Rising, 42, 108–10, 138, 147
Cauld boy of Hylton, 204
Cavendish family, 139–40

Index

Cecil family, 130
Cecily, Duchess of York, 129, 133–34, 196
Chandos family, 45–46
Charles Castle, 4
Charles I of England, Scotland and Ireland, 27, 46, 55, 57, 90–93, 102, 115, 122, 129, 132, 139, 161, 165, 169, 176, 198, 215
Charles II of England, Scotland and Ireland, 33, 38, 81, 92, 118, 177, 199, 216, 231
Chartley Castle, 174, 247
Chaucer, Geoffrey, 65, 90
Chester, 144, 174–76
Chester, Ranulf de Meschines, 3rd Earl of, 186
Chester, Ranulf de Gernon, 4th Earl of, 142
Chester, Ranulf de Blondevilles, 6th Earl of, 138, 174
Chillingham Castle, 214–17
Cholmley, Sir Hugh, 169
Clare family, 73, 81, 85
Clarence, George, Duke of, 117, 154, 196, 224
Claudius, Emperor, 97
Clavering, John de, 226
Cleves, Anne of, 80, 100
Clifford family, 151, 172–73, 186
Clifford, Roger de, 150–51, 160
Clifford, Rosamund, 158
Clifford's Tower, 148–52, 160, 246
Clinton, Geoffrey de, 113
Clitherow, Margaret 'the pearl of York', 150
Coggeshall, 83, 99, 104–06
Colchester, 83, 84, 97–99, 246
Coleraine, Lord, 233
Comines, Robert de, 193
Compton family, 118, 233
Comyn, John 'the Red', 180
Conisbrough Castle, 152–53
Conisburgh, Richard of, 3rd Earl of Cambridge, 54
Constable, John, 100

Constantia, Lady, 233
Copeman, Frederick, 194
Corbeil, William de, Archbishop of Canterbury, 83
Corfe Castle, 25–27, 50, 67, 92, 147, 246
Cormoran and Cornellian, 8
Cornhill, Reginald de, 83
Cotell, John, 35
Courtenay family, 18–19, 22, 229–30
Crécy, 54, 61
Crevecoeur family, 80
Crew, Lord, Bishop of Durham, 213
Cromwell's Castle, 4
Cromwell, Oliver, 4, 34, 50, 57, 61–62, 71, 81, 150, 161, 165, 211, 226, 244
Cromwell, Ralph, Lord, 145–46
Cromwell, Thomas, 35–36, 244
Croxton Abbey, 132, 135, 137
Crusades, the, 103, 137, 149, 174, 235–36
Culloden, Battle of, 181
Culpeper family, 81, 161
Curthose, Robert, 73, 83, 160, 237
Curzon, Lord of Kedleston, 66, 146
Cuthbert, St, 221–23
Cynric of Wessex, 56

Dacre Castle, 241–42
Dacre family, 71–72, 241–42
Dalyngrigge, Sir Edward, 64–66
Dapifer, Eudo, 98
Darcy family, 19, 161
Darrell Family, 87–88
David I of Scotland, 128, 182, 210
David II of Scotland, 53, 212
Dawkes, Richard, 77
Day, Lady Ann, 190
Deincourt family, 188
Delamare, John, 36
Denmark, Alexandra of, 215
Denmark, Anne of, 46, 208, 215
Dent Family, 44–45
Despenser family, 52–53, 121
Devereux, Robert, 3rd Earl of Essex, 21
Dickens, Charles, 1, 12, 66, 86, 131–32, 240
Digby, Sir John, 28–29

Diocletian, Emperor, 53
Dissolution of the Monasteries, 9, 18, 65, 69–70, 75, 120, 127, 132, 136, 160, 163, 206–07, 222, 231
Ditchling, Maude of, 68
Dobson, John, 237, 239
Domesday Book, the, xvii, 13, 16, 18, 30, 37, 43, 49, 95, 112, 116, 120, 142, 144, 149, 159, 163, 170, 231
Dominicans, 41, 177
Donnington Castle, 90
Dover, 68, 73, 75–78, 83, 171, 237, 246
D'Oyly, Robert, 95–96
Dudley Castle, 120–21
Dudley family, 114, 117, 120–21, 235
Dunbar, Battle of, 211
Duncombe family, 154
Dunstanburgh Castle, 160, 209, 211, 217–21
Dunster Castle, 32–33
Durham, 182, 189, 192–96, 210, 213, 221–22, 234–35, 247
Durotrige, 29

Eadgyth (Editha), St, 122–23
Eadfrith of Lindisfarne, St, 222
Earberht of Lindisfarne, St, 222
Edgehill, Battle of, 115, 118
Edmund, 'Crouchback', Earl of Lancaster, 114, 123, 218
Edward I of England, xvi, 3, 27, 54, 61, 81, 85, 100, 103, 110, 111, 113–14, 123, 140, 142, 143, 155, 163, 168, 174, 180, 189, 196, 206, 214–15, 226, 244
Edward II of England, 40–43, 53, 54, 61, 81, 100, 108, 109, 114, 122, 129, 150, 152, 155, 156, 160, 168, 172, 180–81, 191, 198, 206–07, 218, 226
Edward, 2nd Duke of York, 74, 129, 152
Edward III of England, xvi, 34, 41–43, 53, 54, 64, 81, 90, 92, 94, 100, 109, 114, 122, 129, 131, 138, 139, 142, 152, 154, 156, 160, 165, 186, 187, 215, 226
Edward IV of England, 22, 34, 44, 50, 100, 115, 117, 129, 138, 152, 157, 160, 196, 210–11, 224, 234, 239
Edward VI of England, 4, 13–15, 44–46, 50, 100, 111, 114, 117
Edward VII of the United Kingdom of Great Britain and Ireland, 118, 242
Edward VIII of the United Kingdom, 4, 95
Edward of Woodstock (the Black Prince), Duke of Cornwall, 12, 17, 61, 108
Edward the Confessor, St., xv, 9, 16, 60, 206
Edward the Martyr, 26
Eleanor of Aquitaine, Queen of England, 48, 176
Eleanor of Brittany, 26, 191
Eleanor of Castile, Queen of England, 81, 142–43
Eleanor of England, 52, 113
Eleanor of Gloucester, 82
Elfrida, 26
Elizabeth I of England, xi, 4, 14, 27–28, 40, 42, 45–46, 55, 57, 61, 75, 79, 87, 90, 92–93, 114, 117, 124, 129–30, 139, 146–47, 151, 176, 189, 206, 215, 230
Elizabeth II of the United Kingdom, 92, 95
Elizabeth, Princess, 58
Emery, Anthony, 115
English Heritage, xi, xiv, 58, 75, 91, 106, 108, 116, 141, 143, 153, 154, 157, 162, 171, 192, 203, 224, 226, 232
Ennor, 3–4
Espec, Walter l', 153
Æthelburg, 37
Æthelflæd, 116, 121
Æthelheard of Wessex, 37
Æthelred the Unready, 16, 26
Æthelstan, 202, 242
Evesham, 27, 52, 114
Exeter, 9, 16–18, 61, 246

Fairfax family, 81, 150
Fairfax, General Sir Thomas, 22, 29, 81, 150, 154, 229
Falkner, J. Meade, 58
Fareham, 54
Farleigh Hungerford, 34–36

Index

Farnham Castle, 89–90, 247
Featherstone Castle, 200–01
Featherstonehaugh family, 200–01, 238
Felton, Sir Robert, 168
Ferrers family, 123, 129, 140, 142
Fiennes family, 70–72
Fieschi Letter, 43
FitzAlan family, 61, 64, 231
FitzHarding, Robert, 40
FitzOsbern, William, 1st Earl of Hereford, 40, 56
Fitzpatrick, Mary, 151
FitzRandolph, Robert, 156
Fitz Richard, Roger, 225–26
FitzRoy, Adam, 207
FitzUrse, Reginald, 155, 201
Fitzwalter, Robert, 210
Flodden, Battle of, 111, 122
Flower family, 133–34
Flynn, Sean, 77
Forster family, 212–13
Fortescue family, 23–24
Fosse Way, 115–16
Fotheringhay Castle, 124, 128–29, 246
Fox, George, 99, 102, 151, 169, 177
Framlingham Castle, 84, 110–11, 247
Frankland, Edward, 186–87
Frithogyth, 37
Froissart, Jean, 81
Fuller, John, 66
Fursey, St, 106

Gael, Ralph de, Earl of Norfolk, 111
Galeys, William le, 43
Gallon, 219
Gard, Dolorous/Joyous, 209, 211–12, 220
Gaunt, John of, 1st Duke of Lancaster, 34, 64, 89–90, 99, 114–15, 123, 125, 142, 156, 160, 188, 218
Gaveston, Piers, Earl of Cornwall, 116–17, 156, 168, 170, 206
Geoffrey Plantagenet, bishop-elect of Lincoln and later Archbishop of York, 191
Geoffrey Plantagenet, Duke of Brittany, 26

George's Chapel, St, 93–94
George II of Great Britain and Ireland, 181
George III of Great Britain and Ireland, 92, 93
George IV of the United Kingdom of Great Britain and Ireland, 92
Giffard family, 22, 37
Gilpin, Reverend William, 245
Giordano, Luca, 197
Girtin, Thomas, 19, 218
Glanville, Bartholomew of, 104
Glemham, Sir Thomas, 181
Glorious Revolution, 169, 187
Glastonbury, 10, 30
Gloucester, 42, 46, 85, 127, 245–46
Gloucester, Gilbert de Clare, Earl of,
Gloucester, Henry, Duke of, 58
Gloucester, Robert, Earl of, 144
Godwinson, Harold, 70, 152, 206
Godwinson, Tostig, 206
Gonard, 107
Gorlois, Duke of Cornwall, 10–11
Green, Valentine, 137
Greville family, 108, 117–18
Grey family, 54, 111, 114, 117, 120, 131, 160, 203, 210–11, 234–35
Grey family of Chillingham, 214–18
Grosmont, Henry of, Duke of Lancaster, 114, 160
Guinevere, 209
Gundulf of Caen, 83, 86, 98
Gunnor, 60
Gurney, Sir Thomas, 41–42
Guy the Seeker, Sir, 219–21

Hadleigh Castle, 100–01
Hadrian's Wall, 180, 204
Hailes Abbey, 6
Hainault, Philippa of, Queen of England, 156
Hamelin Plantagenet, 152
Hamilton, James Hamilton, Duke of, 177
Hammond, Colonel Robert, 57, 229
Hansard family, 198

Harclay, Andrew de, 1st Earl of Carlisle, 180–81
Hardrada, Harold, 167
Harengood, Stephen, 98
Harrington, Sir John, 28
Hastings, Battle of, 68
Hastings Castle, 68–69, 73
Hastings, Lord, 210
Hatton, Sir Christopher, 27
Haughley Castle, 103, 246
Hawkesworth, Colonel Joseph, 115
Haye, Nicola de la, 144
Hedingham Castle, 84, 246
Helmsley Castle, 153–54, 159, 247
Henrietta Maria, Queen of England, Scotland and Ireland, 115, 217
Henry I of England, xvii, 25, 32, 37, 48, 73, 83, 92, 98, 103, 108, 113, 122, 155, 159–60, 172, 176, 180, 224, 237, 238
Henry II (of Anjou) of England, 40, 48, 54, 61, 69, 76, 89, 92, 98, 100, 103, 104, 108, 110, 112, 113, 116, 122, 123, 135, 137, 140, 142, 149, 152, 155, 158, 163, 167, 186, 188, 191, 193, 210, 212, 225, 237, 238
Henry III of England, xvi, 12, 26, 37, 52, 54, 68, 73–74, 77, 84–85, 92, 96, 98, 100, 113–15, 122, 123, 128, 130, 131, 139, 140, 142, 144, 149–51, 163, 167, 171, 174, 180, 189, 210, 214, 218, 234, 237, 244,
Henry IV (Bolingbroke) of England, 61, 74, 82, 86, 114, 138, 160, 175–76, 194, 196, 210, 224, 227
Henry V (Hal) of England, 54, 72, 74, 82, 86, 114, 227
Henry VI of England, 34, 44, 70, 82, 145, 168, 184, 219, 225
Henry VII of England, 22, 34, 44, 139, 154, 157, 235, 239
Henry VIII of England, 5, 13–14, 17–18, 31, 35, 44–45, 49–50, 54–55, 71, 77, 79–81, 92–93, 95, 100, 108, 111, 117, 127, 129, 131, 139, 147, 153, 161, 175, 187–88, 207, 222, 224, 233, 234, 244
Henry the Young King, 103, 108, 110, 112, 123, 140, 191, 210

Herman of Salisbury, 48
Herne the Hunter, 94–95
Herstmonceux Castle, 66, 70–72
Hexham, Battle of, 34, 184, 220, 225
Heydon family, 232
Heyno, Peter de, 57
Hill, Sir Rowland, 233
Hoby, Lady, 91
Holinshed's Chronicles, 41–42
Holland, John, Duke of Exeter, 61
Holt, Thomas, 198
Hope family, 231–32
Hopkins, Matthew, 98–99
Horne, Richard, 95
Hotspur, Henry Percy, 2nd Earl of Northumberland, 210, 224, 227–28
Howard family, 19–21, 50, 61–62, 79, 103, 108, 110–11, 151, 161, 177, 200, 210, 239–41
Hudson, Dr Michael, 102
Humphrey of Lancaster, Duke of Gloucester, 82, 100
Hungerford family, 34–36
Huntingdon, earls of, 65, 128, 138
Hurst, Hubert de, 68
Hussey, Edward, 87
Hutchison, John, 139
Hylton Castle, 202–04

Igraine, 10–11
Ine of Wessex, 37
Ingleby (Ingilby) family, 164–65
Ingoldsby, Colonel, 96
Ireland, 26, 46, 67, 82, 175, 198, 241
Iron Age, xv, xvii, 29, 47, 76, 78, 129, 131, 167, 170, 174, 218
Isabella 'the she-wolf' of France, Queen of England, 41–42, 53, 81, 108–10, 114, 138

Jack-the-giant-killer, 8
Jacobite rebellions, 169, 181, 222
James I of England and VI of Scotland, 19, 21, 28, 91–92, 111, 115, 117, 122, 124–25, 129, 150, 157, 165, 176, 192, 194, 199, 204, 215, 218
James I of Scotland, 74

James II of England and VII of Scotland, 38–39, 169, 187
James III of Scotland, 129
Jeffreys, Judge George, 17, 39
Jennison family, 198–99
Jews, 112, 148
Joan of Wales, 139
Joan, the fair maid of Kent, 61
John of England, xvi, 9, 12, 25–26, 37, 52–54, 67, 73, 76–77, 83–84, 92, 98, 100, 110, 113–14, 121, 128, 131, 135–40, 149–50, 152, 155, 160, 167, 174, 189, 191, 210, 225–26
Jonson, Ben, 115

Kenilworth Castle, 113–16, 170, 246
Kenninghall, 111
Ketch, Jack, 39
Keyne, St, 8
Kimbolton Castle, 129, 233–34, 247
Kipling, Rudyard, 75
Knaresborough Castle, 155–56, 246
Knolles, Sir Robert, 64
Knollys, Sir Francis, 148

Lacy family, 114, 159–60
Lambert, John, 161, 239
Lambeth Treaty of, 98
Lambton, 213, 220, 235–36
Lancaster, 34, 64, 100, 114, 117, 123, 142, 143, 152
Lancaster Castle, 176–78, 238, 246
Lancaster, Henry earl of, 114, 160
Lancaster, John of, 1st Duke of Bedford, 224
Lancaster, Thomas, Earl of, 114, 117, 152, 160, 181, 196, 218, 220
Lancelot, Sir, 139, 209, 220
Lancelot du Lac, 122
Langdale, Marmaduke, 1st Baron Langdale, 161
Langley, Edmund of, 2nd Duke of York, 100, 129, 152
Langside, Battle of, 147
Langton, Stephen, Archbishop of Canterbury, 83
Lanvalai, William de, 98

Latymer, Lord, 188
Laugharne, Sir Rowland, 102
Law, John, 178
Leake, Sergeant, 94
Leeds Castle, 74, 80–82, 147, 153
Leland, John, 30–31, 117, 129, 138–39, 148, 150, 229
Lewes, 52, 74, 113, 143, 247
Lewis, Matthew, 220
Leybourne, William of, 80–81, 84
Lincoln, 134, 142, 143–46, 238, 246
Lincoln, Aaron of, 148–49
Lincoln, bishop of, 135
Lindfield, Sir William de, 68
Lindisfarne, 212, 221–23
Lisle, Brian de, 140, 142
Lisle, George Sir, 98
Llywelyn ap Iorwerth, Prince of Gwynedd, 139
Loches Castle, 83
Locust, John, 45
London, Tower of, xi–xiii, 18, 28, 32, 34, 75, 79, 81, 83, 93, 98, 102, 138, 150, 154, 156, 160, 182, 184, 198, 208, 246
Louis VIII of France, 52, 68, 73, 77, 84, 98, 112, 144
Louvain, Adeliza de, 108
Lovell, Agatha, 145
Lovell family, 50
Lowther Hall, 242–43
Lucas, Charles Sir, 98–99
Lulworth, 230
Lumley Castle, 194–95
Lumley family, 194–95, 203
Luttrell family, 32–33
Lydford, 16–18
Lyonesse, 1–3, 8–9, 12

Macartney, George, 243
Maelgwyn, 3
Magna Carta, 52, 83, 98, 113, 128, 144–45
Malcolm III of Scotland, 205–06, 237
Malcolm IV of Scotland, 142
Malebisse, Richard de, 148–49
Malmesbury, William of, 242
Malory, Sir Thomas, 212

Maltravers, John, 41–42
Manners family, 132, 154
Marcus Aurelius Carausius, 53
Margaret of Anjou, Queen of England, 54, 210–11, 219
Margaret of France, Queen of England, 100
Margaret of Scotland, 26, 128–29
Marmion family, 121, 122, 223
Marley, Sir John, 238
Marlowe, Christopher, 42, 206
Marsden, Sir Simon, 230
Marsh, George, 176
Marshal, William, 1st Earl of Pembroke, 52, 54, 144
Marshal, William, 2nd Earl of Pembroke, 113, 128
Marston Moor, Battle of, 150, 165–66, 236
Martin, Lawrence de St, 49–50
Mary I of England, 22, 46, 111, 114, 117, 168, 224
Mary II of England, Scotland and Ireland, 199
Mary, Queen of Scots, 61, 109, 111, 124–25, 129–30, 147–48, 161, 173, 181, 182, 189
Matilda, Empress, xvi, 60, 116, 144, 180
Maud Lucy, 224
Maudit family, 54
Maulay, Peter de, 26–27
Mauléon, Savari de, 98
May, Hugh, 92
Meldrum, Sir John, 169
Mere, Peter de la, 138
Merlin, 11, 187, 219
Michael, the Archangel, 8
Middleton, General John, 90
Militon family, 5–6
Milton, John, 8
Mohun, William de (father and son), 32–33
Moine, Berengar le, 127
Monmouth, Geoffrey of, 10, 31, 186
Monmouth, Scott, James, 1st Duke of, 17, 38–39

Montagu family, 127, 138, 233
Montague, Lord, 224
Montalt family, 108
Montfort family, 27, 34, 37–38
Montfort, Simon de, 6th Earl of Leicester, 27, 52, 84–85, 113–14, 116, 142, 210
Montgomery, Roger de, 1st Earl of Arundel, 60
More, Sir Thomas, 117,
Morley, Bishop George, 89–90
Morrice, Colonel, 161
Morrison, Richard, 244
Mortain, Robert, Count of, 73, 153
Mortain, William, Count of, 73
Mortimer, Roger, 1st Earl of March, 41–42, 53, 61, 81, 109, 113, 138–39
Morville, Hugh de, 155, 186–87
Mourdour, 156
Mowbray family, 67, 110,
Mowbray, Robert de, 206, 212, 237
Muncaster Castle, 183–84
Murrell, James, 101

Napoleonic Wars, 55, 77–78, 169
Naseby, Battle of, 38, 161
National Trust, 33, 66, 87, 146, 187, 222, 236
Navarre, Joan of, 74, 82, 138
Naylor, Grace, 72
Nectan, St., 11
Nero, 97
Neville's Cross, Battle of, 53, 212
Neville family, 157, 167–68, 189–90, 192, 195–98, 225, 227, 239
Neville, Richard (the kingmaker), 16th Earl of Warwick, 117, 157, 184, 189, 210, 212–13, 239
Newark, 102, 135–36, 247
Newburgh, William of, 167
Newbury, Battle of, 90
Newcastle, 34, 139, 141, 224, 237–38, 246–47
Newdigate family, 235
Nibley Green, Battle of, 40

Index

Norfolk, Dukes and Earls of, 60–63, 79, 103, 108, 110–12, 124, 231
Nottingham, 42, 109, 137–39
Nowell, Roger, 179

Ockley, William, 42
Odiham, 52–53, 246
Odo, Bishop of Bayeux, 82–83
Offa, King of Mercia, 121
Okehampton Castle, 18–22
Olaf, 208
Old Sarum, 28, 47–49, 246
Old Wardour, 36, 49–51
Oldcoates, Philip of, 212
Orford, 100, 104–06, 246
Osmund, St, Earl of Dorset, 28, 48
Osred II, 205
Oswald of Northumbria, 212, 221
Oswin of Deira, 205–06
Otterburn, Battle of, 227
Overbury, Sir Thomas, 21
Oxford, 9, 27, 50, 94–96, 102, 198–99, 238, 246
Owen, St Nicholas, 165

Packer, John, 90
Parnell, James, 99
Parr, Catherine, 45–46, 100, 187–88
Pearce, Dickie, 40
Peasants' Revolt, the, 85, 111
Pelham family, 69, 74–75
Penda of Mercia, 221
Pendle Witches, 176–78
Pendragon Castle, 185–87, 191
Pengersick Castle, 5–7
Penitone, Alan de, 183
Pennington family, 183–84
Penrith Castle, 173, 239
Pepys, Samuel, 86, 198
Perche, Count of, 144
Percy family, 19, 167–68, 197, 203, 208, 210–11, 224, 226–27
Peter, Geoffrey fitz, 1st Earl of Essex, 233
Petrock, St, 16
Pevensey, 68, 72–76, 82

Peveril Castle, 140–43, 246
Pevsner, Sir Nikolaus, 36
Pilgrimage of Grace, 147, 150, 161, 168, 224
Pitman, Colonel, 27
Playsted, Thomas, 74
Poitiers, Battle of, 117
Poitou, Roger de, 176
Polesworth Abbey, 122
Pomeroy family, 9, 13–16
Pontefract Castle, 81, 142, 159–62, 218
Pontius Pilate, 53
Poore, Bishop Richard, 49
Popham, Sir John, 234
Popish Plot, 199
Portchester, 53–56, 246
Portland, dukes of, 141
Portsmouth, 54
Porter, Linda, 46
Powderham Castle, 229–30
Power, Thomas, 208
Prater, Colonel Richard, 36
Prasutagus, 97
Princes in the Tower, 22, 117
Prudhoe Castle, 224–25
Puiset, Hugh de, Bishop of Durham, 193

Raby Castle, 190, 196–98
Rainsborough, Colonel Thomas, 40
Rainsford, Sir Henry, 125
Raleigh, Sir Walter, 28–29, 208
Ramsay, Admiral Sir Bertram, 77
Rawcliffe, Thomas, 177
Rayleigh Castle, 100
Reade, Bishop William, 231
Redburgh, Reverend Henry, 240
Redhead, Robert, 151
Redvers, de, family, 22, 56
Reynolds, Sir Joshua, 132, 197
Rich, Richard, 100
Richard, 3rd Duke of York, 129, 152, 196
Richard, Earl of Cornwall, 12, 17
Richard I of England, 9, 15–16, 60–61, 83, 137–38, 149, 160, 212
Richard I of Normandy, 60

Richard II of England, 12, 41, 50, 54, 61, 65, 74, 81, 85–86, 90, 94, 114, 138, 147, 160–62, 175–76, 196, 210, 227, 231
Richard III (Duke of Gloucester) of England, 44, 117, 129, 150, 154, 157, 160, 168, 170, 184, 189, 196, 205
Richardson, James, 151
Richmond, 44, 156, 163–64, 191
Ridolfi Plot, 124
Ridleys of Hardriding, 201
Rievaulx Abbey, 154
Ripley Castle, 164–66
Rising of the North, 189, 196–97, 224
Robert I (the Bruce) of Scotland, 85, 181, 233
Robinson, Edmund, 179
Roches, Peter des, Bishop of Winchester, 37, 83–85, 98, 144
Rochester Castle, 82–86, 98, 246
Rockingham Castle, 130–32, 137, 171, 246
Romans, 29, 73, 97, 107, 167, 190, 200
Romille family, 172
Rous, John, 116
Rubens, Sir Peter Paul, 133
Ruffin, Elizabeth, 58
Rufus, Alan, 163
Rupert, Prince, 46, 91, 150
Russell, Lady, 90
Ruthven family, 165
Rutland, earls and dukes of, 132–33, 154

St Albans, 83, 97
Salisbury, 28, 47–50, 246
Salvin, Anthony, 32, 87, 118, 136, 183, 211, 226, 239
Samlesbury Witches, 178
Sandford, Captain Thomas, 175
Savoy, Peter of, Earl of Richmond, 68–69, 74, 191
Saxons, xv, xvii, 1, 3, 9, 16, 26, 29, 32, 37, 42–43, 47, 56, 73, 76, 80, 98, 106–07, 112, 120–21, 123, 134, 167, 186, 192, 202, 206, 212, 222, 238
Scales, Lord, 34

Scarborough Castle, 156, 166–70, 206, 246
Scarfe, Baron Rudolph, 107–08
Scargill, John de, 191
Scilly, Isles of, 2–4, 198
Scot, Reginald, 204
Scotland, 26, 61, 106, 129–30, 138, 142–43, 149–50, 155, 168–69, 172–73, 176, 180–82, 186, 188, 189, 190, 192–94, 200, 204–05, 207–08, 210–12, 214, 216, 220–23, 225–28, 233, 237–39, 241–42
Scotland, Prince Henry of, 225
Scotland, John of, Earl of Huntingdon and Chester, 174
Scotney Castle, 87–88
Scott, Sir Walter, 115, 119, 122, 143, 153
Scrope family, 54, 147–48
Sedbar, Adam, 147
Sedgemoor, Battle of, 38–39
Selby, George, 208
Senlis, Simon de, Earl of Northampton, 128
Seymour family, 13–15, 44–46, 93, 226
Shakespeare, William, 42, 54, 94, 114, 136, 160–61, 184, 189, 227
Sharp, Dr John, 213
Sherborne, 28, 246
Shrewsbury, Battle of, 210, 224, 227
Siberg, 107
Sidney, Sir Henry, 146
Sizergh Castle, 187–88
Skelton, Robert, 203
Skelton, Thomas (Tom Fool), 184–85
Skipsea Castle, 170–72, 247
Skipton Castle, 147, 156, 172–73, 186, 247
Smirke, Robert, 242
Smith family, 239
Smithson, Hugh, 226
Smythson, Robert, 140
Somery family, de, 120
Southampton Plot, 54
Spencer family, 23
Stafford, Thomas, 168
Stamford Bridge, Battle of, 206

Star Castle, 4
Steele, Captain Thomas, 175
Stephen of Blois, *see* Blois, Stephen of
Stewart, Alexander, Duke of Albany, 129
Stewart, Captain Robert, 241
Stirling, 168
Stratton, Battle of, 50
Strecche, John, 114
Strickland, Agnes, 46
Strickland family, 187–88
Stuart, Charles Edward (the young Pretender), 181
Stuart, James Francis Edward (the old Pretender), 181
Stubbs, Bishop, 174
Sudeley Castle, 43–47
Sutton family, 120
Swinburne family, 205, 238–39
Swineshead Abbey, 136
Swynford, Katherine, 156

Tailboys, Sir William, 210
Talbot family, 130, 140
Tarquin, Sir, 122
Tattershall Castle, 145–46
Taunton Castle, 37–38
Tennyson, Alfred Lord, 2, 11–12
Tewkesbury, Battle of, 44, 184
Thackeray, William Makepeace, 12
Thanet, Lord, 65
Thanet, Nicholas 3rd Earl of, 186
Thirlwall Castle, 204–05
Thompson, Peter (potter), 164
Throckmorton family, 28, 36
Thwenge family, 165
Titian, 133
Tiverton Castle, 22, 229
Tolkien, J.R.R., 98
Tollemache, John, Baron, 175
Tom the fiddler, 38–39
Towton, Battle of, 34, 210, 214
Tracy, William de, 155
Trevor, Sir Charles, 23–24
Tromp, Admiral Maarten, 4
Tudor, Jasper, 44

Turner, J.M.W., 19, 86, 122, 154, 163, 197, 202, 209, 218, 226, 242
Turpin, Dick, 101, 151
Tutbury Castle, 123–25, 147–48
Tyburn, 35, 42, 71, 109
Tynemouth Castle and Priory, 205–08

Ufford, William de, 2nd Earl of Suffolk, 111
Umfraville, Robert d', 224
Uther Pendragon, 10–11, 185–87
Uvedale, Sir William, 55

Valois, Catherine of, Queen of England, 86
Van Dyck, Sir Anthony, 133, 197
Van Mildert family, 193–94
Vane family, 189–90, 197–98
Vere, John de, Earl of Oxford, 9
Vernon, Sir Edward, 125
Vesci (Vescy) family, de, 168, 209, 210
Veteripont, Lady Idonea de, 186
Victoria/Victorian era, xvii, 11–12, 17, 32, 46–47, 56–58, 60, 62, 69–70, 75, 84–85, 95, 112, 144, 145, 163, 166, 174, 181, 197, 213, 231
Virginia, 81

Wace, Robert, xv–xvi
Wakefield, Sir Humphry, 2nd Baronet, 215
Walcher, Bishop William, 192–93
Wales, ix, xiii, 14, 102, 118, 139, 215, 227, 245
Wallace family, 201
Wallace, William, 215
Waller, Sir William, 91
Walsingham, Sir Francis, 124
Walsingham, Thomas, 227
Walter, Lucy, 38
Waltheof of Northumbria, 192, 206
Walworth Castle, 198–99
Warenne family, 84–85, 116, 152, 168
Warkworth Castle, 210, 225–26, 228
Wars of the Roses, 9, 40, 50, 114, 129, 132, 138, 146, 160, 163, 181, 187, 213, 218

Warwick Castle, 115–19, 168
Washington family, 203
Waterloo, Battle of, 77
Watling Street, 82, 190
Watson family, 131
Weldon, Sir Anthony, 86
Wendover, Roger of, 83, 171
Westminster, 42, 86, 130, 199
Widdrington family, 228, 238
Wild man, 104–06
William I (the Conqueror) of England, xv–xvi, 13, 25, 40, 48–49, 60, 68–70, 73, 76, 82, 89, 92, 95–96, 111–12, 120, 121, 128, 131, 140, 142, 143, 144, 149, 152, 153–54, 159, 163, 167, 170–71, 192–93, 203, 237
William I (the Lion) of Scotland, 149, 191, 210, 224
William II (Rufus) of England, 73, 82–83, 131, 180, 189, 206, 209, 212, 237–38
William III (Prince of Orange) of England, Scotland and Ireland, 169, 199
Winchester, 37, 50–52, 89, 94, 144, 244, 246

Windsor, 26, 50, 52, 67, 76, 91–95, 215, 244, 246
Wingfield, Sir Richard, 233
Witchcraft, 6, 37, 55, 74, 82, 94, 98, 101, 133–34, 176–78, 204
Wood family, 157
Woodcroft Castle, 102
Woodstock, Edmund of, 1st Earl of Kent, 61
Worcester, 9, 43, 118, 137, 231, 246
Wyatt family, 168, 235
Wyatville, Sir Jeffry, 215
Wydville (Woodville) family, 22, 57, 100, 129, 160, 234
Wykeham, William of, Bishop of Winchester, 94
Wyndham, Colonel, 33
Wynford, William, 50

York, 148–52, 161, 165, 190, 227, 239, 246
York, Elizabeth of, 22

Zennor, 105–06